THE COAT OF MANY COLOURS

... and he made him a
coat of many colours

Genesis

SVEN BERLIN
the coat of many colours

redcliffe

First published in 1994
by Redcliffe Press Ltd.,
49 Park Street, Bristol

© Sven Berlin

ISBN 1 872971 08 3

British Library Cataloguing in Publication Data
A catalogue record for this book is available from
the British Library.

Typeset by Mayhew Typesetting, Rhayader, Powys
Printed in Great Britain by The Longdunn Press, Bristol

CONTENTS

I DEDICATE THIS BOOK TO THE UNKNOWN ARTIST

He who wears this coat puts on
The honour of the law of light
And shines as if a habergeon
Of silver blinds our sight.

He is knight of the butterflies,
Warrior of the setting sun,
Sinks as he lifts his head and dies
Blazing like a holy one.

He who is born but never slain
Is he who lives through death and dares
To recreate the world again –
The coat of many colours wears.

PREDELLA

I, Sven, was christened so
From Svanh the Swan, perhaps,
Or the Knight in Lohengrin.
Now I am a man I know
S also stands for sin.

A favourite uncle bore the name –
A Swedish husar who died young
Manoeuvring an army game:
His horse, Hawaii, by chance stept wrong
And threw him when its leg went lame.

Although from font marked Christ the Fish
Came the name Berlin, man of fate,
It was a drunken Rabbi's wish:
When exiled to a Swedish town
He chose to be a Christian late.

And there by sperm to arctic circle sent –
In snow on everlasting lease
To Beauty's wide encirclement –
I paid for peace the Viking price
And lived with fish beneath the ice.

When the horn-prowed longships sailed
From my ancient father's groin
I crossed again the northern seas
To England's angular green loin
Where only English women please.

An exile from magnetic north,
Descended from a Wandering Jew,
Searching for my origin:
I never found a way more true
Than Beauty on the arm of Sin.

Only four words father forth:
I, SVEN – MY SELF WITHIN.
A lonely single-bodied beast

7

Who strikes an arc at azimuth
And as he turns from west to east
Knows that all is truth.

There is none other left to tell,
No one else to be my guide
Like Odysseus had in Hell
To ride again the azygous tide
And ring the Longing Bell.

A BESPOKE LINING

When I started to write this book it seemed that it was a repetition of all the books I have written over my long life. This is not so. An author can only graze the field of his experience and imagination, but if the field is on a plateau or cliff that extends over a great ocean he becomes like an albatross following his own ship over the same seas he has known and written, but also those unknown, this time to search for and relate those depths indicated by the sighting of a whale or a lone seaman, an uncharted landfall – anything that will give meaning to what otherwise might be a black desolation over which the soul is doomed to glide on the wings of Time Absolute. This is the journey of that soul searching for and finding the original spark of creation from a falling star of a lone berg of ice in the moonlight, the touch of a woman igniting the experience and finally finding a way in which it might be held long enough to illuminate the mind and lock out Time. Therein, and only therein, can the original mind of man function at its most pristine as a visual artist.

The scientific attitude seems to be much the same and was once explained quite simply to me by an eminent biochemist. He said that when he was doing original research work in the laboratory, the moment of discovery was preceded by a flash of vision that bridged the gap of the unknown and presented the truth, which later was confirmed by a process of reason. The artist obeys such a moment of vision and proceeds to invent a language to contain it, if with less reason. The one works for absolute knowledge for its own sake, the other to contain absolute beauty. Both are ways of becoming a useful human being. Both are an attempt to extend consciousness. Both, it is to be hoped, are instructed by truth and goodness. Thus Plotinus:

SO STRIKE AND BE A LIGHT TO MEN!

It is the moment of strike and the flash that comes from it that is the source of creation – the creative act takes place and afterwards there must be no precious nonsense about being in the mood, but tough work at the rockface through unrelenting days till the object is created. To try and extinguish this is the first immorality.

9

There are some men who have this mechanism as though it were slipped in the breast like a secret device by an unknown hand at the beginning of human existence, a shuttle that shoots a magic thread through the moving mind. Some have not got it. Some have it and never learn to use it. To some it is given and they corrupt it. Those few who have it, and go through with the difficult task of learning to use it, show in early life. They are usually set aside as misfits, delinquents, mavericks or those who don't conform – simply because they are not able to do so, any more than a man with platypus feet can make a Guardsman. In the case of the painter, the poet and the sculptor, this means inbuilt isolation and appalling hardship if he is poor; rejection even, because not only does he not conform with the Establishment, but working at the original source of life, what he is about to discover is usually too subjective to be understood. He learns to live through death to create life again. He wears the Coat of Many Colours of which men are jealous. This is what I write about, using my own life as a bespoke lining for my research, and to shield a small but intense flame that will find my way across the universe.

I have started as far back as my personal records will take me, to a violent Europe from which my first ancestor fled carrying his spark into South Sweden from Germany when Goethe was writing his great poem on Faust and showing us for the first time the Mephistophelean nature of his people that finally found its ultimate expression in the emergence of Hitler, the Prince of Evil, 200 years later. I have followed through the dark arctic unconscious of the long dead, whom I found more disturbing than the living, until the present time, and have found no artist among them save a little old lady, named Charlotte Berlin, who taught music in Ystad and possibly composed. But my ancestors have included one great explorer who did fine topographical and portrait drawings and wrote books on his remarkable journeys of discovery in Asia, and one master of the horse, several priests and philosophers, bankers, engineers, chemists, and one scholarly cousin who helped me to understand and recreate my 'First Father', guiding me from the gloomy wood, through unknown territory.

All the way through, even when I got to England's angular green shores, there seems to have been a life-force already established and creating patterns of sometimes inexplicable behaviour, directing destiny over which one has little or no control, snatching up individuals like the giant Polyphemus, testing them, breaking them, casting them aside until one with the strength of bronze appears and

10

is able to do the immense task of expressing the nation's soul – like Sibelius – or a single human destiny, like Van Gogh who was destroyed by fire.

Nothing is known of this invisible but unique part of the human psyche. It cannot be studied in clinics or laboratories. It is elusive like Ariel and like him can brave the storm, has a touch of magic for Prospero the poet. The Violet Man always at the elbow never letting things go logically, but guiding the great work. Nowhere can it be studied but in the artist's daily life: the uncertainty, the sacrifice, the joy and love and mystery of the journey from nowhere to nowhere, as a whale migrates into unknown waters. My father bringing me to England opened the icecap in which I would otherwise have been trapped and unable to make for the open sea, and later, harbour my longship in Cornwall.

To present this journey is the task with which I am now faced. I shall attempt to do this without betraying the secrets of a drunken aunt or the private follies at the wells of youth. Not to disappoint or hurt one's loved ones or offend the memory of a noble ancestor by telling too much truth, is almost impossible. To avoid the embarrassment of a devoted wife by writing about the ones before her. To exclude the political deceits of one's enemies or the carnal weakness of one's friend. To reveal the secret love locked in the stone of one's heart. To eschew harming persons unknown or being mean enough to spit in the soup while serving it to the Minister of Arts at dinner. These are all things I wish to exclude, once having had the joy and humour and anguish of not excluding them and being faced with fierce reprisals afterwards, though I might now be brought to task for leaving them out.

I am not putting out the black refuse bags for each passing rat to tear open and am external only when it explains an internal equation, for it is a book from inside, to tell the secret processes of the mind and sometimes the heart. It becomes a sort of *I, Claudius* of the spirit. I, Sven: the Vagabond Jew in search of his soul and finding in the end a Coat of Many Colours. This has made it possible to pass through death and recreate life: become king of the rainbows, for a moment master of the setting sun, until I take out of my side the leaping shuttle put there by an unknown God – or Devil, perhaps?

If in having passed through disturbing traumas I have troubled the ghosts of the dead or those of the dear defeated who are still alive, by breaking up megatons of experience ossified by the years to try and extract a little radium, I have also done it to set a small saucer alight in a chancel to keep away the Angel of Darkness and pay tribute to the receptive genius of the woman who keeps vigil, without whom creation cannot be completed.

If God there is it is he who is in me that I am and I grow as a tree as I die.

SVEN BERLIN
DORSET 1994

A CREDIT ACCOUNT

In the first instance, on the Swedish side, I thank my nephew, Steffan Berlin, who supplied me with photographs of his grandfather, Sven Berlin, after whom I was named: also extracts from Sven's personal diary when he came to visit us in 1922, with other information that has been helpful. After that, owing to pressures in his own life Steffan passed the task on to my cousin, Gunhild Aberg, who quietly took it up with a trained mind which proved invaluable, crossing the language barrier and researching back to mid-eighteenth century Sweden and Germany to make a vivid account of Abraham Brody – the Wandering Jew – who became the first Berlin from whom this unique family flowed. Gunhild, whom I have never met, also did research on Sven Hedin, the Explorer (cousin to my father, Karl Gustav Berlin) at the Ethnological Museum and the Sven Hedin Museum in Stockholm, the Charlotte Berlin Museum in Ystad in South Sweden, and the House of Nobility also in Stockholm. She sent me photographs and references I could not otherwise have obtained. She also sent me new sections of the Berlin pedigree going back to 1772 which clarified those I had in my archive – in Swedish, which I don't speak or read. Unfortunately no portrait of Brody-Berlin – in either painting or drawing – exists. He seems to have been caught in a violent destiny and a brilliant account of his behaviour was recorded in the *Memoirs of Aaron Isaak*, the first Jew to legally enter Sweden. Gunhild has translated this for me. So for all the early part of my history, my thanks and gratitude are due to her and to the historians and scholars she consulted but not known to me: and to Ruth Gyllensvaan (née Berlin – Lt. Sven Berlin's widow): also to Hans and Ragnar Berlin for 'two pompous portraits of our great grandparents', which take us within 30 years of the appearance of Brody-Berlin in Malmo, South Sweden. What I have always thought of as the icy archives of arctic Sweden have suddenly given out a warmth and life by which I am enriched. The frankness and accuracy of the information I have received is a credit to any scholar.

In the second instance, on the English side, it has been more difficult because of the lack of records and photographs which have been consistently destroyed, either by destiny, poverty or personal

13

decision. I found a letter from my Aunt Dickie Slade who had sent me several good letters before she died, but in one she says 'I throw all old photographs on the fire.' My sister Alma Berlin also says she destroyed all the early photos after my father's death. Perhaps it is a family trait. I have never liked photographs and although I kept many with files of letters from all manner of people my archive has been continually etiolated and eaten by rats over the years because I have lived in such meagre conditions as you will see, and have had as many as 16 places of residence since I set out to be an artist – being sold up most of the time.

There is one family tree with no dates, going back to my maternal grandfather, Joseph Hughes, who gave his wife, Mary, 20 children, 14 of whom were reared: what a walking archive they would have made had any of them been alive today! But I have an unusual memory, we all have, so I can remember a good deal. The only photograph of grandfather Hughes has been destroyed and no one in the family will admit to having a copy. It has almost given me a persecution mania trying to find one. It has been due to the kindness of another cousin whom I never see – Geoffrey Haslewood, Professor Emeritus of London University and former biochemist of Guy's Hospital – that I have a few fragile notes written down by my maiden Aunt Mabel before she died, very angry and disappointed with the world. These fit exactly into shards of memory which have helped me to build most of the original shape of an ancient vase that was once shattered by internal madness, drunkenness and tragedy, but with an unexpected flint of genius that never seemed to find the right stone to strike and make it give spark. Thus poverty dogged us and disappointment, but giving in return a certain wisdom, intelligence, humour and humanity that saved us from being lost in the sargasso of the mass mind – uniqueness which makes for originality, perhaps. What we did, we did well: it was not always pleasing to others, but we insisted that that is how it should be, so there was no conformity: only richness, but not riches: and we completed it.

My brother Jack and my sister Alma have been helpful with what photos there were and with checking points by memory. I don't think any family wants to be written about in case the laundry basket is opened too far: it makes them nervous and activates the family neurosis. But that is not my intention or wish, since this book is not about them but about me and my struggle to become – or to realise my capacity to be – an artist, which is far more difficult and certainly more rare than one would expect. To do this it is necessary to look at the nature of the ground out of which I grew and what obstacles caused my root to grow in one direction or another. Such things as the love of literature and philosophical thought my brother and I shared almost as a birthright, and the excitement of the professional stage in the days of the old Music Hall on which I worked as an adagio dancer, and shared with my sister, who was also in the same profession with her greatest friend whom I married. All such things are not only precious memories but part of the fabric of one's life and psyche as it expands into becoming an organism as complicated as a tree. So to them, loving thanks and apologies for disturbing the dung heap. My children also – sons Paul and Jasper and daughter Janet – a declaration of profound love before I fall off my own tree. By them I am increased.

Cousin Marjorie Foote (née Slade) for information and for passing the only copy of the family tree on to me. It has been very useful, and curiously sad. And to the ghost of her brother Anthony Slade, a beautiful and lucid painter who died young. He influenced me with his gentle and patient thoughts when I was a raging boy tearing at the curtains of the future.

I started late in life to write this book, when most of the key figures had died, and as there are no archives I have drawn largely on long talks I used to have with my mother, who could make the past come alive around her when she told me about her drunken father and her loneliness in Northern Sweden when she first married. About her brothers and sisters and the kind of life a large Victorian family had to lead in order to survive. She was a very small person with intense vitality which she would use up to the point of death from heart failure but return miraculously after a dose of Digitalis or Bella Donna, sit up in bed and say : 'I'm all right now dear!' and carry on with life as though nothing had happened. Sometimes, in the morning, when my father had already gone to catch his train and I was drinking my last cup of tea, she would suddenly say, 'O, come on, Sven, let's have another cup of congo and talk!' This we did. It was then that I was close enough to feel the love and devotion she had for us all, and the extraordinary courage with which she faced the loss of her home and endured shortages of food, which people today cannot conceive. Yet she was excited that I wanted to be an artist and encouraged me by talking about Whistler and Wilde whom her father knew and Augustus John whom her sister Dickie knew – even though no one had any idea how this obsession had come upon me or could be channelled so that I could learn the first prerequisite of the visual artist – to draw. It was the light she gave out that mattered. The unquestioning belief and the energy she transmitted ignited the first spark and I experienced the extraordinary sensation of seeing things in a new and unique way. For this and for that affection she pronounced by being at the fountain and giving me gold, I shall remember her in the distant kitchens of the past, under the South Tower of the Crystal Palace drinking tea, when there was no bread to make toast.

My father was less of a communicator, but spoke always of Sweden and his favourite brother, Sven, when it snowed in Sydenham and he would fly down Peak Hill with us on our Swedish sledge. He showed us the beauty of the ice flowers on the nursery window and the mystery of the stars on winter nights, which he loved secretly like a man who would go on an expedition to some high mountain if life had treated him differently. It was all these conversations with them both, which were the off-record things that make up a poetic structure in a separate slipstream of time, which helped me to understand them even when things were at their worst and torn by rage and nervous tension within a framework of starving respectability. They are top of my statement of credits, not for a photograph or for copyright permission, but for being what they were. Unique people. Which is the only way each of us can make a lasting contribution to the human scene. The greatest thing they gave me was the magic shuttle without which a man cannot create and that long silver cord of memory upon which I have relied to write this book. So to them, resting like sculptures of a King and Queen cut into a hill at Brighton I whisper my thanks.

Somehow a more dishevelled family fortune comes out of our London past than that of our Swedish relations, because they had risen from the depths created by Brody-Berlin to become the intelligentsia and nobility of the Swedish hierarchy. But in spite of our amputated education and hard rearing – or I think because of it – the dyke gates were left open enough to flush out any pretence and give a chance for any original force to activate. Many unknowns from the London streets and alleyways added to the voltages required for this, more than I could have generated. Even the snobs who tried to switch off the power added a positive tension by trying to defeat us.

Out in the field so much was given by such as Dr Turk, former Reader in Natural History at Exeter University, Jack Wilson, metallurgist of London and Arthur C. Hambly, painter and teacher of Cornwall. I can do no more than thank Dr Turk, the only survivor, for photos of all three of these wise persons and for anecdotes and information I had not recorded, correction of some that I had, like dates and places, and hope that in return for their influence my later pages on them are adequate. David Philips for friendship with himself and family at the Treleigh Vicarage when I was very poor and unknown and for a transparency of my first serious portrait in person, painted downstream 1939.

On the technical side concerning the hard task of finding photographs, records, permissions of copyright, Sarah Fox-Pitt and Adrian Glew of the Tate Gallery Archives have patiently contributed. Also the Keeper of Paintings at the Victoria & Albert Museum, the Keeper of Drawings at the National Library of Scotland, the Curator of the Musée de la Bataille de Normandy, Bayeux, France, the Keeper of the Ovar Museum, Portugal. John Coulter of the London Borough of Lewisham Archives for Sydenham, the Penwith Society of Arts in Cornwall, the St Ives Society of Artists. Roy Ray, Principal of the St Ives School of Painting; The Barbara Hepworth Museum, St Ives; The Central Office of Information, London; The Wills Lane Gallery, St Ives. All these people and organizations have contributed generous help to my long continuum – my Makemono – of research.

Richard and Beatrice Dopita took on the task of making photographs of my work for this book over two years.

Other photos are also credited individually where it has been possible. When I have been able to trace the photographer I have written for permission. Only in a few cases I have had no reply and unusually, when the photograph has been taken many years ago, I have accepted that they have gone away, gone missing, presumed dead. In that case I have used the photo and given credit in print, wholly contrite if it turns out that I am wrong. Some I might have overlooked, but not intentionally.

Among my special contributors are Gilbert Adams for permission to use the photographs he took of me in the forties outside my Tower at St Ives, and the sculpture of the Unknown Political Prisoner I carved in 1950, both full of Adam's magic. John Wells for the beautiful letter he wrote to me when I was in an Army asylum in 1945; used and abused by others it is now famous, but as far as I know has never been seen in its entirety as I received it among those broken men being repaired like ancient sculptures from a bombed city. It was as though I had had delivered to me in Hell by special messenger a private message from the Gods, which I was able to re-live later when I went to stay with its author on the Isles of Scilly.

It is now preserved in the Tate Archives. Dear ghosts such as Naum Gabo who so inspired me before I went to war in 1942 and to whom I owe my life by obeying the magic spell and advice he gave me when I went in as forward observer on the battlefield: I returned to thank him. In conjunction with the Tate, the St Ives Studio has been helpful in allowing me to reproduce the photograph of Gabo in his bungalow workshop at 'Faerystone', Carbis Bay, as well as one of Guido Morris inking the forme on the Albion Press which I called his 'Iron Soul' when I arranged a way of getting it sent from London to start up his Latin Press in St Ives in 1945–46, and with Bryan Wynter with whom I started a friendship of almost sinister humour and affection we fixed it for Guido to take over Carn Crows as his workshop, which then belonged to 'Gillie' Gilbert's father. To Hyman Segal I touch my white forelock for his cartoon of Endell Mitchell from his burlesque *Art Colony*; and Eric Quayle, a friend of later date, for his allowing a quote from a letter telling me of the death of Barbara Hepworth in 1975: a unique, private account.

Denis Mitchell gave me several stories I had half lost or forgotten, two of which I have used from recent letters. He and his brother Endell were good friends from these severe but inspired times. I thank Terry Frost for his great encouragement with my 'Autosvenography' and long friendship which, like a train, disappears and appears in the landscape of time, long enough for me to salute 'my first student' and he to sign himself 'love to my old master and friend'.

I thank Irving Grose for supplying photos taken by David Brown and a colour transparency of my painting, *Man and Woman with a Flower*, and others which still haunt me like the starving years when it was painted; David Edmunds, for a photo of my painting of *Nancemellin*; Alice Lenthall for *Treswithian Orchard*; Danny Andrews for photocopies of *Field Drawings*; John Polglaze for photos of Dr Frank Turk, Jack Wilson and Arthur C. Hambly; *Cutting the Lion* by Murray Hardy; Terry Frost by Dean Wilcox; COI for Crypt Group; Atelie Klang Sweden for Lt. Sven Berlin; photo and poem of Alfred Wallis, Nicholson & Watson 1949; drawings from *I am Lazarus*, Dent 1961; drawings and photos from *Cornish Review* 1949, edited by Denys Val Baker; also *Art Colony by the Sea*, Denys Val Baker 1959; Paul Elek for drawings from Peggy Pollard's *Cornwall* 1947; my drawings from *Dark Monarch*, Dent 1962; quotes from my book *Pride of the Peacock*, Collins 1972. Also my article, *Aspects of Creative Art in Cornwall*, Facet 1948. 'Joke Grimm', my poem to W.S. Graham written after his death in 1986, was first published in *Cornish Scene*.

A CREDIT ACCOUNT

I thank David Brown for his chronological grittern of dates in the Tate Gallery Catalogue St Ives Exhibition 1985; also to Rosemary Lloyd for checking my statement about teaching from her own experience; Polly Walker for her notes on her father, Alec Walker; and not least, Clara Sansom who had the difficult editorial task of fitting the Coat, so that the chalk marks would not show, and of preparing the index.

More latterly, I wish to thank, for his interest and encouragement, Michael Tooby, Director of The Tate at St Ives.

There are so many more not on my list but the groundswell that a book of this nature sets going has washed them temporarily from my mind. But not the image of Julia Berlin who has borne the silence, the isolation, the neurosis and secrecy a writer's wife endures as an inbuilt part of her endless task of providing coffee and shepherd's pie with equally endless devotion; and her vital insight, before which I kneel.

As the names go down, the patterns fall into place, the words and events weave their huge moving tapestry of colour and form and sound and feeling and sensation, intuition and thought that have made up the continuum of my horizontal image, flowing like a river into the sea, I am bewildered that so much has been caught and so much lost, so many faces of loved ones, and of vital enemies who tried to stop the flow, have been involved in my destiny so far as I have been able to take it, and, with the Gods in favour, I might be able to continue writing into the 30 years' exile until the present time when I prepare for a new and final exodus.

Above all, I am thankful to the Spirits who are always with me and who guide me in my work: among them the Muse, that enigmatic woman by the well who draws water from a deep place – making a poetic statement possible when nothing else will do. Who knows how?

My 'Oscar' nominations are: John Sansom for publishing the book and making it beautiful; Austin Wormleighton for introducing me to John Sansom; David and Tina Wilkinson for devotion to my work, and the vital art biblio control centre at their splendid Book Gallery, and Irving Grose for ending my exile of 30 years with a covenant of colour.

Other names of people vitally important to me, will be recorded in the second volume of this story: *Virgo in Exile*.

AUTHOR'S NOTE

An event is like a force passing under water: it causes a wave that lifts the swimmer on its surface, while he and the water itself stay still: it breaks where the water ends.

In some cases it is possible to divert this energy by building a wall so that it breaks elsewhere or passes us by, using up its strength as it goes.

Sometimes I have been able to do this with a serious event to save it shattering the lives of innocent people still living, which delays history for that one purpose. This I call the ethic of understanding the truth – knowing that a happening cannot unhappen once it has happened – or be denied: but it can have the destructive force taken out of it by using up its own strength and be diverted by silence unless the dykes are already broken.

PART ONE
THE WANDERING JEW

What rough beast, its hour come round at last,
Slouches towards Bethlehem to be born?

W.B. Yeats

Magnetic North

I believe that everything I paint is a self-portrait because it is part of intrinsic experience: so, too, with sculpture and writing. So it is difficult to make a book out of and about these three activities, without being charged with conceit, though I know vanity is fruitless and it is a first law of making a work of art that the ego must take off his shoes before he enters the temple. Virgil said of Charon: 'He was half a God and the old age of a God is tough and green!' Everyone who is touched by the Gods has vision and is touched also by the Goddess who belongs with them and inspires them to create, whose spirit reaches down to the wells of history, and of Sydenham Wells where I was born. It is from this source that I write my book.

I, who in old age am tough and green, come of a sudden to the crest of a hill and turning back see it all laid out before me, a vast landscape in which there are civilisations, cities, temples, minarets and palaces which I have discovered and created myself so that they are all part of my visual history. The history of my face, of my spirit, of my body, my hands, with which I worship life and transform it. To turn away from this task and leave it unfinished is death.

I have been for a walk through a ruined city with a tiger whose name is Time. He is a man-eater.

I met him first when I was a boy in Wells Park at Sydenham. It was raining and the nursemaids with their borrowed children ran for shelter. The soldiers wounded in the First World War, in their borrowed uniforms of cobalt blue with red tie and white shirt, hobbled to shelter, followed by the rancid tramps. All had been walking by the two ponds where the well sprang from the Norwood Hills and where they fed the ducks and flirted with the nursemaids in search of the goddess who would stir their manhood again and touch with poetry the iron reality that hemmed them in, demanding their lives.

The rain grew heavier making spiked German helmets on the surface of the pond. The tiger roared. I looked up and saw him staring out of the spotted laurel bushes. I pulled my mother's long skirt and pointed. She looked down at me with her gentle blue eye from under the shade of her grey velour hat with a red woollen rope around it. 'A tiger, Mother! Look!'

'Yes, dear. I know. But he won't hurt you. I expect he is a nice tiger!' She rushed me to the shelter where we stood with the randy soldiers and their nursemaids. I kept on but no one would believe there was a tiger. Their smiles were compassionate. 'What's 'e on about anyway. 'E must be dippy!'

Ever since that day I have been trying to tell people of another life and convince them of its existence. 'It's all imagination!' they said. Well. That's what I mean – penetrating our daily bread. But it didn't make any difference. They went on laughing and winking at one another until quite early I became maverick.

Now, as an old man, I stand on the hill with my tiger, who in spite of all has walked at my heel through forests of love, furnaces of war and the stark plains of starvation, far from those ruined cities of childhood, and I suddenly realise I know him better than my own mother or the man next to me in the pension queue. He is my self. He knows as I do that my life could not have been different, because of him. That had I turned from my purpose he would have struck me down. That I would have been destroyed if I had betrayed him to the powers of evil. That I would have been lost in the maze of lunacy if I had not held his eye with mine when no other could give help. That I would have been expelled forever if I had taken the coin so that I might eat the oat instead of a stone, when false prophets beckoned.

When he roars I am without fear.

Having written so many books about my experience of life, it is as though I write this book in reverse – I mean inside out and backwards – for you will know about people and things before they are said, sometimes just before they happen and will have time to consider what happened at the beginning because I have already been able to tell you at the end like a theme constantly recurring as a variation in a symphony. In this book I am like a sleeping man who is dreaming it all from the end backwards, but with experience, feeling, sensation, thought and intuition woven into the images that I created during my life by following the destiny of my own soul and deceiving time, which I shuffle like a pack of cards. It is quite a new way of looking at things perhaps and might point to insanity, but it is not that – it is simply outside reason – as a self-portrait is part of a horizontal continuum like a river: the personality also.

Mac Axel Christian Berlin, Order of the Polar Star. Lecturer in Mathematics and Philosophy at Uppsala University and Jönköping. Married to Alma Carolina Christina Scholander, of which union my father was the fifth of six sons, all of whom my father told me were beaten till the blood came. It is for this arctic rage which blew also through my own childhood I have named him Mad Mac and not from any lack of respect for honours bestowed for his talents.

The sons were all professional men. Mac, a medical doctor; Axel, a stockbroker; Erik, an apothecary; Alan, a civil engineer; Karl, a timber merchant (my father); and Sven a lojtnant ind Smarlands Husarregemente.

They were all born at Jönköping by Lake Vatten and lived respectable and successful lives. The strict upbringing included punishment for self abuse to a degree that my father tied his own hands behind his back to avoid being found guilty, the warring forces being left to work themselves out later, though he and his favourite brother, Sven, emerged as persons of some charisma. It was Sven after whom I was named. The darkness and oppression of our Victorian age did not begin to thaw in Sweden until well into the twentieth century. It was a miracle of fortune I was not born there.

Yet it was not Mad Mac Axel Christian Berlin, not my father, Wild Kalle who started the Berlin family flowing from the North, but a wandering Jewish rabbi who preached the Talmud through Europe at a time when there was great discrimination against his race. David Abraham Brody, born in Frankfurt an der Oder in 1742. Although Jewish liberation was to start in 1789, the anti-semitic disabilities were strong. There were pogroms. Many thousands fled to America, among them probably those who were exiled already from Russia and the Holy Land itself. In 1771 the young Brody travelled north through Schlegwig Holstein into Denmark, by ass or horse or on foot, to cross at Helsinger where the channel is frozen over in winter to Halsingborg and settled in Malmö in south Sweden.

In 1771 a strange and unexpected thing was to happen and I first thought it was as much to do with the Ice Queen of the North as with the inhuman pathological hatred of the Jews in Europe. He changed his name and his religion. He was christened in Caroli Church in Malmö, taking the name Johan Christian Berlin. Berlin, no doubt because it was the capital of the country in which he was born and had wandered studying and preaching the Talmud: and of which also Frankfurt an der Oder was almost near enough to be a suburb of that great city. In reverence also for his people who would have come from the Holy Land through the Czech countries to Berlin, hoping for sanctuary, as indeed the gypsies did from India, significantly marking a point in history where two wandering races met, later to be almost exterminated by the Prince of Evil: some going on to Sweden and to England, as would my father later. It could well have been that it was because Brody openly preached the Talmud that he became a marked man and fled to Sweden, where he changed his name and religion to save his life: also to marry. It was as though the life-force had swept him there, but instead of becoming a great writer or painter out of this rich experience, as I had hoped, he is recorded as marrying Sofia Elisabeth Wendt and settling down as a grain merchant. Never mind, I told myself, both Constable's and Rembrandt's fathers were millers – a vital enough trade to be significant, broadcasting his seed in Sweden. Here I was going to leave it, when I got a letter from Gunhild Aberg of Bromma who was helping me with research. She had spoken to a Jewish historian who said that 'Jews who wanted to immigrate into Sweden had to fulfil some conditions, 1. a testimony showing he had a profession in the country he left, 2. recommendations from an employer, 3. a lot of money, 4. a protecting Jew who would take care of him and control his employment. Our forefather did not fulfil any of these conditions. How could he then get into Sweden and stay there? 1. He joined a great group of travellers: the suite round the German Prince Heinrich. In Malmö he left the group. Because he did not fulfil the conditions, he ought to have been ordered out of Sweden. But he solved the problem. He became a Christian. Smart but not quite honestly.'

I insert this factual information into my original text for it is also my belief that he was a lone traveller otherwise and would have mingled with the Prince's cortège probably from Helsinger to Halsingborg. The two accounts fit perfectly together.

'The Swedes have always seen him as a Sloven.' This came also from my cousin Gunhild Aberg of Bromma. I had started the research late in life and was anxious to get a clear light on the arctic wastes of my ancestral past before it was too late. Gunhild Aberg, daughter of my father's brother Erik, made it possible. We had not, as far as I remember, corresponded before, but patiently and kindly she took up the story in Sweden, researching into the achievements of Sven Hedin at the Ethnological Museum in Stockholm which contains the Hedin Museum, and at the House of Nobility to check the honours bestowed. Also the tiny Berlin Museum in Ystad, her original house set up by Charlotte Berlin and left to the nation. But most revealing and valuable of all was the research into the behaviour and life of Brody-Berlin, the arch-villain. It was triggered by my defending him when she wrote that 'the Swedes looked upon him as a Sloven'. I had said that whatever he was I thought he was a man of originality and courage in preaching the Talmud in a genocidal Europe, then crossing the ice as a lone *illegal immigrant*, to change his name and religion and start one of the famous families of his adopted country. After some weeks of silence Gunhild replied with the following letter in which she had transposed into English for my benefit passages from the *Memoirs of Aaron Isaak*, the first Jew to *legally* immigrate to Sweden. By the quite clearly written truthful prose of this Swedish lady I was suddenly shocked into understanding what kind of man Brody-Berlin was: how he appeared, like Mephistopheles and, quite as mysteriously, disappeared. Here is the letter.

Dear Sven,

In order to describe our 'first father' as exact as possible, I have read the *Memoirs of Aaron Isaak* and also a book on the Jews in Sweden. Berlin and Aaron met in the street in Malmo and Berlin said: "Scholaum Alekham, Rabbi Aaron" (Peace be with you). Aaron asked: "How do you know me?" and Berlin told: "For about four years I was a wandering Talmud student and stayed with you over the Sabbath. My name was then Abraham Brody. Now I am a Christian and my name is Berlin. On Sunday I went begging as Talmud students always do. I came to your door and knocked and stepped in. Nobody was there. A pair of black silk stockings were hanging on the chair. It was 1769 in Butzow. I took these because I needed them very well and went out. On the way out I met your wife and said good day and asked her for money for travelling. She gave me four skilling and a piece of bread and butter. I went away together with a friend. None of us could get a job."

Berlin insisted to invite Aaron to his home. Aaron was irritated by obstinacy but when he said he had a great house (probably belonged to his brother-in-law or to the Vicar) and that his wife would like to meet another Jew because she had only met one Jew till now, Aaron decided to follow him. He found Berlin's wife pleasant. They had a child of about four weeks, their second born in 1773. (Parish register).

According to Aaron Isaak, "Berlin had got his wife in a strange way."

Brody-Berlin had decided to convert, but as he could not understand Swedish, he asked to be instructed by the Vicar of the German Parish. During this time he lived in the Vicar's house. The Vicar had no wife and no children but a niece who helped him with the housework. To cite Aaron Isaak: "Brody and the young lady met and he made her pregnant". She had a sister who was married to a wealthy merchant and they urged Sophia (born Wendt) to leave Berlin, who still had no job, but she answered: "The man who has taken my honour shall give me my honour back."

People said that the Vicar had plenty of money. Berlin took care of him while he was ill. This must have been between the baptising of Brody and the wedding in 1771. The Vicar died of a heart attack the day after the wedding. When he died it was evident he had no money left. This fact might have changed B's and his young wife's lives. Berlin still lived a merry life; he was every day in the wine-house; treated anyone and let money run away. He bragged of his life but still had no job. His wife and little son lived by relatives. He bought "licence for commerce" but never practiced as a business man.

When Aaron Isaak was planning to go to Stockholm, Berlin insisted to accompany him. He said that he had 6000 Daler in a bank in Stockholm, and that he knew the Duke Karl very well and could introduce Aaron to him. His wife asked Aaron to persuade him to stay at home: she was anxious because of his extravagances. By that time Aaron had begun to distrust Berlin and tried to shake him off. "He was a bad man who every day was drunk and fought with everybody." On the tour to Stockholm Aaron did not mention anything to Berlin about his plans.

In June 1774 they arrived in Stockholm. At 9 o'clock Berlin left Aaron waiting and went to look for lodging. Two hours later Berlin was back and said: "Stockholm is a very unsafe town. Of course you can find a lodging, but you can also get murdered. Here is very dangerous for foreigners." He would be back in half an hour. He was not back by two o'clock and Aaron had found himself good lodgings with two rooms. After two hours yet Berlin came. He was drunk and said he had been seeking Aaron the whole time. "I thought you were murdered . . . Every

day someone is murdered in Stockholm." When Aaron
came home the host called him and said: "You may stay
here but I have kicked out Berlin. He said so indecent
words to my wife that I will not mention them. He ought
to have a thrashing, that indecent man." Next day Berlin
was waiting for Aaron at the gate. He had found a new
lodging by a kind widow. After a week she came to Aaron
and complained about Berlin. "He is a debauche and does
not leave me in peace. He must out of my house." Aaron
gave Berlin 100 Daler. He drove round town and when
the money was consumed, he (as Aaron believed) went
back to his family. But he never came back to his wife and
she and the two sons afterwards lived at the Poorhouse.
Where were the 6000 Daler? Sorry, I have not found
anything good to say about Brody-Berlin.

The letter from Gunhild, except for a few notes, ends here. Berlin-
Brody disappeared altogether. There is no record of his death. He
was a drunk and the worse, because he did not seem to eat, and
probably died of malnutrition. Also amoral. It is thought he may
have been murdered. It is the kind of make-up that has often gone
with a man of great creative power, like François Villon, Lord
Byron, Gauguin, Verlaine and Dylan Thomas. But genius needs
three things to survive and express itself: freedom of personality,
talent and self-discipline. Brody, like an eagle with one wing, had
only the first of these. He could not take flight and smashed up
everything around him till he was destroyed. I still think he was a
man of original force and power and lived to become the conscience
of the family he created producing one of the great explorers of our
time. While Goethe was beginning to write *Faust* in Frankfurt Brody
was a living Faust. I wonder what his family would have thought of
their 'First Father' if he had been the poet himself instead of the
subject of the poem? They contain all that he was, and all that he
failed to become. Moi aussi.

Carl Jung was convinced that Faust was the answer Goethe had
given to his time and quotes 'Two souls, alas, are housed within my
breast.' Out of this has come good as well as evil.

Brody-Berlin's son, the half-Jew, Johann Ludwig, was born in the
Poorhouse where he lived with his mother till he was 16, then got
employment as a clerk to the district Judge. He was clever and
worked hard. He became upper clerk and finally bailiff. Then he
left to become bailiff at Marsvinsholms to Count Piper.

One of Ludwig's four sons, Gissel Berlin, rose to be Dean of Balkakra. He married Anna Catharina Nordström and was awarded the Order of the North Star. It was through the marriage of their daughter Anna Berlin to the Town Architect of Stockholm, Ludwig Hedin that Gissel and his wife became grandparents to Sven Hedin the explorer, born in 1865 in Stockholm. Anna Berlin (his mother) and Mac Berlin (my grandfather) were brother and sister, making Sven Hedin cousin to my father, Karl Gustav Herman Berlin. So bringing two great families together by the advent of a great explorer.

A note on Sven Hedin is relevant because, although I never met him, he was a major influence on my early life. I risk a grain of boredom which will grow later in the warmth of my book if I plant it here, and become meaningful.

I quote from the *Encyclopedia Britannica*.

SVEN HEDIN was educated at Stockholm High School and Uppsala University. Studied in Berlin and Halle. 1885–86 he travelled through Persia and Mesopotamia and in 1890 was attached to King Olaf's Embassy to the Shah of Persia. In the same year he visited Khurasan and Turkestan and reached Kasligar in 1891. His travels in Tibet placed him in the first rank of modern Asiatic Explorers. In 1902 he became a Swedish Noble. In 1909 the Indian Government invested him with the K.C.I.E. He was one of the 18 members of the Swedish Academy. He wrote many books. Was honoured worldwide with gold medals from Ethnological Institutes of 12 countries.

Sven Hedin was also awarded the Order of the Polar Star 'with brilliants', twice, as a personal gift from King Oscar II – the second time as Knight Commander and was the last Swede to be made a noble, which is significant because it will have marked the end of the old feudal system and the domination of the army classes, to be slowly replaced by a greater leniency toward the peasants by Gustav V, who came to the throne in 1907, and a much needed evolutionary move toward Socialism.

Of the many books Hedin wrote about his explorations in Asia were two thick red volumes published in English by Macmillan in 1910, titled *Trans-Himalayas*, as well as *Overland to India* and *Pole-to-Pole*, all to be found in my father's book case. Besides the text they were illustrated by fine, precise topographical drawings and portraits by himself of peasants and tribesmen of central Asia and Sherpas. There are also photographs of him in deep snows and being charged by a wounded yak or fighting his way in a blizzard through an unknown mountain pass. He was an explorer emblematic of the spirit of man questing the centuries, entering forbidden cities, finding new continents, unearthing forgotten temples, discovering images of art, climbing mountains, crossing unknown oceans and deserts. I read the books avidly. I wanted to be an explorer.

For some reason of his own Sven Hedin was pro-German in both World Wars. Because of this, his books were taken from the shelf at home and hidden in a cupboard. His name was not mentioned, which I as a young boy found it difficult to understand. The Swedish colony in England no longer boasted of him: they seemed ashamed. 'He knew the Kaiser!' it was said almost in a whisper.

At the beginning of the First World War Sweden was erroneously believed to have entered into a pact with Germany until her King made a declaration of neutrality. Her fleet tried to prevent military operations in Swedish territorial waters. There were great food problems: 280 of her merchant ships were sunk by German U-boats and mines. It was known that a 'small group of activists' urged intervention on the side of Germany, but most Swedes wanted neutrality, which was maintained.

My father carried on business in London and even travelled to Sweden in a cargo ship to see his family during the war. No one troubled him. The only indication of his being an exile, which he proudly remained all his life, was that his business notepaper read: K.G.H. Berlin (Swedish). When the war was over, Hedin's books came back to the shelves and the Swedes swanked about their countryman, the Explorer. As with Rubens it was a mistake to have played 'the Little Statesman'. To have entered Lasha when it was still a forbidden city and to have crossed the Gobi Desert, was far more important. His genius was for finding unknown places on earth. It is a fitting tribute that a mountain on the moon has been named after him.

The one thing lacking was imagination. Explorers are logical, scientific people: they seldom write great books. Think if Thor Heyerdal's *Kon Tiki* had been written by the author of *Moby Dick* what an excitement it would have been! Apart from good painters and writers, two great women artists who have come out of Sweden during my lifetime and influenced me: Greta Garbo as Christina of Sweden was one. Mai Zettering, whom I knew and loved, proved her greatness in *The Master Builder* and *The Wild Duck*.

I say this with caution because inherent in every great race is the spirit of at least one great artist every century. It is not surprising that the Swedes got the balance wrong to allow this to happen if you look at the pure Viking (the ocean traveller, the Fjord Man) and what he was: a wild man controlled by the need to form communities for he had only the wood, the herring and the iron to sustain him to build beautiful and safe ocean going ships which demanded high craftsmanship in wood and metal to produce a longship like part of a great bridge or building – a construction by Naum Gabo. It is for this they are renowned as great seamen and engineers. I have long believed the engineers were for centuries ahead of the abstract artist. Concorde is the greatest sculpture in space made by man. The wild fury with which the Vikings plundered the Western Isles was the obverse side of the creative spirit. When they got themselves under control finally and became Christians they still cut off the heads of those who kept allegiance to Odin. It became an oppressive force and a strict orthodox morality to hold down the wild man who is not only the destroyer but he who creates. In each of them remains the icy blast of rage from the arctic ranges which I instinctively recorded as a boy coming from my father and grandfather. When such a fury is harnessed to the single rogue Rabbi Brody-Berlin it was not without sanctuary – a troubled sanctuary at that. Henry Treece has written the best sentence to cover this wild race of men who were never fully tamed. 'Vikings are tied to salt water as a prisoner is tied to chains! No, there's no understanding them! They are either madmen or heroes!'

Although I was early to realise I could not become an explorer I was led by Hedin's influences to discover the ancient tombs of the mind which visual images awakened in me and with which their secret chambers are filled. The living Gods and Goddesses who guard them in those ruined cities through which my tiger has led me down the years have taught me to weave them into the fabric of daily life through the rare and extraordinary processes of art. It is because of this kind of deep influence on the spirit and the mind that I single out any unique person among my forebears, believing as I do that the power of life impinges on certain ones to transform it into creative force, in one form or another, which finally widens the consciousness of man and advances evolution. If this does not come about the force becomes destructive and erases the individual, even a whole epoch. So it is not for emulation that I cite them, but to indicate the forces that have directed me in my search for beauty and truth. Since I was rather unwillingly spun into writing this book

34

about myself by the centrifugal force of someone who had already started to do it and abandoned ship, I had to turn quickly on my own axis and recentre gravity or the energies released would have destroyed me, and I now am compelled to do it in the only way I can, by talking about these things of which so little is known, because that is why I have lived as I have and become what I am. I want to catch, if I can, the moment of contact, be it God or man, with whom I am mysteriously engaged as was Jacob with the angel, wrestling through till dawn and walking away with a limp, not really knowing what had happened. That is the reason for my work and for my being. Within that moment is hidden the radium of truth which might give out a small but intense light when I have struck camp and moved on.

Sven Hedin was a questing person, alone, never married, giving out that remoteness I remember coming from Ernest Shackleton who used to live in a house at Sydenham next door to the church where I was christened and confirmed, St Bartholomew's, which Pissarro included in his painting of the *Chain Road* when he was in England with Monet in 1871 as a refugee from the Franco-Prussian War. But I was not named after Sven Hedin, who seemed a morose melancholy sort of man, though I am assured otherwise.

I was named after Sven Berlin, sixth son of Mad Mac and my father's favourite brother. There was only three years between them, Sven being born in 1888 just 100 years from the moment I write these words.

They grew up together in the small town of Jönköping beside Lake Vatter not far from Stockholm. They used to swim out to an island as young men and walk together and ski in the forests. Like my brother and I they were friends for life and, by my guess, a good deal after. When in later years my father Karl, or Kalle as he was known, came to visit me in the New Forest, where for a time after leaving Cornwall I was living rough with the gypsies, he vanished for a long period. After searching anxiously, for in those days he could well have been lost in a bog, I found him under some ancient but very tall pines, marching up and down singing Swedish songs – ones, he explained, he used to sing with his brother Sven when they walked in the forest in Sweden as boys.

Sven was a soldier. He studied military matters and was instructed in the horse at St Cyr L'Ecole Special Militaire en France, and at the Military School at Somyr. It seems that great things were expected of him and Sven Hedin was particularly interested in his career. But as his grandson, Steffan Berlin, writes to me

He was pretty young in the beginning of his career with a great potential (35 years of age), it is always easy to give him a 'saint-status', if you know what I mean. Nevertheless he must have been a quite remarkable man with lots of friends and supporters. All people who have met him always tell very positive things about him.

He, Sven, visited us in Sydenham just after the First World War in 1922. In his diary for May of that year, 8th–31st, he writes that he found my brother Jack 'pretty hard to get contact with and, according to Kalle, pretty objectionable to his mother. Sven was much more easy to approach. Alma served me tea at the bed every morning and was like a quicksilver ball, pretty tall for her age (about 7) and very well grown. Kalle didn't dislike to return to Sweden if opportunity were given. Billy also seems to accept.'

Billy was my mother's nickname: a great Swedish obsession. She could not return of course because of her weak heart. That remained the lock on the chain that kept Karl exile. I have often wondered if it was Sven's mission to bring about his return.

I remember Sven as a tall good looking man in a well cut suit, wavy black hair, carrying a black ebony stick with a silver top embossed with the three crowns of Sweden, his bowler hat in the other hand, as he walked with my father, Karl Gustav, up the suburban hill to our Victorian semi-detached house with peeling stucco. They were laughing and talking together and the anxious look that usually haunted my father's face because of money matters was gone, showing his naturally fine features and broken nose done when skiing. These visits from Sweden were an extension of another life that was dreamlike, curious and well-to-do, to us young boys already feeling the screws of reality as my father's business faltered and finally went into bankruptcy.

Unbelievably, a year later Sven Berlin was dead. He remained crystallized for me as that tall charismatic figure who was never able to finally express the gifts that the life force had put upon him or even know how they would finally emerge. There is no doubt he had all the prerequisites of an explorer and it could well be that Sven Hedin hoped he would extend his own discoveries, but that is only surmise on my part. The interesting thing is that the negative theme announced itself so suddenly in the unfinished symphony and destroyed him. My brother, Jack, did seem to take to him. 'I remember a rather arrogant, dashing man,' he said in later life. 'A brilliant young officer!' Alma, my sister, was reserved, slightly enigmatic. 'He trod on something of mine and broke it. Then he pushed it aside with his foot without saying anything, as though it didn't matter. So I never quite got there!' She didn't say what it was he broke. And what if we had gone back to Sweden?

All this might seem like family gossip and probably is, but it does also show this little group, like a clutch of different shaped stones and how they related to one another for just that one fleeting moment in a bygone age. For me it struck a spark which is quite illuminating and helps me to present my story, and to respect the devil at my elbow.

Sven Berlin was on a military manoeuvre in the Swedish Forest, acting as assistant to the inspector of cavalry, General Duke Reinhold Von Rosen, which was an assignment for three years, given him two weeks before the fatal accident. He was riding his horse, Hawaii, who threw him and he broke a rib which, it is now thought, pierced his liver. My father told me he insisted on resuming command until the exercise was complete. Details in research always vary, so I take the middle path and present it as true. The resulting damage caused a septic condition which penicillin would have cured. After 11 operations he died at the Sabbatsberg Hospital in Stockholm.

I remember his mother, Alma, writing to Karl saying Sven was shrunk almost to the size of a child before he died. This beautiful person was destroyed by his devotion to duty which might have still been avoided but for the same obstinacy that enabled Abraham Brody and Sven Hedin to reach their targets. In this case it was a negative result, whereas, had it been in battle, it would have been positive. Yet it is this that perpetuates the memory of an unusual man. I never knew what it was that caused Hawaii to throw him: at what moment of tension between man and horse.

His wife Ruth received a letter of condolence from the Swedish Queen Victoria. Sven was given an 'honoured funeral'.

In 1923 Ruth visited us in Sydenham on her way to the middle east to get over Sven's death. I remember a very beautiful woman with a black veil who gave me my first £1 note.

I had a curious Jewish friend whose hobby was conjuring. Whenever I had any money, which was not often, he used to borrow it to practise a new trick. He took the £1 note Ruth had given me and made it disappear. When I asked him to make it come back he said he had forgotten how. I never saw it again. This created in my mind the truth that money is a myth, which has lasted all my life. It never comes back. Art remains.

The theme of destiny persisted on the male side of this unusual family. I remember two of the brothers suddenly dying, reported to Karl in letters from his mother, who sat there like an old snow eagle by the lake at Jönköping crocheting mandalas for her large family, as though she were using the threads of their lives. Mad Mac had long ago died, though his thunder, followed by lightning from those snowy mountains, reached us when my father was in a rage.

The eldest son, also bearing Mac's name, a family doctor, was going on an outing one day in 1928. He left his family outside in the sleigh while he went back in the house to get something he had forgotten and hanged himself on the mantelpiece. He had not slept for three years.

Axel collapsed in the street in Hamburg in 1926 with a heart attack.

My own father died quite suddenly of a ruptured aortic aneurism in 1973, and I myself skidded across the vortex with a sudden haemorrhage in 1985 caused by rage at a sculpture of mine being vandalised at Poole College of Further Education in Dorset, which reduced me to a reclining figure in white alabaster in need of a huge and immediate blood transfusion. I recovered to write this.

It is not by chance that these moments of violent death have come about. That becomes clear to me as I write. And now I know how the machinery works I can even tell when they are near because, as an artist, one learns something more than most people about one's own processes. It is sometimes the obverse side of the creative act that brings them about as in the spoiling of my *Madonna and Child*. They are not all on the Swedish side as I will show later, but at this point I think it worth saying that in the Swedish connection there is inherited a pulse of manic depression which is an unconscious condition of the Swedish race, perhaps because they have not been able to release themselves in war or art as a complete nation for centuries, their economic and geographical needs demanding that they become men of reason. Great engineers, seafaring men, priests, philosophers and teachers – only in early time great fighters, seldom, it seems, great artists. The sanctions imposed by Mad Mac on the creative impulses of his six sons seems to be emblematic of this condition, which even filtered through to myself and my brother as children. I can remember my father chasing us with a cane down the suburban hill where we lived to thrash the lives out of us when we were caught, which, thank goodness, was not often. And even if we were and sustained scars, humour dissolved it into a domestic comedy at which we laughed when it was over. For my father, like Brody-Berlin, loved life and the ladies so much that he could not be serious about any delinquency for long, even though he was a highly responsible citizen and family man: not an alcoholic or lecher.

We finished up saying our prayers to compensate. 'God bless Grandma in Sweden. God bless Uncle Sven and Auntie Dickie and Jack and Alma and Dad and Mother. Amen.'

Entering the dark palaces of my arctic ancestors – and indeed of the Ice Queen herself – has not been easy or without fear of the unknown terrors being awakened: anguish of souls unfulfilled or spirits tormented by love. If one enters too far into the family psyche or the psyche of the race out of which one grows, it means entering a vast unconscious continent of whose forces nothing is known. It brings about fragmentation of the mind which in turn could lead to insanity, and like Theseus one would not be able to return. They are regions which should be explored but only with serious purpose for short periods or you grow into the rock.

I have therefore stepped with reverence and respect toward those who are in the keeping of their God, lest I should stir his anger at disturbing him, and the Goddess who presided over their lives. Sven Hedin did not ask the blizzard if he could go through the unknown mountain pass. Nor have I asked permission and have ventured only to throw light on those who have themselves lit the way for me on a journey of the spirit through the universe though it be no more than a single crystal of snow dissolving in the spring sunlight. I know I have created it.

Out of this experience there is one thing of which I am quite certain. Under the silence of the ice of Sweden there is a great symphony waiting to be born and her own Sibelius waiting there also to create it. She must not prevent him by the negative anger in her soul when he appears a little drunk and wayward in his behaviour. He carries the genius of the race.

My father, Karl Gustav, trained in the forests of North Sweden at Umeå, just below the Arctic Circle, to become a forester and a timber merchant. He seems to have loved it well up there, perhaps because he was a misfit in an organised and pre-destined family. As part of that training he came to London as a young man to work on the wharfs of the Thames and the timber yards of New Cross, having travelled from Sweden by cargo boat, repeating without his knowing the history of Abraham Brody in taking his seed to generate in another country. There he gained experience in an unobtrusive way among the British workmen. The Cockneys loved

him right away. His honest, naive personality was the exact foil for
their rather piss-taking humour which made him laugh and pleased
that he was singled out for comment. They affectionately called him
'Bloody old Charlie!' or 'The Dook!'

'Look art. Ere comes Bloody old Charlie!' they shouted when he
arrived in the morning. It was always like that, even when he got
on; or later was very poor. They helped him and made fun, which
in turn he understood and laughed like a silver chain – at himself
and the things they said.

When he arrived in England, quite alone, as his forefather the
Wandering Jew had arrived in Sweden, the pivot he turned on was
also a simple religious one. He went to the Swedish Church in
London and asked the Vicar to recommend lodgings. The Vicar sent
him to an address in Beulah Hill in South Norwood to the family of
Joseph Hughes.

I don't know how destiny arranges these things, but if you watch
a bull take cow in a field you will realise how accurately evolution
fires its arrows.

Joseph Hughes was born at Stalybridge in Cheshire, the son of a
poor Welsh ironmonger, probably from Tonypandy. They had a
hard time but Joseph seems to have had an inborn brilliance and
passed a scholarship to Westminster College. He became a distinguished linguist with seven languages and set up as an
educational publisher in London, writing and publishing his own
books on mathematics and language. He married Mary Locking of
Cottingham, Hull, from a family of Quakers who even wore the
bonnet and shawl of that simple but unique sect. In the churchyard
at Cottingham there is one Locking who was physician to the King
of Sweden, so the destinies had already pointed a finger in the right
direction. Joseph gave her 20 children, 14 of whom she reared. But
hardship, following like a great pike, snipped off the rest of the
young as they trailed behind mother duck: a sweet, gentle,
exhausted soul who died at 60. But when Joseph came to London
and set up his business in Pilgrim Street he became prosperous, even
keeping his own parents as well as his huge family. He published the
London Teachers Magazine, at which all the girls were expected to
correct proofs and their mother to write the monthly article for
women, signed Marie Louise. Before he started to publish he had
run his own school, Pontefract College for Boys in Yorkshire, which
no doubt gave him experience in handling large numbers of children
to the best advantage. He was terribly strict and some of the
daughters hated even kissing him.

I have a small family tree which records 17 children but no dates. With my Swedish research I had large pedigrees to call upon with highly accurate tabulation, which in itself speaks of a certain wildness and disorder in the Hughes family. There may have been more or less of them. One thing seems certain, even though Joseph became relatively rich, the gradual deterioration seems to have started when someone conned him into buying a magazine on the theatre and the arts which proved to be on its last legs and it broke him.

At this time they lived in south London in a Georgian house on Beulah Hill where my mother was born in 1882. It was there also that the leading people of the Victorian art world came to see Joseph. He was friends with Whistler, Wilde, Sydney Grundy, Frank Harris, Ruskin and Charles Spurgeon, the controversial preacher who built a tabernacle at Southwark and privately christened one of Joseph's favourite daughters. A mixed bag. As always with the artists they got him drinking after being a total abstainer. The daughter they called Dickie, because she was born between the two boys, Tom and Harry, remembered sitting opposite Oscar Wilde in a horse bus. He was dressed in checked trousers, a cloak and a wide-awake-hat holding a walking stick between his legs. He smiled at her. Later Dickie married into Augustus John's family and thus the curious charisma of the artists flowed into my branches.

At the centre of all this was the little Welshman, Joseph and his wife, Mary from whom he expected so much, such as coming home at 9.30 or later with a large joint of pork and insisting it was cooked that evening, even though she was pregnant. He is recorded as being mad on water and baths, had a good singing voice and was a wonderful dancer. No doubt there were parties when the artists were around. Mary, though so suppressed, must have had some command in the bed because there were at least eight beautiful daughters around with heavy lidded blue eyes and long hair. Except, that is for Hannah, who herself said she was called Dickie because, when she got ringworm, they shaved her head and made her wear a lace cap, which made her look like a boy. She was dark and next in line to Mary Louise who was fair and blue eyed. What a net to be caught in! Dickie was a painter from early days. A generous colourful person who influenced my life greatly by injecting imagination that was missing from the arctic wind blowing down from Sweden and which brought Karl Gustav Berlin to the Thames and London.

The meeting of the artists was important because it is they who carry the chalice of the human spirit in every age even though it is nearly always half-full of whisky: not bruised or beaten back at birth as in the north. It is poured forth. But where this happens there is also disaster, for the coin of creation has a dragon on the back whose name is death. Joseph Hughes, who was a dynamic personality, had not the alchemy to deal with this. The phoney magazine sank. The tiny Titan had hit an iceberg.

One day he disappeared. There was no organised searching in those days and a week of anxiety was lived through until a hansom cab turned up at the house, a body was tipped out on the ground and the cabby drove off. It was Joseph, not dead but deeply drunk, dressed in workman's clothes; his own clothes, his rings, his gold watch, his wallet all gone. Some thoughtful cabby who remembered Joseph's big tips, past generosity and friendliness, had found him in a back alley and brought him home.

This happened again – and then again – as he got drunk out of his mind. At first it was said to be only beer. Later it was brandy, the Golden Lady whom you must not hold too lovingly or lie with for too long. She is insatiable and has the tongue of a viper. He died penniless at the age of 96 in the poorhouse, drawing an uncanny parallel with Brody-Berlin and his wife and sons.

I met him once. A small man with a silver beard who talked to me about mathematics with a voice like a ringmaster, shrouded in cigarette smoke. There is no longer a photograph of him extant.

So it was his kingdom collapsed and Mary needed help. The vicar told her of a young man from Sweden looking for lodgings. She took him in.

Karl was always a woman's man who sauntered between the girls with gallantry as they came and stood aside to look at him. He always loved them. But for six or eight to be casting a fly was abnormal choice and temptation. Dickie took a shine to him but no doubt her shaven head put him off. The others were interested in the handsome young Swede, not with the flaxen hair and blue eyes of the Vikings, but with the black hair and brown eyes of the Wandering Jew. Among the other girls who would have been eligible at that time there was Lottie, who later married a surgeon from St Thomas' Hospital, John Henderson Bell, but she had her father's predilection for drink, bringing again great tragedy in its wake. Flossie, too, who later gave me my first experience of the country way of life at her Apple Tree Cottage in Suffolk, a life to which I finally returned, and Margaret (known as Maggie), who remained unmarried and was an assistant matron at Guy's Hospital,

and went later to America to nurse the film stars, Will Rogers and
Alma Talmadge among them. For me, the most notable was Buster
Keaton, the great comic of silent film who enchanted my childhood,
because later I was to meet and work with the great comedians of
English music hall like Max Miller, Nervo & Knox, Charlie
Naughton, Bud Flanagan, Eddie Gray. They were a race apart who
contributed to the human scene far beyond the perimeter of their
calling: artists of timeless laughter.

So I end my posse of young ladies. Although there were more I
have enough to show that when the whole orchestra is gathered
together the pulse of destiny still throbs under the themes of love and
death, hatred and desolation, joy and happiness, with the emphasis
first here, then there and every now and again choosing a victim to
take the penalty for the others. I was the Family Madness -

> I am the family madness
> Who comes and goes
> In each generation:
> In me fantasies press
> For exultation of the rose
> And truth.
> No one can understand
> Why, in the junk shop of the heart,
> I rape Dol then, to perplex,
> I write with blood-stained hand
> A poem of exquisite art on sex.
>
> I am the maniac who, out-priced
> At auction of the family things,
> Looks out from the face
> Of uncle and aunt in painted lace
> To break the image in old mirrors,
> Crack the countenance,
> And thus my father's law deface
> In lunacy without disgrace
> Until they turn the key
> And I am locked away
> And once more again am poor:
> The vagabond in the workhouse
> Who waits the Guardians to eke out an oat
> Or fill my golden bowl
> And silver spoon.

I am my mother's teaset
On a Sunday afternoon.
Behind that mad look
I love gentleness and peace
And things of great beauty:
One day I will write a book.

None of those young ladies was the one who was to carry my life like a fragile glass into the future. It was to be little Mary Louise, with her delicate health and frail stature, heavy blue eyes, now recovering from rheumatic fever and wanting to be a sculptor, who struck Karl in the solar plexus with a tension and strength from which he could not escape. When a woman has done this to a man, like the falcon who was the bird of the Goddess Circe, she has made her kill. The transference is complete. Her image is the image within him after which he longs. No other woman can intervene. I believe he had to take her from a young Indian who was paying his attentions and followed the pair about the residential roads of Norwood. But this was a foil. She turned and struck. They were in love. They got engaged.

After this he returned to Sweden to tell his family, arrange a wedding and to continue his work in the Northern forests. No one of the Hughes family but Mary Louise thought he would return. Even the vicar had his doubts. But Karl, being a man of truth, did return and took her to the great frozen north which was his homeland, right up to the little town of Umeo on the Gulf of Bothnia just below the Arctic Circle where Lapland begins. There they were married and soon after they were settled Mary became pregnant. She found the cold and the isolation, intensified by her lack of language, the silent wooden buildings painted red oxide or black and white, yellow ochre with flashes of red or blue, and only the sound of the silver bells of the sleigh horses, almost unbearable: also the Swedes, whom she found insular and inquisitive with little humour. There was a family nurse called Fastra who seemed to have looked after her. There was a feeling that the family in this small village of Sweden resented her as of different class and a poor outsider from England, not suitable for Karl. But Fastra was her lifeline and gave her great love.

One day she was out for a walk alone. It came on to snow heavily and she fell down a pit half covered with pine branches. Probably an old bear trap. She was too short to reach the top and being pregnant could not climb out. She was there for several hours until

44

a gang of foresters, Karl among them, came by on their return home from work. She was just able to attract their attention and they rescued her. As a result of this experience she became very ill. The earlier attack of rheumatic fever, from which she was recovering when she met Karl, had damaged one of the valves of her heart. She would be an invalid and probably not survive the winter if she remained on the Arctic Circle. The doctor ordered her to return to England, in time for my brother Jack to be born.

I don't think Karl's family were pleased about this, but he was very good and reversed all his plans for the future and took her back across the North Sea to become an exile for the rest of his life. They settled in Beckenham, Kent. I don't think they had any money and while Karl was picking up the threads of his business on the Thames and in the City of London they became very poor and moved to the slums of Lower Sydenham where, on September 14th, 1911, I was born, missing Haley's Comet by a tick. After fishing through the ice for so long, I was landed on life's huge bank, pointing magnetic north.

The Glass Palace

While all about us the world was thawing into the reality of hardship for Karl and Mary, not the least was my brother's jealousy at my appearance.

Through his contacts in the City – where for half a century he was to be known and loved – Karl made an intuitive trip to Paris where he met up with a M'sieur Colan whom he had known there in earlier days. Colan was looking for a business partner. They came back to London and set up in Laurence Pountney Hill. I don't know how long this lasted but Karl did well and even had a Jewish secretary named Miss Bird who, with her blonde hair and black suit, is part of my Goddess-imago to this day. The first woman I wanted to have – when I was ten.

As our status improved we moved on the vertical scale to Upper Sydenham to 'The Link' in Silverdale Road and reached the halfway in a house on Peak Hill where but a century earlier Lord Byron had visited the poet Campbell at Peak Hill Lodge, and Blake had passed near on his way to visit Samuel Palmer in Shoreham, reporting that he had seen the angels among the reapers of the corn at Sydenham. We had arrived. And because my mother had indeed been left with a weak heart by her experience in Sweden, as well as for our new status, Karl employed a young girl in service to run the kitchen and look after us children. She was a tall, simple girl who was with us for many years. Her name was Ethel and had a great influence on our lives as Mother-Goddess. She died of cancer when I was 16. Never forgotten. I married someone much like her in late years. At times of pregnancy a Nurse Charlotte came: an English equivalent of Fastra.

I record all the seemingly unimportant things as well as those of obvious significance, because no one knows how a child's psyche really works, or how it grows when it becomes a bedding out plant away from the womb. Thoughts and memories hang upside down in the mind like bats. It is not till they take flight and home on the unexpected that their meaning is revealed. It is in this growth of the mind and the spirit that I am deeply interested, even more than physical fact and events, for it is from there the mysteries emerge and give majesty to our art. I am an artist: it is up to me to understand my business. If in doing this a small area is illuminated or a fragment of beauty is held, even for a moment, then the purpose, or part of it, is fulfilled, for every fragment has a spirit which will light the world if skilfully revealed. Every image is part of a mystical brotherhood which is invisible until it is lit by the mind. No insect is too lowly, no person too sinful or ugly to be included. For the artist, only the aggregate is the truth. He adds to it. Teachers are different: they are factual and know what they are talking about. I am an explorer and do not know what I am talking about or where my journey will lead or what it will reveal. To talk is for others: it is a talking world. Stay silent and know the truth. With any luck it will be fathered forth in a language that has been invented specially for it – a language of form and colour which might even be beautiful. That is the work of art.

Before Sydenham became a place of importance it had been an unknown hamlet where the orchards of North Kent apple country were not yet overrun by the expanding metal of Greater London, and the people were still country and not town: a distinction I first noticed between two ways of life when I had that short but dreamlike visit to my aunt Flossie's cottage in Suffolk as a boy. The smell of the trees and the grass was the same and that magic of gold in the sunlight held its secrets, which meant the spirit still lived there. When that goes before the advancing builders and their machines, the inner energy and stillness dies.

The Crystal Palace was moved to Sydenham in 1854 from Hyde Park where, in 1851, it housed the Great Exhibition. This fantastic Palace of Glass appeared on the West Hill of the North Wood dominating Sydenham, Penge, Dulwich, Anerley and Lower Norwood. It was a mecca of the arts, visited by great musicians like Dvorak, Schumann and Liszt.

Although I did not realise it, it must have been this influence that brought a family of Jewish musicians to live in Sydenham and with whom we became life friends. The old man was a composer and played the violin, the sons and beautiful daughters played also the banjo, piano, flute and viola. It was a terraced Victorian house in Venner Road that was never silent. Out of it came one beautiful girl named June who played the violin at the Rink Cinema and whom my father called 'the loveliest girl in Sydenham'. With Margaret Isobel I was in love all my young life from the age of 4, but it was Marcus, one of several sons, who took my £1 note given me by my Swedish aunt and made it disappear with other silver coins at different dates and upset my finances for life. My sister was also in this friendship. Margaret, with whom I once danced all one night, was her companion en tour as a chorus girl. We heard of another daughter dying of drink, a son conducting the Carla Rosa Opera Company. Indeed knowing them was like knowing a company of strolling players who enriched our lives without ever becoming deeply involved. As if the Crystal Palace had drawn them together in a dream of great art to be performed in its precincts and afterwards left to find their own lives in the vicinity, but never quite being people of genius.

The Palace was also a place of science where Blériot used to go and John Logie Baird had his studio. The Towers were designed by Isambard Kingdom Brunel like huge phallic symbols by Hepworth. The building itself was a construction of great beauty, like an enormous quartz crystal in the moonlight, foreshadowing Gabo and the Constructivists by nearly a century. A dome of glass which became a magical umbrella to our childhood. It also housed the Imperial War Museum and had not only aircraft that I could recall fighting over London, but huge searchlight reflectors which, when you looked in to one of them, was like looking into the well of eternal life with the illusion of a circle of light suspended two or three feet above the surface so that it enclosed me as I gazed downward. It was an experience that never left me and could have been the impulse I handed on to Bryan Wynter and sent him in search of his IMMOS – albeit unconscious to us both, for we carry experiences of a unique kind like fish spawn in the claw of a bird, which will finally germinate in someone else's lake without our even knowing. It is a service we do for each other. As we were such close friends and worked later near one another this is most likely and was a two way ferry.

But the Palace was dying. All that happened in the last half of the 19th century, several decades before my growing up was complete, its influence on the area was over. Pissarro and Monet, Schumann and Liszt, Elgar and other great men had left their footprints. I have written about it in depth in my book *Ben Blossom: A Secret Childhood*.

Joseph Paxton's Dream of a Glass Palace – an extraordinary complex of culture and engineering – was presided over by Sir Henry James Buckland who lived in a Georgian house at the top of West Hill under the North Tower. Throughout the twenties my brother and I had a season ticket for the Palace for our main Christmas present which covered our early quest into the mysterious art of fishing as well as going to the Great Circus run by the Ginett family, hearing the mighty organ at the Handel Festival, attending the Crufts Dog Shows and spending hours among the Egyptian, Moorish and Greek Temples. As well we played less admirable games of stealing chocolate and fireworks. The firework display was a weekly performance of great beauty and, when reflected, the Palace itself became the 'dome of many coloured glass' that is the umbrella title of all my books. Threading through this and through the years was the figure of Henry James Buckland, dressed in full morning suit, spats, with top hat and wax moustaches walking like a man in a Dali dream through his Palace of Glass to see that all was well until it was burnt down in 1936. I was away dancing in Dublin. It was not only the burning of an age, a fire without sacrifice, it was also the burning of that fragile Palace of Childhood which each of us builds secretly in his imagination and which has influenced my whole life.

The firework display is also precious to me for the image of my sister Alma peeing down the neck of my Uncle Ludwig as she sat on his shoulders walking home from watching it during his only visit from Europe. A slender happening that probably quenched his desire to put some money into my father's business while he was in England.

What happened I don't know but Karl who was not a libertine had done well and was most likely over spending. He sent us to a terrible boarding school at Kenley in Surrey when I was only seven. I suffered anguish and humiliation when my brother turned on me and went on the side of the bully boys who singled us out as Filthy Huns because of our name. As a result I lost my dignity by wetting the bed and my tonal hearing from a bash on the head with a book during singing lessons from the master. I all but lost my left arm from a stab with a pen full of ink from my brother which turned septic, my confidence by forgetting my lines in a play and was dyslexic from being beaten for bad reading. So I became an outsider at an early age as a form of protection, and because I simply could not go along with the injustices and obscenities, the falsehoods and brutalities of the crowd. There was a secret life to be found and followed which I was sure contained other things of greater worth, even if it was only silence.

A gentle art mistress showed me the wonders of painting in watercolour. The headmaster's mother showed me the Old Testament poetry of the Bible. The matron, the harsh kindness of moving my bowels with castor oil, cauterizing my poisoned arm with boiling water and sudden slash with a scalpel from the doctor. But no one seemed to have a cure for that ache in my heart which, I learned later, was for love. A secret Indian friend who played to me on a green pipe he made out of an elder branch in the woods was the only source of comfort I can remember, probably because I was unable to stand up to the coarse and sometimes obscene behaviour of the other boys. It was a tiny unexpected spring of poetry which I touched by chance and it gave something to me which seemed to have a new reality that was not all the time in conflict. He taught me to make a pipe for myself out of an elder. I loved scooping out the cakes of pith oozing with sap, but when it came to playing it I could get no sound.

'That doesn't matter,' he told me. 'You can hear the sound inside you if you listen.' I listened and I could hear it to my surprise. Try as I did, no sound came from the pipe.

'Don't worry. The sound does not want to leave you,' he said. 'It will later on. Music is like a butterfly that takes its own time and flies where it will. Later perhaps, it will come outside and you will hear it being made with your breath into the pipe.'

He was a slender person in a green suit who always seemed to be alone. There was a gentleness and kindness the other boys hadn't got. When I asked him he said he wanted to be a poet. I was not quite sure what that was, but the statement stayed with me and at different times I have been able to refer my own experience to what he had said.

Otherwise it was a long period of walks in crocodile formation on the North Downs among autumn leaves, wearing wet woollen gloves that gave me chilblains of appalling size like caterpillars. Back to honey on dry bread with a mug of tea and after evening prayers, in which we thanked God for his bounty and protection, there followed the misery of weeping for my mother under the bedclothes until the warm friendly fingers of urine crept over my loins and sent me to sleep, soaking through the mattress on to the floor.

In return for this my father was paying large fees. It was a status signature to go to good schools where we were taught to talk properly and behave like the sons of gentlemen. Karl would turn up with mother on sports day, bringing Uncle Axel with the heavy eye and a very broken accent, over from Hamburg where he operated on the Stock Exchange, travelling back and forth to Sweden. If he was in London he stayed with Kalle and Billy, as my parents were known. They hired a large Daimler for the day and came in style among the Rolls Royces and Hispano Suizas, Axel having footed the bill. They watched us with delight running the obstacle race, doing the high jump and sack race. At all of these I excelled because I

50

wanted my mother to say how clever I was and to show the other men what a success I was. I felt like a Greek God when I went to collect my prize for the hundred yards sprint and they clapped and slowly went away like people in a dream waving from the big Daimler. Afterwards the other boys, having noted my prowess imitated my lazy eye which was inherited from Uncle Axel, whom they called a filthy Hun with a German accent. They jeered and my brother jeered with them, calling me Boss Eye. Though so trivial the incident gave me great anguish and the fleeting presence of my mother at my side was only long enough to make me more unhappy, and she was asked by the Headmaster not to come for a time. How long that period was I cannot tell for time gets squashed by the pressure of the years, but it all ended quite suddenly with an announcement at morning prayers. 'The war is over. There will be no more work. Term will end today.' By some magic the playing field was filled with swings and sideshows and roundabouts. It was a celebration which ended with the arrival of the cars, the Daimler among them and being driven off between mother and father and Uncle Axel in a whirring silence of a beautiful machine, never to return.

I did not really understand the significance of the war ending, or only in terms of the Devonshire boy who delivered milk and eggs and with whom Ethel was in love: he no longer came to the door and she was often weeping. There was terrible news of my Uncle Sydney dying of his wounds at Gallipoli. Men appeared in the streets with arms and legs missing, begging for food and money. The Crystal Palace had become a great demobilisation centre where the wounded and dying were discharged and the dead kept in great cylindrical refrigerators with labels tied to their feet till their loved ones claimed them. Then they were hauled out and taken off to be buried.

Karl could no longer afford the fees at the posh school in Kenley. We were sent to another school on Sydenham Hill where we were beaten into ignorance. The hidden virtue of poverty came upon us. In the early twenties Karl went into voluntary liquidation and filed his petition of bankruptcy. Again he could no longer pay the fees. We left school. I was 12.

The plan had been to send us both to public school and then on to university, from which evils I was thankfully protected by destiny. Although I did pass the entrance examination for the City of London public school I was not able to go. My brother got as far as Merchant Tailors in the City for a year but was withdrawn. We were casualties of society. Later in the century it has been everybody's privilege to go to university if they could pass the exams. In the twenties it was a bonus for nouveaux rich or the upper classes. The tensions set up by this snobbery were very destructive to the mind and spirit of a young person, especially when they crash landed half way. To be poor and common was a noble thing even though it could mean to be barefooted and starving. To be rich and snobs was another situation which blinkered the mind from all hardship and carried with it a kind of decadence. To be in between these two states quite suddenly was bewildering and I had to grow eye teeth and claws to deal with it: a terrible realism on one hand and a false heaven on the other.

The only way out my father could find was to make us 'improvers' at the Crystal Palace School of Practical Engineering, a tall Georgian house on Anerley Hill under the South Tower, where we scrubbed the floors, cleaned the brass, carried the coals in return for a half-crown every three months and our training as mechanical and civil engineers. We were looked after by an old Indian Army sergeant who beat us on the head with his hard knuckles when he was drunk, but who was a kind and lonely man at the centre. The paying students were mostly boys from the posh schools we were once attending. This awakened a certain humiliation and made us at once proud and ashamed. This was no fault of my father's. He had sent us there to be sure we had a trade in our hands. He had always overspent when he was doing well and liked to hold his place in a very suburban society but there was a streak of wildness under his bowler hat that was hidden from the world, and made him an unusual person who was never quite tamed. Also he retained a certain innocence and was a man of truth, which forestalled his ever becoming a good businessman. I think his family in Sweden helped him quite a lot but I am of the conviction that had he stayed in Sweden they would have seen to it that he was properly established and a credit to the Berlin family, which his equally wild ancestor had founded.

He carried that bloodline to England and although it has never been of high office here it retains a certain nobility of spirit and eloquence of mind which I consider a mark of great value. He had the courage and originality to become a person in his own right though he thought all artists to be mad and could not understand what they were up to. He loved the stars and showed me the glory of their constellations hung over the suburban roofs of Sydenham on a night of snow and ice. He loved beautiful women, drank brandy at Frascati's and read Dickens in English, was proud of being related to Sven Hedin and thought everything Swedish was infallible – like using Swedish cartridges to exterminate rats, which nearly gassed the whole family. A man of paradoxes who became unique because he had no way to solve them and would take the bailiff for a drink with his last money rather than tolerate him in the house. It was therefore sad to see him when the furniture had gone, the electricity cut off, standing in the candlelight eating caviare on Swedish harbröd because it was the only thing in the house left over to eat when he had spent a day carrying heavy cases of tinned food round the City to flog to the Swedish colony and earn enough for our meal the next day and his train fare to continue with his work as the Uncommercial Traveller. He lost everything, then moved us to Upper Norwood at the top of a Victorian block of flats called St Aubyns Mansions. Here my brother and I set up our first studio and studied painting and writing and philosophy and poetry as our great passion, which drove him nearly mad because we should have been out looking for jobs. In the end we stayed up all night working by candlelight so that he would not know.

Out of my father's dream to make of us middle class gentlemen, equivalent to the modern Yuppies who have foundered on the rocks of financial ruin, our real friends emerged – those whom up till then we had been told were common, and were referred to as street urchins, some of whom had no shoes and the arse out of their trousers. Gradually as the soles of our own shoes came off the uppers and the arse out of our trousers, they took us more seriously and we made new friendships with boys like Jack Wilson, who was a lone strange person with a hooked nose and furtive piercing blue eyes. Chris Goodall, a tough merciless fighter of the streets, Eric Alexander a cut above the others with a motor bike. Chris had beautiful sisters who came home on the evening train from work in the City and we used to hang about to watch them, especially Violet who had lovely eyes. From these people who were simply real Londoners of the time, we learnt a new set of rules among which was to fight for ourselves and steal for survival, to have sex as an act of living, to rob factories and swear. To run like deer and ride bicycles with the skill of trick cyclists. Ride on the backs of brewers' drays and get away before the driver caught us across the face with his whip if he could. Climb trees better than Tarzan. In all we did in this amoral life we expressed ourselves with freedom and without fear. Our proper English changed to honest Cockney.

There is but one incident I have never come to terms with and which has haunted me all my life. One day when we were ranging the streets looking for trouble one of my mates dared me to go into a chapel where there a single light burning. 'I bet you wouldn't go in and blow it out,' he said. I stole in quietly on my own and blew the light out. It was the Eternal Light, lit there by a sacred hand. This I did not know till later and I was deeply troubled. An irreversible act which could have destroyed my life. Ever since I have been trying to relight it. Perhaps I have now done so.

Probably it was this that helped to define the existence of a more profound area to life. The artificial partitions of society were made so transparent by what had happened to us that our earlier school friends walked by us in the street, ignoring us for the urchins we had become. The effect on myself and my brother Jack was to heal the schisms which earlier dethronements and betrayals had caused and bring us close together in a friendship, like Karl and his brother Sven, which lasted the rest of our lives: an unexpected jewel on the yoke of poverty which cannot be found elsewhere. And the thing that made the bond so strong was a thirst for learning. We did not want money and did not become millionaires like so many young Londoners did from those hard times – we wanted to learn the *meaning of life*. Earlier, there had been a fight to the death: I won.

A good deal of the visual side of our education came from the Palace: not only the firework displays which I was to see performed on the Western Front later, the miraculous feat of engineering construction of the Palace itself, or even the Christmas Circus which gave me more insight into the balance of the human figure, behaviours of animals, love of showmanship but the Egyptian Galleries with a reproduction of the columns at Karnak, and of the Moorish temples and palaces of which our Master of Mechanical Engineering later spent all his spare time taking rubbings and copies in colour of their abstract designs and talked about it incessantly to me because I had told him I wanted to be an artist. This was a source of real information and enrichment which excited me far more than the dry lectures on The Permanent Way of Railway. His name was Hodson and he was himself an artist but between the tensions of teaching and the agonies of art he developed a drinking habit which finally won. His work on Moorish Art remains with me as a vital contribution in my glass university of learning.

After the adventures in the ruined civilisation of the Crystal Palace, with its prehistoric cast iron animals – robbing the chocolate machines, working in the circus, breaking into the firework sheds – we found ourselves on the brink of great danger with no jobs, no schooling, no money. The bailiffs in at home and caviar for lunch and tea and supper till we were sick. Two things turned me in a new and positive direction.

The first was my friend Jack Wilson taking me on the No 12a bus to the National Gallery and showing me the paintings of J.M.W. Turner. On the way back on top of the open bus we saw the sun setting over the Thames.

'There you are Berlin. There it is. Capture that!' he said.

For a man whose whole life seemed, until then, to be obsessed with making explosives in his kitchen and trying to blow up a derelict lorry to get at the metal, this statement was a revelation. I can still hear him saying it.

Another of the chance treasures of our environment was that, on a walk I took twice a day with my brother along the Crystal Palace Parade, over Sydenham Hill, down Cox's Walk and across the golf course to Dulwich Village there was a quiet gravel road that contained a long building with a lantern roof. It was Dulwich Gallery, watched over by a man in tailed coats with gold brocade and a golden cockade on his top hat, white hair, an immaculate figure who charged sixpence to go inside and see paintings by Rubens, Rembrandt and Andrea del Sarto, Rembrandt's son Titus in a scarlet coat, Carlo Dolci's *Tear* about which I was to upset Augustus John many years later. A de Hooch courtyard, Ribera's locksmith turning the key of destiny. Gainsborough, too. All silently watching from the centuries to see who was coming. Had I known that Van Gogh had visited I might have seized up with awe to know that such a one had come here to learn with his eyes the problems solved in paint by other painters before him. There is no way to tell of the silence, the wonder and sense of miracle I felt upon me as I came out into the sunlight of 70 years ago realising that art was a dream it took men all their lives to translate for the human psyche, into beautiful, truthful and eternal forms.

The other event which altered my whole life was in 1922, when Howard Carter and Lord Carnarvon discovered the tomb of Tutankamun. Their findings were published by Hutchinson in a magazine called *Wonders of the Past*. My father bought the first copies for me. They were the first colour photos of the great sculptures, the Golden Mask, the sarcophagi, the wall paintings and furniture for the after world, even to grains of corn that grew again after 3,000 years. This experience was an exact parallel to the discoveries of my Swedish uncle, Sven Hedin, locked irreversibly in my young mind. I knew I could not be an explorer, but I realised at that moment I wanted more than anything in this world to be a sculptor and a painter. I had not only discovered the entrance to past civilisations, but I had found the way into the deep inner mind of man which I was sure had always existed. When nearly 50 years later I opened the first edition of Jung's *Man and his Symbols* and found that he had used a photograph of the entrance to the tomb of the Egyptian Pharaoh Ramases III for his opening chapter, 'Approaching the Unconscious', I was astounded that the mind of a young boy should have so accurately stumbled on the same thing in discovering the entrance to the tomb of Tutankamun. The same strange feelings rose in me again, as though the last footprints left in the sand when the chamber was sealed 3,000 years before were my own. Although I knew nothing about it whatsoever I had found my way by the same route into what Jung came to call the Unconscious Mind. It was a form of self identification, as though I belonged to something larger, more timeless, going on behind daily life, which I had always known. It is that world of which I am endeavouring to write. The rest is only the roundabout on which we swing from century to century to the sounds of war, political wrangling, intellectual claptrap about art. What art is cannot be told: what makes art cannot be known: what art says cannot be written: only the essence can be transmuted by the soul in a flash of intuition.

In writing this I am covering areas of experience I have used in depth in other books. I have become like Time the lonely albatross taking flight over my own ocean, in an effort to see and relate events that are a pointless tangle, a Sargasso of weed and monster, and spawning elver that will seek their own rivers eventually and be given meaning. That is why life, especially in youth, is so bewildering: we don't know what is happening and it is a long time before any meaning can be given to events: without meaning life has not purpose and this is where being faithful to one's own centre, where truth is resident, becomes of paramount importance.

After the final run-down of Karl's business in Sydenham and our removal to Upper Norwood there was a period spent in Brighton. Here the troubles seemed to dissolve in the bright light from the sea, which we had known on holidays and for a time in the First War. Brighton with its beautiful Georgian buildings had a dignity of its own. The smell of the sea and fish, rotting wooden breakwaters and hot pebbles was a new garment for our senses. The life in rock pools, even to catching a great Prussian blue lobster with my hands and wondering at its articulating body as a marvellous construction, which at one time was made by God and is now made by evolution

– the firm has changed its name, that is all. In the Blue Lagoon, at that time outside my Aunt Dickie's house at Hove, such creatures existed and were sometimes cut off by the tide, but the dream was broken when my Aunt popped the lobster into a cauldron of boiling water and I heard it give out a primitive scream. This was the proper way to do it she told me afterwards. For all that she was a kind soul and gave a lot of time to seeing we enjoyed being with her. Instead of the destructive and violent games with my London street friends there was something different, another world of greater joy and intensity, added to by the colour of Dickie's half-gypsy way of dressing, which came from Augustus John with whom she had travelled in waggons and lived at Romney Marsh where Dick Innes was working and others such as Epstein and John Masefield were about. A romantic movement which proved to have a creative reality behind it worth considering. Dickie made beautiful fierce dolls out of rags, fragments of dresses, broken jewellery. They were like sculptures coming out of some unknown tribal culture. Her son Tony and her daughter Marjorie were both artists and Marjorie excited my young imagination by having an affair with Leon Bertron the great master of the sword who ran a School of Fencing. And it was here that one day when I was watching Tony Slade drawing that I suddenly realised you could be an artist as a lifetime occupation which fitted exactly my moment of *satori* when I first saw the treasures of Tutankhamun. It was he who had that inbuilt loneliness of the serious artist. He spent most of his days walking the smooth contours of the South Downs, painting the light caught between them in an ever changing variation like that fragile translucency which plays over the body of a woman. He did this with an unassumed fluency and was as able as Dick Innes whom his father knew: had he lived, he would have been placed with the great watercolour artists. Anthony Slade had several one-man shows at the Leicester and Redfern Galleries which I and my brother attended, meeting such incredible people as the psychologist Metrinovitch: he lectured for Lilian Slade who ran a Psychological Society in Gower Street at which Carl Jung also lectured. At 33 Anthony Slade died miserably of cancer brought on by a motor car accident.

I understood by watching him work that I could live by using colour and form to make beautiful things instead of the grey oily world of engineering and the rancid tramps of Wells Park. I did not know how hard it would be. I did not know what sacrifice the Gods would demand when

The prison walls begin to close
About the growing boy

or that it was this magic 'apparelled with celestial light' that I would all my life struggle to regain – not even knowing when it happened.

Frank Slade, father to this little family, was always away. A strange friendly but sarcastic man, who as with Dickie, usually left you with a sting that went on for quite a time: otherwise kind. He was usually out fishing in his dinghy where he caught a huge conger that barked like a dog. Although he was colour blind he did delightful watercolours of the white cliffs while he sat on the great waterbed that in some way gave him the answers to this life on land. It was his brother Lobin who married Dorelia's sister Jessie O'Neill that provided the link with the John family. He was also a Fellow of the Zoological Gardens and looked after animals at Horniman's Museum at Forest Hill near Sydenham at that time. The importance of this to me was that he sent me green tickets for the Zoo at Regent's Park with which, for years, I used to enter free and draw the lonely members of that lost legion, the animals; also learn the structure of insects and enter the mysteriously beautiful world of fish and birds.

Another point at which I brushed sleeves with the world of artists in those early days was through my mother's sister Charlotte: my own dear aunt who had married a doctor – a surgeon at St Thomas's Hospital – and was always pissed out of her mind. We used to walk across London to see her at her house in Cadogan Square in Chelsea, with the Sitwells as neighbours on one side and Sybil Thorndyke on the other. She gave us teas with exotic cakes and jellies and I danced endlessly with her beautiful golden haired daughter, Joan Bell. I not only saw the Sitwells sitting in their glass studio at the bottom of their garden, but also the young Augustus sweeping down the King's Road in black sombrero and cape after some new crumpet he had seen but not yet tasted. I met Forbes Robertson in a pub. Eddie Morrow, an Irish cartoonist for *Punch* who was my aunt's lover, gave me my first oil painting brushes. All seemingly trivial events which helped to awaken the unique machinery which composes the soul of an artist. The little pattern of people came to ruin through Charlotte's drinking, which probably started with her father, and dear little Joan Bell was overtaken by a terrifying mental affliction which turned her into a monster after the death of her father. I watched him die of a brain tumour in a candlelit room in Smith Square. With my cousin Geoffrey Haslewood and others I went to his funeral, my first, and was deeply moved by the process of cremation behind embossed doors, like the entrance to an ancient tomb, at Golders Green. I wrote my first short story about it. I was on my way to being an artist.

But again the unexpected happened and altered the course of things. There was a period – almost in parenthesis – which I could not have planned or achieved if I had wanted. I spent a whole decade on the music hall as an adagio dancer and in a mysterious way this was another method of gaining the experience I needed, during the late twenties and early thirties, before I went to Cornwall. Here again it was one of those changing of the points by an unknown hand that caused it to happened.

After causing an explosion in the City in my first job as an engineer I had spent six weeks at the Art School to try and get enough work in to pass for the Royal College. This was at Beckenham under a sound teacher and solid painter named Henry Carr RA. He thought I might do it if I worked day and night for six months. After a lot of distressing rows with my father, who was almost sinking under the strain of my wanting to be an artist, but support from my mother who held everything together by working like a shrew in spite of her fragile health, consent was given. Karl had come home one evening very excited because he had secured a job for me at Hambros Bank in the City. I was to start on Monday. I refused to go and left home, making for the Thames Embankment where I intended to sleep and draw on the pavement with my coloured chalks next day. But he sent someone after me: a friend of mine I shall call Horseface, who knew where I was likely to be. Horseface found me in Trafalgar Square at midnight outside the National Gallery where I had spent so much time when I was working in the City as an engineer, but now watching the rows of derelict humans asleep under the fountains and the pale green sodium lights, wondering how many of them had set out to be artists or musicians or writers and had failed. There it was. It was worth a life I told myself. 'Your Dad says you can go to Art School and try for the Royal College if you come home!' he said. I returned with Horseface.

But the next morning the door bell rang and a telegram was delivered from a ballet dancer for whom my sister worked, asking me to call. I went to see the lady and she offered to train me as an adagio dancer to fill the place of her partner who had just walked out on her. Fifteen shillings a week retaining fee till I was trained and £3 a week when I was able to appear on stage as part of her act. I had often seen her dance with her partner and was caught in the Valentino-like atmosphere of the apache dance where they were surrounded by beautiful girls while he threw her about in a French café. I had also looked longingly at her lovely niece who was her understudy and would take over as soon as I was trained. The enticement added to the small fee which meant freedom from rows at home and a lot of time to keep up with my drawing was enough. I accepted the offer against all reason and good sense and was now to quarrel with my father for NOT going to Art College.

The principal dancer was Gladys Groom who had been a good performer of her art for some years but now at 45 she was finding it difficult and saw this as a chance to step back and let her niece, Phyllis, take over.

I had been interested in Phyllis Groom from an early age. On one occasion I had walked into the West Country to find her where she was staying at Lyme with her brother who was a wing commander in the RAF. This journey was significant for another reason. It was on my way through the New Forest that I followed a dark girl into the trees and came upon a lost civilisation, a band of nomads living among the trees. The dark girl has vanished but the haunting magic of this experience in a green wonderland stayed with me. It connected with tales told me by my Aunt Dickie Slade of gypsies at Romney Marsh and Augustus John, and Dick Innes. Like other significant happenings it presented itself but faded till later except for using some of Brahms' Hungarian gypsy music in the dance. When it did return, it and the Dark Lady took over my life for a time.

Phyllis was my sister Alma's great friend and the link therefore was great for me because I was also able to see more of my sister, who was away touring most of the time, as well as get to know a beautiful woman with blue eyes and arched nose with hands and feet like Pavlova. This part of the experience worked out, because although Gladys did not want to give up when the time came and I was a proficient at the dangerous art I had chosen, we made secret plans and broke away to work together and finally to marry. From the moment I accepted the offer I became a dedicated dancer: my entire person was taken over. But I did not consider that I had given up the obsession to be a painter in doing this: it went on like an underground river and the new course only turned out to be another way of arriving at the same point, much more fruitful and enriching than being stuck in a college gathering facts. It took longer but what I did learn was learned with a strong content of feeling and sensation and I developed as a human being.

As with Abraham Brody, I had done the unexpected and crossed the ice floe to a new life.

This was a great experience because it was not only directed by the Goddess, but also contained a discipline of considerable severity and truth in which I had to learn the groundwork of classical ballet as well as the dangerous mechanics of acrobatic dancing, for the adagio dance was the bastard child of the union of these two. Swinging, lifting and throwing a woman depend on perfect timing and strength: because I was a naturally strong person, these things were slowly but painfully mastered and I arrived at those hidden virtues of awareness and quickness of mind which know the centres of gravity in relation to the body and the behaviour of natural forces, the value of harmony, rhythmic vitality, density, weight, levitation and elevation, all of which were a profound contribution to my drawing and later, but at the time unforeseen, a unique understanding of the solid image in space which is the first law of sculpture. So really I was learning, through unknown and secret sources, the laws of nature that never even show themselves to most artists. I had been admitted into a secret society where I became a highly tuned instrument, never letting up because to do so a pain-barrier of greater intensity than an electric fence had to be crossed to get back. Likewise the degree of skill achieved in one performance must never be less but more than the one that preceded it, or the quality of performance was forever lost. No drink, no cigarettes, no sex, only work. All this training was given by Gladys Groom and her niece who were highly skilled ballet dancers in their own right.

Not that these things alone contributed to my evolution, which made me feel I was experiencing a second life built within the first. I had also been admitted into the greatest profession on earth – show business. I learned to be professional in all I did under any conditions or get out. That is the rule. There is no short cut to being a good performer because what you do is done under the eyes of the world and there is no room for mistakes. This lasted all my life. There was no room either for those unskilled amateurs who stalk through the art world and indeed the great museums and galleries writing the history books, calling the tune but making no sacrifice to enrich their lives, and little contribution to enrich ours.

I met some wonderful people like Léonide Massine with whom I worked for only one week as an unpaid instructor. I was working the Hippodrome, he was at the Alexandra Theatre in Birmingham.

He came to the Hippodrome to ask if they could rehearse there while his stage was being used for creating decor for his new production. I was at that time also rehearsing and I found that the young men in the ballet could not lift their ballerinas over their heads and hold them there. I showed them the timing: kick, and lock when they were up. It is simple if you know how. They did not, so I taught them. I realised even then that to work so close to a man of this calibre who does every movement however small at the supreme level of genius, was a transforming experience and I was never the same again, or ever gave up until I had got each move right. He seemed to search endlessly for the exact moment when the spirit activated itself and the artists worked at all levels in perfect unison. It was a painful process. I have seen Massine with his fine bird face, white and taut with concentration under a Trilby hat, until the unspoken message passed as if to a flight of swallows about to turn on the wing. He was producing his *Les Presages*. I was deeply moved by the poetry that emerged as he welded the choreography into Beethoven's *Fifth Symphony*. I, an unknown dancer of the music hall, had the privilege of working on the fringes of this very great art of the ballet with one of its finest exponents. The experience taught me the meaning of art and it might well carry a message for others. I think Tom Cross was wrong when he wrote that the dance was only to entertain: particularly the dance I practised, as a professional. Whatever is wrong with it, it was choreographed to the great artists in music – Brahms, Sibelius, Ravel – with complex patterns and harmonies that demanded considerable skill and mental prowess to perform if any attempt at beauty was to be attained or the passion of the human syzygy to be expressed. Even at the risk of our lives each night we appeared in this very difficult and dangerous art. It took no less a genius than Diaghilev to show how it combined with music and painting and sculpture by employing Stravinsky, Gabo, Picasso and Cocteau to design his sets, write his music and such as Nijinski to dance it, for the entertainment of the lovers of the dance, and give beauty to meaning. It was on the advent of the adagio dance as well as the Russian Ballet that the entire reorientation of dance came about and formed within itself the conception of 'modern ballet' as an historical step forward. I was fortunate enough also to work with Alexander Zass, the strongest man on earth.

The comedians are the parrots, the brightly coloured macaws of the profession, always laughing, exploding a pretence, undermining pomposity and destroying snobs. They are the funny men who make you laugh whatever they do on or off stage, not men who say funny things only. Comics are a tribe who can't help laughing and although they are a joy they are also as sharp as a sword, as quick as a snake, as ruthless and fierce as a tiger, even to themselves. They have minds that move like piranhas and tear you open. They invent an answer in the face of sudden death. Their timing is impeccable. They are great to be with because they extend everything into meaninglessness which gives new meaning to ordinary things. All this comes, or came in my day, from years facing brutal music hall audiences who would not be palmed off with slick routines, but needed and wanted to roar with laughter because life was so hard. It is one of the sad things in the profession now that most of these men of inherent comedy have gone into the blockhead business of hosting quiz games or God slots. I wonder what George Robey would have thought – or Grimaldi or Grock? To see Grock at the London Coliseum, was to have seen a man of genius as also Carl Georges. Robey playing Menelaus to Evelyn Laye's Helen was to experience laughter and beauty interlocked. Working with Max Miller, Nervo and Knox, Charlie Naughton, Bud Flanagan, Rob Wilton, Jimmy James, George Formby, was like drinking whisky. The world changed into something mad and strange. Pretence, snobbery, conceit were cut through with each laugh from a rapier tongue. And however important or grand or beautiful you thought you were, a prop cabbage dipped in a fire bucket and thrown at your head when you were dancing before 2,000 people taught you once and forever to laugh at yourself. Messengers of the Devil and buffoons among the Gods.

Even now, after so many years, I miss their humanity, their cruelty and courage under any conditions, remaining always classless and lovable. They are the people with whom I feel more at home than anyone else and for whom I have so often longed to be when I have found myself caught in the precious but false world of the artistic cognoscenti for whom my work and my personality has an unerring attraction. Laughter is a prophylactic for all ills: humour the sabre edge that cuts open the pumpkin truth at a single slash.

Travelling with a music hall company in the thirties was to be in the same secret world as the strolling players of medieval times, save that they travelled by horse and we by train. At train call on Sunday morning we met on the platform in our actors' great coats and hats, our faces often with traces of make up from the last show of the night before, or a late cabaret done for charity. We travelled in reserved carriages, and were a world within a world going from city to city, sometimes the length of England in a day. Band rehearsal on Monday morning in the new theatre where we were booked and two shows a night and two matinees a week was our work. In my case it was necessary to rehearse every morning and on Monday in the afternoon to get used to the rake on stage, the dimensions and set of the footlights, the position of the strong limes and the surface of the boards upon which we were to dance. All important to save having an accident and working to the highest of our powers with a new musical director each week. When non-stop variety came to the Windmill and Prince of Wales Theatres in London we worked 12 shows a day from 11 am to 11 pm. A hard life for £10 a week.

Leaves of Myrtle

Yet once more, O ye laurels and once more
Ye myrtles brown, with ivy never sere,
I come to pluck your berries harsh and crude
And with forced fingers rude
Shatter your leaves before the mellowing year.

Milton

It has always seemed to me, and even at that early time it was becoming apparent, that where the forces of creation were active in any degree so also were the forces of destruction, that one interacted with the other; or else it was that if the pristine force which drives us all was not transmuted into creative or constructive work it expressed itself in tragedy and death and that often the two forces met in a single personality.

This was so with Jack Wilson. He was the friend who first showed me Turner's painting of *An interior of a room at Petworth*. He also blew the face off another friend with a magnesium bomb. He was into radium which finally destroyed him. He lit a spark in me that has never gone out. But at this point I only want to say that he was the one who brought me to meet another young man who greatly influenced my life and, in turn, through him I met the man who was to teach me to draw: that all important aspect of the visual arts without which the highest point of expression cannot be reached, unless you are that rarest of all things, a pure primitive.

The first was Frank Turk. Not a man but a mind.

> 'Many-minded Turk
> Mad as the mist and sea . . .'

we used to say, parodying Yeats on Homer. Meetings and learned discussions at all times were illuminated by flashes of laughter, which, like shooting stars, crossed our delighted minds, often to be the touch needed to let fall, suddenly, apples of understanding. For me that was the most valued thing I could have wished for. A tall person with high shoulders and head set forward with wide-set eyes and a flat bridge to his nose and full mouth, much like the young Yeats by Augustus John. He was married to a lively little Egyptian woman named Aza. They were both at London University. He is retired Extra-Mural Research Fellow and former Reader in Natural History and Oriental Art at Exeter University. Thus it was that the university which I had sought and lost came to me in this form: not an academic process of learning but an intrinsic experience of knowing, understanding and, most valuable of all, forgetting. It was he who directed the scattered threads of my searching into a tapestry to be achieved by my own life and led me into the paths of knowledge few men can boast, leaving me to interpret in my own way what I had learned from his guidance and forgotten. Like Dante, when Virgil found him in the Gloomy Wood and led him to the point where he beheld the stars, I was enlightened.

By this happening I am convinced that destiny brings to the seeker a man of wisdom to act as Cicerone.

My searchings with my brother in those long days walking the hills of Sydenham discussing what we had read during the night before by candlelight, from Plato's *Symposium* to Bergson's *L'Evolution Creatrice*, Homer's *Oddessy* to Shelley's *Adonais* or Blake's *Gates of Paradise*, Samuel Richardson's novels to those of Thomas Hardy, brought us learning but also enrichment and freedom of mind because our enthusiasm made each work we read also an exciting experience, rather than a gathering of stale factual knowledge. We visited the museums and art galleries.

We also made visits to Shoreham in Kent not knowing it was the place where Samuel Palmer had lived and worked and where Blake visited him by waggon drawn by a team of oxen. We slept in the open and knew that strange mystical moonlight of those translucent hills by our own discovery. At three in the morning the sun rose on the stones of the little Saxon Church, turning them to rose and gold. Here I did my first serious drawings from nature. It was like wrestling with an angel and I came off worst, with my mind limping as I walked away. But it was a start. I knew I had the tenacity if not the skill to continue. An added bonus was an early contact with country life. I learned the silences and secret sounds of waking birds and of insects moving in forests of grass. Another world to investigate and discover.

The third of the three wise men whom destiny sent with their gifts of frankincense and myrrh, was to come later, when I first went to Cornwall. Before that happened, after I had passed out at the

Engineering School, and before I went dancing I spent a period in the City travelling by train every day dressed in a 50 shilling suit, Trilby hat, rolled umbrella as an assistant engineer to a heating firm. I finished up by undergoing a slow metamorphosis to a velvet jacket, red trousers, black sombrero hat, spending every moment I could in the National Gallery, eating my lunch under Holbein's *Duchess of Milan* or Turner's *Fighting Temeraire*, because this was the only way I could experience the great painters. There were no grants to aid young painters or any means of becoming an artist otherwise, except as I found later, by starving. In fact an artist was usually considered a useless member of society and an outcast by the mass of people.

I had finally got fired from my job as an engineer by causing an explosion in a bank in Bishopsgate. I had miscalculated either the oil or the air intake of a boiler I was converting from coal. It blew off the fire door and sent the fireman through a brick wall into the street, scalping him as he went. I never really believed it was my fault because he told me one day that if you burnt potato peelings in the boiler the alcohol in them could build up and cause a sudden explosion. Never on any account to do it. But the kitchens had sent in refuse the day before when we were fitting the new burner. I was not there when the accident happened. One of the unsolved crimes of the City of London. 'Anyway,' he said to me. 'What the fuckin' 'ell do they want to burn bleed'n oll for when we got coll. Don't make sense and it will corst me my job. You see!' which also set me free to follow my destiny on the stage.

The value of the engineering experience to me was that I got to know every painting and every brushstroke of every painting of which I was interested in the National Gallery and the Tate. I studied Rembrandt's drawings and etchings in the Print Room of the British Museum and the eighteenth century English watercolour artists in depth at the Victoria and Albert. It was worth an explosion. I no longer wanted to be an engineer, although I was later to value the structural draughtmanship it had taught me and the laws of construction contained in exo-skeleton beauty with which living inside and outside the Crystal Palace my young mind had been permeated ready for St Ives 20 years later.

One of the pleasures and comforts of working on the stage in the same business as my sister and her best friend Margaret had been that it gave a homeliness to the harshness and to such sickening disappointments as when Charles Clore, then an impresario, docked £2 off my pay of £10 because my contract was not through, in the show *Les Nuits de Paris* at the Prince of Wales Theatre from the Moulin Rouge and Lautrec. We now called Phyllis Groom Helga, from the film *The Rise of Helga* featuring Greta Garbo. Even my daughter called herself Greta in later years. The name had stuck. Such are the metamorphoses of stage life. Thus Sven and Helga. We became famous. Our names were in lights and paraded up and down Piccadilly and Regent Street by sandwich men. Although that was a thrill, a distressing sight was to see the Welsh miners cruising the gutters with their faces haunted by starvation singing their beautiful songs to save the mines for their people.

At the back of things when we went on tour with the same show I was painting in the dressing room, watching the landscape all over England and Ireland, learning the movement of forms in light and colour from the wings when other acts were on and, fortunately, the human figure, for there was a nude tableau in which the girls had to remain motionless by law. I did drawings. I wrote huge unreadable romantic novels when we were out of work. The underground river flowed incessantly from the original spring.

During one of the rests between bookings my friend Turk came to stay at our digs in Penge and we went by train to London each day to see the great Chinese Exhibition of 1936 at Burlington House, or to the Tate or National Galleries. All the beauty that had haunted me earlier now renewed its influence like a woman that gets inside you and you can't forget her image day or night. At the Chinese Show I saw the great Makemono down one wall of those giant rooms. It was called *Ten thousand miles on the Yangtse*. I understood the continuity of drawing for the first time. Since then I have not stopped and from the acceleration given by seeing and reading the Japanese Hokusai I have become Gwakio Rojin Manji – The old man mad about drawing. All indicated by Turk, the Orientalist. It was after one of our visits to the Exhibition that, riding back down Whitehall in a 12a bus, we suddenly saw George Bernard Shaw walking in the crowd, a tall white bearded pink faced man to whom I never spoke but by whom my mind was influenced through the magic of words. Turk stopped me jumping off the bus to talk to him. This way everything was exciting, in spite of the poverty. Even earlier, one summer, we were out of work, caught in the hot back streets of Brixton with no contract till we were to return to work with the Crazy Gang in the autumn, which was to be our best booking yet, the Palladium. But our money ran out before then and I had a torn muscle in my back which prevented our doing cabaret in the West End to fill in. I wrote to Turk. He answered at once. 'Come down and bring a tent. You can stay in my field.' We bought a small tent and travelled by train to Cornwall in 1934. Once we crossed the Tamar it was all over. That curious opiate drugged our minds and we did not care what happened. It was the beginning of my first real break to become a painter. It was as though a force had hold of me and whichever way I tried to direct myself it saw to it that I went another.

Turk's house was inland with mine workings for our landscape, which was disappointing when we arrived except for the hospitality we were given by our friend, his wife Aza with their two children Stevie and Ashgan, the pet monkey they kept in the kitchen as an emblem of evolution, and his old mother, who was an image of patient suffering drawn up in a chair with an arthritic condition that daily enclosed her like an invisible boa constrictor. We set up in the field helped by a young friend named Edward Parsonage, who cut away the grass for us and helped put up the tent. It was not long before we had walked through the Tehidy Woods and come out suddenly upon the Atlantic ocean spread like a dream in the sunlight beyond the North Cliffs and looking south we could see the blue hills of Zennor behind St Ives, that little gathering of houses by the sea, that tiny Bethlehem, that Unholy City.

The first thing to do was to search out the art school and I found it at Redruth in an old Victorian red brick building under the control of Arthur C. Hambly, the third of the Three Wise Men sent to guide my destiny.

He was a shorter man than I, with blue eyes and a fair moustache, hair neatly parted, later to be fitted with a beard, and wore a tweed jacket and flannels. Nothing of the unconventional artist about him. He was the son of a bank manager and that fitted also. Headmaster of Redruth and Camborne Art Schools, later to be head of the whole of art teaching for Cornwall. An artist of honest intent himself and a devoted teacher. Member of the Royal Society of Painters in Watercolours. International award for etching and other honours. He died aged 73 in 1973 at Downside Vicarage, Bath, where he spent his retirement with his close friends, the Reverend and Mrs Greenwood. That is an ordinary enough obituary for an ordinary man, but the special quality of integrity as an artist and teacher made him a unique person: a man of truth. In as much as he had this ordinariness, so also were his ideas simple and straightforward.

In 1942 he wrote this to a student:

> The whole life of an artist is full of discouragement in one
> form or another . . . either from without or from within
> because we aim higher than we can achieve . . . a pale
> shadow of the glory that was in the mind . . . There must
> be enthusiasm for more than the technique in pursuing
> the illusive achievement of an idea, forcefully and
> beautifully stated to others. There is an argument for as
> much skill as possible but more and more technique is not
> an end in itself. . .

His vision was a poetic overtone of pure beauty arising from a
conjunction with nature – the glory that was in the mind. There
seemed to be a lack of personal daring that prevented him from
allowing that moment of glory to take over and invent what it
would demand of him to find its full expression. Inspiration is a flash
of the human mind that must not be hindered by logic. He was
caught in his own trap as are most of us. When he did not care it
happened. He cared a great deal too much and remained a fine
artist but a great teacher. I was the one who gained. He did not
influence me but taught me all I know and that left me free to
break the rules and create for myself. An artist is remembered not
for what he knows but for what he invents to speak the glory of the
mind.

At that period, which was the 1930s, teaching was not the high
powered profession it was to become after the war and it was still
possible to keep the passion of the heart, 'the glory of the mind' and
yet deal with the exigencies of being a teacher – or almost: Hambly
had his work cut out and in the end the contest negated him. A
good deal had to be sacrificed and when this happens the aggregate
sacrifice demands expression which, if there is a physical weakness,
can be lethal. He got TB.

After the war, when the Arts Council came to make people
conscious, everyone wanted to be an artist. Many trained on grants
as teachers, but found afterwards that a professional life in teaching
art had killed any vision they might have started with, and they
could not get back because it made them too conscious of what they
were doing – or trying to do – unless you were as tough as Terry
Frost, who was an artist first and ruthlessly used teaching as a
vehicle, or later as an overtone of his gift. I would not touch it: it
was too fierce.

The lost army that wanders about afterwards is usually absorbed into the Corps of Art Officers who know too much about Art and have to borrow the genius of those who stayed out to create. Arthur C. Hambly is to be respected and remembered for never losing his own vision as an artist and never losing sight of what Michaelangelo called 'Beauty's intolerable splendour.'

The strain of his teaching and the administrative work and responsibility that later went with it, long after I was with him, brought on the condition of tuberculosis and for a while he was not able to teach or paint. It would seem the spirit of so gentle and valuable man had not the stamina to deal with the forces he set going by his pursuit of beauty, and was ruthlessly sacrificed on the altar of logic. He left a stained glass window in the church at Redruth as his memorial and, perhaps a significant colophon, the sensitive little etching of *The Great God Pan Dancing in a Wood.*

Turk writes of Hambly:

Arthur was a most excellent and devoted teacher and wholly loyal to his students. I consider the teacher needs three loyalties –
1. To the subject he teaches. This must be paramount.
2. To the student, which is equally important and containing.
3. To the professional body to whom he is responsible – and this last one, the third, is a long way behind the other two.

This fits exactly my experience as a student of Arthur Hambly. As a *not-teacher* I would add a fourth.

4. To understand that the 'glory of the mind' cannot be taught.

Saying that his drawing was conventional means that it was opposite to the growing forms I had learned from Rembrandt and the flowing forms of Hokusai, the instinctive forms of Lascaux. It was a static, academic and constructive edifice set up before nature transmuting natural forms into their logical equivalent, a method which emerged from Greek culture and the Italian Renaissance. It was this I needed and this indeed was the thing I was after: this truth of the *conscious* mind: as Cézanne and Sutherland have both said, the confrontation right up in front of nature. This I got. The

71

honest transposing of forms as they existed to the eye before nature. It is painful. It needs endless application and self-discipline.

I kept my own free method of drawing alive and when the grafting process was over I had a living tree that could be allowed to grow in its own earth and make its own interpretations in its own way. When the satori came, as always unexpectedly, and one had to confront the unconscious mind the whole process was forgotten and trusted to work. For it is not until the mind has forgotten, that the glory can come through and the imagination interpret spontaneous invention.

It might be right to say that our ways forked at a point where I went off on a quest of imagination and searching which every young artist must do as a means of growing, but it was always my commitment to go all the way with nature first, for unless you do that you don't even know your own evolution. Like Hokusai I drew every sea-shell, flower, insect and bird I could find. Like Rembrandt I drew in the streets and the fields, on the moors by the sea, everything that moved and all objects that did not move but composed the setting in which all things lived. It was an attempt to be able to say with David, in Browning's poem, 'Saul',

> I have been the whole round of Creation; I saw and I spoke!

for the drawing *is* the voice of the eye.

In setting out to draw the whole of Creation I did not think that a drawing was worthwhile if it was altered by the nosey interference of an india rubber which destroys the quality of line, excavates the surface of the paper and breaks the concentration of the mind, stems the flow of the spirit. A direct, unaltered drawing in pencil or ink was the rule. Wherever I showed my work for years later, one person was sure to turn up – 'to see the drawing'. It was Arthur C. Hambly. Although he said of me, to a fellow student, Marion Hocking, that I was the best and most hard working student he ever had, I never knew if he realised how much it was due to him that out of many thousands of drawings there were a few that were worth keeping.

In his quick, preparatory unfinished work in watercolours which I like best he showed me how an untouched area of paper was the foam of a wave held between a shadow and a film of light drawn there by the wind. How it happened I don't know – nor did he. But such was his poetry in pursuit of beauty.

Drawing is the voice of the eye and the signature of the human spirit. The act of art is something that can only be performed on a platform the artist has invented or made his own. Without this act the performance is at best high craftsmanship or at worst a stilted emptiness. Because they knew this secret the old masters from the first cave artist still live, thundering down to us through the centuries. Thus my master of the violet shadow.

When later I found myself in the battle front of St Ives where the sea turned red with the fierce contest, I was completely confident because so few of the artists could draw. When it came to abstract construction I excelled because I was trained as a civil and mechanical engineer. When sculpture confronted me I was able to take on the third dimension like a coat because dancing had taught me the laws of mass, volume, gravity and density in space. I entered the third continuum like a neophyte priest.

It is an interesting point to record that Naum Gabo and W.S. Graham, the poet, who were both vitally affected by the Constructivist movement, were both, like myself, trained engineers.

Turk opened the East for me when I attended his lectures on Oriental art and literature and comparative religion. The religious awakening was of particular value, especially in Taoism and Zen Buddhism of the Japanese which is derived from Chan in China. A whole reversal of the conscious mind seemed to take place so that the unconscious was outermost and understanding was suddenly rife. The vitality of the spirit started to be transmitted through my arm to the paper on which I was drawing so that everything had real and pristine life. What wonders to behold. Even with a dry crust. I used Turk's library, his microscope and his field. My only disappointment was that I could not find a dead human body to dissect as Michaelangelo did. I taught myself anatomy from diagrams and an intimate acquaintance with my own body and its articulations through dancing. I even invented a skeleton, undreamed of by God or Darwin.

Finally the money ran out and we were forced back to London to work on the stage for another four years. This was arduous and fruitful as all such experience usually is if you meet it head on. We had quite a lot of difficulty getting started because we had stayed in Cornwall too long and missed our second contract with Nervo and the Crazy Gang. With it the final accolade of the music hall profession, a Royal Performance at the Palladium. Otherwise we held our level and worked here and in Ireland where I sought out the spirit of the Irish poets I so loved, and Scotland where I climbed

Arthur's Seat. I did paintings of Inchkeith Island and Loch Lomond. It all fitted together, but now I had once touched the ocean bed and seen its wonders through continuous work in Cornwall with my two masters of destiny, I came to a point where I knew I must choose, and one day on top of a bus in London, I knew what it had to be. To consolidate this decision more cross fire directed my life. On my 27th birthday my brother gave me Horace Brodsky's book on Gaudier-Brzeska and Helga gave me the Phaidon book on Van Gogh. Both these artists did it alone. That was it. I gave up everything and started penniless from scratch in a basement flat in Thicket Road, which connected Anerley and Penge along the south fence of the Crystal Palace.

Nothing meant *nothing* – nothing else. Starvation is a woman with one blind eye who always says NO.

In no time we were at rock bottom. I queued up with the rancid tramps of my childhood who lived in the park on the Poor Law and drew 12/-. I made nude drawings for 18 hours a day with Helga posing. We used kitchen paper which came in a roll of 18 yards for sixpence. We lived on scraps of food from the shops like bacon bits, broken biscuits and stale bread. Stealing fruit from the orchards, vegetables from the allotments, roses to paint, even eating them, from the gardens and wood from the fence of the Palace to burn. Life and work were just possible. I one day saw a great fire in the grate which filled the room with orange light, but when I got to it there was nothing but the cold light from the gas lamp in the street outside.

How I had paints I don't know or even pencils. Nor did I know what painting was. I tried endlessly for a year and nothing happened. Then one day almost without me knowing it began to happen. A painting started to work. It was as though an invisible hand had taken over and showed me how to do it, after heart-breaking months of trying to find out what made a painting into something else different from nature – a whole image in its own right. There it was for the first time. A self portrait. I called Helga and we looked at it, watched it in wonder, as the Curies watched their circle of radium.

Somehow we realised that this was the sign that we should go on. We were pretty worn down and there was otherwise no direction and no hope. I had permission from Sir Henry James Buckland, who was still the manager of the Crystal Palace although it was burnt down, to go in free to the grounds and draw the Greek sculpture, which I did continuously because it helped with my disciplines and gave me access to a private landscape where I could draw trees and lakes, old farm vehicles, boats and ornate buildings. And on Saturday watch the exciting new dirt track racing and the motor bike races with side-cars. All an experience of the human form in mobility dealing with velocity and gravity with daring.

One evening during the week I sat with Helga by the lake where I used to fish with my brother as a child. There was an evening mist and the water was quite still, save for a fish nosing the surface here and there from underneath. We were both very slim and her dancer's feet and hands were very much the same, not spoilt by our experience, her eyes as luminous.

'Do you miss the stage?' I asked her suddenly. She looked at me and smiled.

'Heavens no. What after all those years teaching for that old bitch? I grew to hate it. It's only since we have worked together it's meant anything. But, I don't know. I don't want to work that hard and be in that kind of danger all my life. That is, till my looks go and you get someone else.'

'That's not likely.' I laughed and was silent. Then in a little while I remember saying, 'It's strange but I have a feeling we won't be here much longer. We are going to leave soon.'

'I know,' she said 'Me too. It's over. We are going to move.'

Both of us felt relieved at this inner knowledge which came at important times unbidden, because I suppose we were living at such a low level of existence that instincts long forgotten came back into use. There was nothing mysterious about it and we did not question its validity. On the way home to our basement flat we collected some struts of wood from a broken part of the fence to make a fire. We had no idea what was going to happen.

The next morning I answered a knock on the door hesitantly because I thought it was Drages come for the furniture payments or the landlord for the rent, neither of which I could meet. I opened the door. It was Jack Wilson standing there with the sharp beak and piercing blue eyes of a falcon.

'How would you like to go back to Cornwall?' he asked.

It was a particular moment, never forgotten, because it seemed to have been triggered by the self portrait smiling back at me from the easel. Looking back I can see that I was caught in a set of forces I could not control. They were far stronger than I and were making me do things of which I would never have dreamed, like moving my furniture to Cornwall without any money, living on the very ossified jaw of poverty. Yet the portrait was not afraid. It had a naive faith, innocence even, and knowledge that it would be all right if I did not falter. I had my father's Titanic health, we were both strong from the dance and was I not descended from Sven Hedin the Explorer? Helga did not hesitate. 'This is what we have been talking about!' 'Yes. I know. Isn't it strange? But how?' I said. 'How are we going to do it?'

When I rescued Helga from teaching for her old aunt it was a kind of Robert Browning situation. I had snatched her away from someone who had been using up her life as captive since she was a child. The release had been tremendous and was one of the factors in making us work so well together. But the dance is a hard taskmaster – perhaps the hardest of all – and, as Alexander Zass said so succinctly, and I am never tired of quoting: 'Zee body go on till 'undred, but zee visage, she crinkle!' Especially was this true for a woman. And then the dedication to a life in which one was always tired and keyed up was also a wearing factor. She wanted me to resume my work as a painter, even though progress was slow. I think I knew that if I turned away this time it would be for good and the talent, which was strong enough to nudge me this far, would die. If a man turns on the voice which directs that talent he will himself slowly die. Once awakened it is his responsibility as much as is the birth of a child or bringing up a kitten that turns out to be a tiger. We knew that we were well established on stage and fame awaited if we returned. It seems odd, perhaps even rare and certainly foolish, to choose a way into life at the simple entrance door of stark poverty when better things were at hand, but it was something in both of us. We each knew that we could not engage on it alone, even though we did not know the severity of the sacrifice to follow. For Helga it was her Everest as much as it was mine, her K2 as it was for Julie Tullis, the mountaineer. It also cost her life. She did not flinch. Forever Helga!

I looked at the self portrait, trying to compress all these thoughts that came welling up into one single thought that would be the impossible answer.

There is one thing in common about all painters – they are men of the eyes. They know the mysterious trick of remaking things they see, giving them their own image and spirit, the same spirit which identifies the hand that paints it: it is a passion for the continuum of the personality recreating through the imagination and even the emptiness of watching when the soul is no longer there, has left the body from exhaustion and too much seeing. With the ageing Rembrandt we see the dignity of the great painter who has gone through to the end, who has given up everything, lost everything for a simple brushful of wisdom seen in a single stroke on his sleeve. He knew – and perhaps he was the first to consciously realise – that the face of a man is not a static upright image as supposed, but horizontal like a river that is always flowing, changing in form, light and colour in every moment, as is the personality from which it emerges – a perpetuum a thousand years long. A self portrait is a fleeting section of this horizontal face.

Innocence, which is a slab of salt licked by the grazing tongue of Time, might well lie in the grass longer than we think and appear in the ancient horned visage of a last self portrait. Thus my first self portrait, with considerable innocence and surprise, seemed to say: 'There is your answer!' as Wilson walked into the room. But Wilson, not being a man of the eyes, did not even notice it was there as he acted messenger of the Gods sent by Zeus himself.

'What have you got in pawn?' he asked.

'My typewriter, my gramophone and records, my watch and our wedding rings!'

What did it add up to? Unwritten books, unfinished symphonies, unused time and love that was not anchored by a golden chain. The tools of my trade, unpainted pictures, uncarved stones at the bottom of streams, civilisations to be built, Gods to be worshipped, and somewhere a Goddess directing the soul as though she had a silver harness on the nerve centres of the spine, guiding me to new circles of experience, perhaps to reach the final vision that is too powerful for the eyes of man. Whether that has yet been enshrined I don't know.

Wilson calculated our fares to Cornwall would be £11, which he gave me. The furniture was a further amount. I gave him the pawn tickets. And I thought he would want the self portrait as well. But he went to the wall over the fireplace and started to cover a nude with his handkerchief. It was in very strong colour and he looked guilty.

'A nice bit of Prime Canterbury, Berlin. That must be worth a shilling or two. But I don't think I could deal with so much as that. We will settle the matter later when you are on your feet.'

When he left I stood in the middle of the room with a fist full of money and tears in my eyes. We looked at each other hardly able to believe our moment of precognition by the lake the evening before. We had our first meal for days and then started to pack everything up. I don't remember how the rest of the money was staked or if it was all paid back. I recall asking for the typewriter back on payment, but Wilson would have none of it. The deal was never worked out to a conclusion, simply because I never saw Wilson again.

In a few days we had packed everything in boxes and a plain van called after sunset, loaded up and took it to Paddington. On the way he dropped us off at Sydenham to say goodbye to my mother and father, but they were so distressed I wished we had not done so. I quelled my mother by giving her the self portrait and my father took us to Paddington in time for the night train, in his 1920s Trojan motor car with solid tyres.

Next morning we crossed the Tamar under a double rainbow, tired, hungry and uncertain of our future. Turk had secured a cottage on the North Cliffs. After a few days at his home sleeping in the attic at much inconvenience to himself and Aza, we went there. The furniture arrived. We set up home by the Atlantic Ocean, a venue for martyrdom if ever there was one. Standing in the little garden watching the brittle leaves and flower of the myrtle – the flower of aphrodite and of death – I wondered what was going to happen: there was no turning back.

Later, in 1943 when I was on leave from the Army before going on the invasion of France, I had a card from Turk which said simply:

'Jack Wilson is dead. He was 40.'

I have learnt since from Turk that he became chief metallurgist for Shell-Mex at their Wirral plant. Thus this unknown man of instinctive genius who found both radium and gold in Cornwall, passed without other mention, as the result of cancer of the stomach and liver.

Turk writes to me in a letter:

> Almost certainly he acquired that from radiation emitted from several sackfuls of powdered pitchblende he took from the Old Red Moor Mine near Callington, a mine derelict after being abandoned by Pochin and Curie a quarter of a century or so previously. I kept it in my outhouse for years. After that he kept it, I believe, in his bathroom. For years too he paid for his Cornish holidays by collecting specimens of pitchblende and other uranium materials from Wheal Owles spoil heaps and selling them to Gregory & Botley in Chelsea.

I remember the specimens because it was these that gave me an insight to the beauty of crystal formations and the colouration of stones. For many years I had a matrix turquoise stone he had given me. He showed me also pitchblende from which the Curies first extracted radium and in doing so opened up for me the structure of stone and hidden forces of the earth and a whole world of wonder by which he was completely obsessed. He not only showed me Turner, but first quoted Shakespeare, Byron and Shelley to me and introduced me to a beautiful blonde Goddess who lived next door to him. I fell in love. For this he offered to kill me. He threw a knife: it stuck in the wall between us. It was right that the Gods chose him as my Cicerone to Cornwall. Creation and destruction met in him at a point where they ignited the spirit while they tore apart the shrine that contained it. The flash lit my vision and never went out. Although I missed out on going to the palaces of learning, what I might have learnt there would have been as chaff on the wind without that fierce incandescent light that can transform dead matter into creation or kill a man. Unknown to any this man, who was the illegitimate son of a London Hospital osteopath, scratched his name with a diamond on the window of our time.

It was by Jack Wilson's influence we now stood together in the stark empty granite cottage that was to be our home, with the open moors and the vast blue window of the Atlantic spread about us. The land of mermaids and raging gales, of brittle sunlight that struck sparks of radium from the rock – the evil as well as the healing and the beautiful locked in each speck of sand blown by the north wind. And beyond, under the blue hills, the little town of St Ives holding my destiny. It was there in 1939 that Hambly first took me on Show Day when all the studios were open to the public and the traditional painters at their height – not knowing how Jericho would fall about them a decade from then.

That was a memorable day for a remark made by Hambly when he pointed out the first celandine blowing on the verges in the March sunlight as we whizzed across the moor to Gwithian in his car.

'When you see the celandine you know you are safe!' he said. Simply that. The thought returns to me every year and with it the memory of the winter which that particular Spring was terminating. Our time in the wilderness, of which he did not know – thank goodness. It was about this time that I painted the *Shah of Persia* self portrait. There was no money, no food, no tea for the pot. I took the tea cosy made by my mother and stuck it on my head in defiance and painted myself pouring an empty teapot. I went regularly to his classes when I was not working in the fields and when I was I cycled afterwards to the evening class at Camborne. Turk picked us up two or three nights a week to attend his lectures on biology, psychology, philosophy and Oriental art and literature. Over three years I packed in a formidable amount of learning, not with any idea of taking a degree but with an overpowering enthusiasm to know about life and art and the human mind, how they worked and what meaning could be given to the processes of nature, the imagination and the spirit of man on his long search to evolve higher consciousness. Nothing was done for fame or money. They were alien to our purpose.

There was a whole new world of survival at the centre of which we now stood: the ancient farming community of Cornwall which had started with early man. In the thirties the farming methods and life on the fields were at the stage we read of in Thomas Hardy, who was one of my great writers. I gave a lecture on him in 1934, arranged by Turk at Murdoch House in Redruth – originally the cottage of William Murdoch who invented the method of distilling gas from coal and made it in 1792 the first building to be lit by gas. The feeling was that all one was doing was within a community of learning in which one met ordinary men and women who cared about the mind and spirit and the improvement of humanity for its own sake. Hambly was part of this. So also was Turk. No razzmatazz. In my opinion Turk did so much for the culture of Cornwall with his WEA lectures linked to Exeter University that the aggregate residue of the work should be valued as discovery of a small but rare seam of gold.

Working on the fields when it came to it was like putting on Hardy, much as Paul put on Christ, and likewise much harder in its reality than in its word. I was strong enough to carry the load and using my body again in work as tough as that of a ballet dancer, though not so sensitive, was certainly nothing new or difficult. I surprised my work mates by being able to stand up to it for as long as 14 hours a day at harvest time.

Everything was still done by human hand and the horse, the only full machinery being the steam thrasher which went the round of the smallholdings. There was the horse hoe, the horse harrows which, in Van Gogh's drawings done only 50 years before, was pulled by a man. Horse lift and pulley for building a rick. Horse reaper and binder. Horse rake. Horse plough. Otherwise it was Jean François Millet all day and the only angelus was the lone sea-bell. Man bent over the fields for 12 hours a day hedging, hoeing, gleaning, stooking, planting and milking, the farmer riding through the morning mist on his horse giving orders. Of all this I did drawings when he was not looking.

Again, as in the dancing experience, I was close to the way in which men used the body to do the simplest or most difficult jobs by procedures evolved over centuries, like skating dung from a fork, building a rick, planting broccoli. Also in unison with animals, particularly with the horse rake and milking by hand. All these things made me aware of a common spirit and also of a marvellous natural machinery at work – as in a dance or a sculpture.

It must be said, in all truthfulness, that although this period on the North Cliffs working on the fields, and later on the Zennor Moors over St Ives, was the hardest time I ever went through, except perhaps some nasty moments on the battlefield, it was a time of great enrichment. Today the fields are quite empty: then they were crowded – especially in summer when the families of each smallholding came in to help the harvest along, the women gleaning and stooking the corn, turning the drams of hay to dry with the men and bringing food to eat at croust time. Here was a beautifully woven, but simple rough cloth, with no embroidery but hard work, good humour, trust and kindness. We had no phone, no electricity, no motor car, TV, radio or money to grace us but the aggregate was an unspoken love that made survival and life possible. When I wonder what is absent now I can only say the strength of uncorrupted poverty and its brutal truth.

I knew nothing. I was a city boy who, as the farmer said, 'belonged to the luxury trade!' They thought I would not stand it and tried me out at 6½d an hour (about 21/- a week) for the summer, probably thinking I had money anyway. But there is no one meaner or harder than a farmer forcing his living out of the Cornish moors, because that was the only way to survive. I was given the toughest jobs, like pulling charlock by hand from a ten acre field, hedging and ditching in a northwest gale coming in from the Atlantic. We served the steam thrashing machine till midnight and then milked 30 cows by hand before going to bed to get up at six next morning. But the worst experience of all was to be kidded into jumping off a lorry into a lime pit, which blinded me for a day with agonising pain and injured my lungs forever, while the others laughed at me floundering and falling about like a drunken man. I hung on and gradually I began to love the toughness because it was on the granite edge of life and gave to my spirit a tenacity and strength that enabled me to know this new plan of experience. How to handle a long Cornish spade, reap corn down the headlands by hand-scythe, dig a ditch, handle a horse, milk a cow, build a rick. Yet best was to work alongside peasants who had been there for centuries and be accepted among them.

I was so poor that I was dressed entirely in sacks. I wore a hessian sack poncho which Helga stitched with string, hessian leggings, hessian bound over sandal for boots, a hessian hood for the storm. This was a warm wind-resisting outfit which made up for the lack of food while we were working the first days to get our pay and buy food. But if it rained when we were pulling mangolds or cutting the thorn hedge and ditching during a storm the water soaked through and became a lethal load to carry.

The great support which enabled us to survive was from our neighbours in the other half of the cottage: Bert and Mabel Tremayne who were of pure peasant stock, strong, unpretentious, beautiful people. Their friendship was gold in a stream of gravel. Mabel helped Helga with cooking, teaching her to make a pasty, a saffron cake, a heavy cake and a starry gazey pie, which came as a fortification when the Cornish slab in which the cooking was done was mastered.

Bert showed me how to milk by hand, how to harness a horse, take cow to bull, throw stooks of corn to the top of a rick, horse-hoe the broccoli, skate dung by shovel, shear a sheep, cast a ram, – all with a silent friendship not met with more than once now and then. There was no pretence. The brittle leaves of the mauve myrtle quivering in a hard wind had that kind of beauty. I worked alongside Bert most of the time.

One day I was put with the cattleman to draw hay from the field. The horse whose waggon was overloaded got stuck in a deep rut and could not move. The cattle man, after raging and kicking the mare with his steel capped boot tore a branch of gorse from the hedge and lit it under the mare's belly and kicked it again with his steel boot till the animal screamed and reared on her hind quarters. I raged and took the branch of fire from the man and threw it far into the field. I then faced him but he said nothing and turned away till Bert returned with his horse and waggon and they made a team to shift the load quietly, efficiently, slowly from the axle-deep mud. Bert told me after that this was a custom to shift a horse because if you got one lazy animal in a team the rest were no good. But I, having nothing to go on and caring for Bert's word, remained silent.

The result of this incident which was stamped like hot metal on my mind forever, was that, come winter, the farmer sent for me after dark. I crossed the field and found him standing under a tree in the rain outside his house. He told me in broad low tones that he wanted the cottage for the cattleman and his family. I must move out. I was stunned.

'But I have no money and nowhere to go!' I said. He looked at me sideways through the rain. 'There are places a man in your position must go for help,' he retorted.

This meant the workhouse and all its merciless charity. The words had fallen like stones. I was silent. I turned away and walked across the field to the cottage. At that time I did not know about Brody-Berlin or my grandfather Hughes. Had I done so I would have realised that destiny had once more sounded that deep beat on her timpani drum as in an unwritten symphony.

During all this time I had worked hard with the belief that the farmer would keep me on for the whole round of the seasons and let me learn more about the job. It was not to be so. But I did find a cottage to go to which would be vacant in the Spring. I was given grace. So we entered the time in the wilderness which it seems was a purification of the soul necessary to achieve my purpose. I shudder to write about it. At first it was quite good because I was free for my studies. I had not stopped drawing. I carried small notebooks in my sack pockets and drew everything in sight from a poppy's seedcase to a man working the horse-rake or a bus stopping, to record its entire structure in two minutes. Rocks, crystals, birds. Now I did not work on the fields I could paint – but not eat. I painted a Chinese student from the Camborne School of Mining, Mr Fong. Also in landscape and memorably, a place called Nancemellin where Turk ferried us for the day. It had a ruined mill, a trout stream and sunlight of that eternal quality left over from another century, given time to go mellow and slightly brittle like a palimpsest of amber. I also did my first sculpture from a small block of sandstone I found in a stream: *The Head of a Sage*. Not having developed a sculptor's vision I was not able to break through the third dimension and pluck the image from the centre of the stone, where indeed it slumbered had I known, but carved it on the outer wall of the stone like primitive man. I also carved a few pebbles and composed an abstract sculpture out of a sea-worn lump of quartz which I hauled up the cliff face alone, and a large steel ball-bearing by SKEFKO, of which firm that childhood love of mine, Margaret, had married the director. All this in 1938 was well in advance of my time as it was of my powers, particularly as I had no contact with the contemporary art scene of that period – no wireless, no television, no art reviews of any kind, for what they are worth. I was to learn later, when I returned from the war and sculpture came in upon me, like meeting a stone man at the entrance to a temple on the road to Bethlehem, that it was also the entrance to the profound mind. That I had come in truth to the doorway of the unconscious, most likely awakened by the mine shafts and engine houses everywhere like the entrance to the Pharaohs' tombs in the Valley of the Kings.

In the evenings, three times a week, Turk still called in his car to take us to his lectures on philosophy, Oriental art and literature, psychology and biology – or on one of the writers such as Robert Browning, James Joyce, T.S. Eliot. I worked also with Hambly at Redruth, now with all this extra experience. Like Helga's mother, who looked just Rembrandt as an old man and was the sweetest of women I have known, sent us five pounds with which we bought clothes and entered the winter with 12/- a week from the Poor Law. I had been before the Board of Guardians at the workhouse, who threatened me with expulsion from Cornwall and, because they could not give hemlock but only slow death by starvation and insanity from social disgrace and the mind's dichotomy, I squeezed my paltry shillings from their hands. Since a cottage some way off and nearer Camborne was found but would not be vacant till Spring, we had to stay on the North Cliffs whether the farmer liked it or not. But he would not, we thought, cast us adrift in so stormy a place with no means of survival. He did not.

On December 4th, 1938 I wrote in my journal: 'It is the anniversary of our wedding. It has been a hard day. We have not eaten since the beginning of the week save for a cabbage I stole from Mr White's field, which we had hot, then cold because we could not heat it again having no fire. . . The headaches which come on the third and fourth days without food were ours today: a steel band at the base of the skull and neck. I cannot paint, having no materials left. Outside the mist comes in from the sea with snow driving horizontally across the moor. The low wind whining in the telegraph wires all day is whining now as I write by the light of the last candle burning low in my room. Always it is like an idiot playing the cello, screaming with the gale that comes in from the Atlantic and rocks the cottage, flooding the lower floors. While there is no creation there is also no destruction. This is as dangerous as it can be: augurs death.' The strange thing was that we could stand on the frontiers of life and death feeling perfectly happy and unified. Nothing had brought everything to us in the fullness of love.

On the sixth day I awoke and after lying for a little while, called Helga. We slept separately not wishing to take each other's life but to stay strong and give out strength to each other. We had gone past the groins of sex – so beautiful and so deathly. Her voice was weak when she answered. We had reached a state of exaltation: a mystical state as I understand it. We belonged nowhere, came from nowhere.

> I am like a cockled star
> Blown by the wind
> Washed by the changing tide
> Drifting afar
> A cockled star
> Wandering in mind.
>
> Anchored to no sea bed
> Or the uncharted sky
> As seems is the oyster moon
> But drifting instead
> Unpiloted
> Living I die.
>
> I am like a cockled star
> The tide impels
> Sunk in the silent seas
> Drifting afar
> Scraping among shells.

I was chanting this to myself as it came into my mind when I heard a hammering on the door downstairs. I remained quiet. The cottage stood listening. Then quietly to Helga: 'Hear that?'

'I expect it's the coal man come for his money – or the farmer come for his fuckin cottage back! Perhaps the old bastard has come to chuck us out. I haven't been up there to work off the rent lately. Sod im.'

The knocking continued. Always the door was open for there was no fear unless the gale was blowing. We heard the caller shout. 'Anyone there?' But the voice was unfamiliar. We did not stir. The footsteps receded down the garden path on the moorland road. A car revved and was gone.

'Wonder who that was?' I said. 'I tell you what, let's get up and pinch a cabbage from Polly Widden Field, some sticks from the woods if we can make it that far in the snow, and perhaps we will find something like a clutch of eggs if we keep an eye open.' It was like freezing: the will power was paralysed. All our energies pointed in one direction with great intensity so that our eyes burned with a new light, our faces were shining, but I don't think we realised we were dying. I rose like Lazarus and started to dress myself in my sacks. I stood for a moment looking in the mirror. I was tall and very thin with a long neck and sunken eyes, hollow cheeks. Helga looked pale and beautiful, her eyes luminous. My head swam. I felt as though I was levitating. 'I shall get a job in a factory. We can't go on like this,' I said. Helga moved like a spirit, looking at me. 'You're raving mad. Who do you think is going to take you on to work for them. You look like a ghost in those bloody sacks. Talk about 'When the ghost walks!' On the stage they'd pay you big money for that. We'd make a good double act.'

Slowly I went downstairs, fragile, as after illness. A friendly shaft of sunlight falling across the flagged kitchen floor fell also on the wooden table where there was a box of provisions. The grocer had left the order for the week even though we owed him money.

'Christ! The ghost *has* walked! Food. Bloody fucking food!' We danced a strange ludicrous dance as we had never danced before, like the Dance of the Consumptives in Kirk White's poem, until we nearly fell over. Together, breathing hard we filled the lamp with the oil he had left and boiled a kettle, drank hot tea made with evaporated milk and ate a little cheese as though it was a holy sacrament, smoked a cigarette as though it was the incense of inward spiritual grace. We felt our bellies burn, our bodies grow warm, our silent hearts start up like great turbines shaking us. We were drunk on bread and cheese, laughing as our stomachs unknotted. When our strength had returned we went across the snow field and gathered twigs from the floor of the wood and with the paper bags from the groceries, lit a flame which leaped like our new life through the scaffold of twigs and caught the larger wood in orange galleries of fire from the green ash, which sank as it burned and squeezed out its white spunk like life blood sizzling in the cold grate.

The next day I collected my money from the Relieving Officer whom I found in a baggy suit and Trilby hat dispensing a meagre stipend to the very poor from a Gladstone bag; a kindly old gentleman who did this office with sweetness and grace, making me feel tall like the sun. I could now buy a stamp and write to my brother in Persia, tell him of progress with my work. And when we went with Turk in the evening to hear his lecture we said nothing, but lit a candle in the side window of the cottage so that it would burn till we returned home and ever after was kept alight. Otherwise none were to know of the strange journey we had taken to the frontiers of physical existence. Who would want to know? No one. It was our secret. Something to carry about and make us unafraid and put a light in our eyes: the light of hunger and the light perhaps of those who search for truth, for this it seemed was a time in the wilderness, a time of purification. We had written a legend on the sea. We had seen a reed shaken by the wind and could not now be corrupted.

We had found the invisible companion to be ourselves. More I will not say: more I do not know. It was like having searched for a crystal and found gold. It was out of this chance experience that I knew what the source of life and creation was. I learned also that the artist and the poet can cross the frontier but cannot complete the journey because, by the rules of their vocation, they are bound to return and invent a new way to interpret the experience. I learnt also that if I saw an experience through to the point where the inner and outer interact, it was followed by a period of extra-spiritual clarity when the whole thing was presented with all its opposing forces resolved into a harmonious pattern and immediate simplicity of meaning. This mystical stamp was always upon me from the beginning, though the moral portmanteau I carried might well have been judged to be made of carpet as much as of sackcloth.

I think now in these later years of my ancestors as I write. They are like ghosts about me, for there is something in the dark north of my soul that understood them and was perhaps trying to complete for them: to be part of, and express, an impulse of transcendental nature which the moral implication of their upbringing had prevented them doing. Starting with my First Father, the Wandering Jew who fled to the pure North and gave birth to a flow of pastors, rectors, priests, teachers, professors, explorers, soldiers and merchants, and I believe one archbikopican, he spawned the Berlin River flowing south, but was unable to deal with the forces that destroyed him, as surely as would a man-eating tiger. He just disappeared without trace, probably murdered.

Another aspect of this which helped me to survive was the lore of the East of which I had taken hold by following the Noble Eightfold Path to the cessation of desire and suffering. Perhaps the whole of this is perfectly condensed in the TAO TE CHING when it says: 'He who is without desire shall know the secret essences.' I don't know if

Sven Hedin understood the mystics of Tibet when he entered the Forbidden City of Lasha. Probably not. But he might well have passed down his unique power of endurance for me to draw on in my own journey of discovery. Otherwise I did nothing remarkable: only that I was out to become a good artist and I learned in this way that the God or Goddess I served would not take second best. It was up to others how they dealt with this problem. I would say that of many who ask to be called so few are let through the frontier gate because most of them have run away: it is too tough. But to create a new image is the silent reward — if you stay.

I might have had an easier time if I had killed for my meat, but being a neophyte Buddhist and an unorthodox Christian at that time — but never a practising Jew — reverence for life precluded my doing so. Helga was the same. We were not puritanical. We were unable to conform. We remained silent about our privations even when friends started eating hot pasties in the car when we had been days without food.

Then an extraordinary thing happened, by some secret working of society, perhaps through Hambly or Turk or both. Even through the tough farmer who wanted my cottage. I don't know. But I was offered a one man show of my work at the Camborne Community Centre, by a local worthy, C.V. Thomas who had made his money on the Rand and in Cornish tin. He was a very elderly man with white moustaches and came to my cottage driven in a huge Daimler to look at me and my work. He consented to do this with no payment for the room used as gallery and laid down certain conditions which I observed. Then he went away, I feeling subservient and grateful but unlike Caliban, I did not say 'Yes, my Lord. Can I lick thy boot!'

He also paid for the frames. He had built and owned the community centre. My father printed the catalogue, Turk wrote the introduction. The show opened in May of 1939 with drawings, paintings and sculpture priced from 5/- to 10 guineas. I sold one drawing for 7/6. When the show closed I gave away the remaining works to my friends. Two things mark this event. One was that I had created an entirely abstract sculpture without knowing anything of contemporary developments in art, which I titled *A prolegomenon to every future metaphysic* — from Emmanuel Kant. Secondly and perhaps most important, I had established myself as a working artist for the first time — no longer an amateur. It was as though I had pointed instinctively ahead at what was to come. I felt for the first time some of the exultation, the heartbreak, inbuilt loneliness and isolation that attend the visual artist – especially if he is a pauper. There were no grants.

Dressed in my actor's lounge suit, still with a dancer's figure, I was proud to stand there and make comments to the worthies and unworthies of the town who came to see my work. I felt it a special privilege to be an artist and felt I had secretly passed the spiritual tests of the soul that initiated me.

After this we complied with the farmer's edict to vacate his cottage. He lent us the old mare I had saved from burning. I hitched her to the same hay cart and loaded our belongings and ourselves for the slow journey to our new home at Treswithian.

The apple blossoms were in full bloom.

I was in time to make a kitchen garden and get planted up. To do this the new farmer, a younger and less ambitious man, took the single share horse plough in to the top of the orchard and turned the ground for me, which we broke up together and got some late potato seed in as well as other vegetables to fortify us later. It was a tiny family smallholding. Next door had eggs and milk and an old man still alive whom I used to talk to and do drawings in the evening by lamplight, which gave deep shadows and mellowness to all I painted. They were kindly and took to us. The son also and the unmarried daughter in her forties. A relief after the brash farmer and the cruel cowman. We missed Bert and Mabel but they were near enough to visit by foot and we were near friend Turk with whom my sister was staying in an adjacent valley, and only three miles' walk to town.

That summer was one of the most unexplained and intense periods of happiness and wonder I have ever known, before the murmuring of war could be heard and the premonitions of darkness were upon us.

By going down a track and crossing a granite stile we descended into a wild and unkempt valley at one end of which was South Crofty Mine and at the other was Nancemellin and Gwithian Bay with St Ives beyond. The two points were joined by the Red River, so called because it was stained the colour of hot cocoa by the oxides from the mine workings. All along its length were ruined surface works with rusting machinery given over to vetch, toadflax, convolvulus, purple loosestrife, foxglove and orchis and meadow-sweet, the smell of which was intoxicating mixed with the salt wind from the Atlantic. A heron stalked the clear pools and streams that ran into the Red River, one from Nancemellin where I had painted as early as 1934. The river itself ran into the estuary at Gwithian turning the sea red. It could not have been toxic for I never saw dead creatures about. It was a living organic theca of creation filled with that orchestra of summer, the insect world – dragonflies which are accipiters of the lower air, bees, grasshoppers, butterflies, golden rain beetles, antlered stag beetles, mayfly born for love, gnats and hornets – a playing symphony which has long since become too distant to hear, victim to toxic sprays. Of all of these creatures I did drawings and was so in harmony with nature that I could take a dragonfly out of the air with my thumb and forefinger and hold it by the undercarriage while it flashed its anger with a thousand lensed eyes as I did my drawing, able to see the flailing action of his wings backwards and forwards in intersecting arcs slicing the light into almost invisible membranes of colour that compose the spectrum and play soundless music to the eye. But I did not know that this experience would be hidden in the caves of the soul for years to come and because the sun shone for a moment and gave warmth it would complete an evolutionary cycle and emerge from the same hand that once held it from flight.

Indoors I set up a room for a studio as I had on North Cliffs where I had painted the bewildered Mr Fong: here I painted a young man with whom I had made friends at my show, listening to the Nevada Rain Chant on a gramophone between visitors. This was David Philips, a sensitive person with a tubercular arm which he managed with extraordinary dexterity so that it gave him uniqueness instead of awkwardness, even though he had to wear it at right angles to his body in an aeroplane splint. He was the son of the Vicar of Treleigh the other side of Redruth and one of a family of sisters, Ruth, Stella and Mary, all of whom I coveted and none of whom I conquered. They had an exacting but whimsical father who put the wireless pips right by his grandfather clock in the hall and a sad but once beautiful mother. David was a student of languages and wanted to teach me French but I resisted because it took time from painting and drawing. It was his love of poetry and his family that made the friendship so valuable to me and I painted his portrait with all the concentration I could command. It was my first journey into personality and perhaps the painting still holds some of the magic of that time.

As the summer ended and with it the enchanted days I spent with Helga working, talking and making love in the Golden Valley, the premonitions of war, like summer lightning, flashed over the low hills that protected the valley of our dreams, until we woke one day to realise that it was all over – the glory had departed. The winter came on. The hardship returned. It was a full stop. War was declared and with it I was called before a tribunal in Bristol, headed by Judge Weatherhead, to defend myself as a pacifist. I stayed the night with the Quakers who were very kind and quite fearless people. My mother's people were Quakers in Yorkshire and their simplicity and lack of flourish particularly appealed to me. They seemed not to care about the authority of the State which I had to face in the University and even heckled the Judge and Professor Field and a third member of the tribunal when I was being questioned. I got a verdict of exemption from military service on condition I worked on the land. But the papers in Cornwall took it up and reported it in full as 'Pacifist faces Boomerang Argument'. I was derogated and the goodwill my show had built up was gone in a day. Public opinion turned against me, especially as I was living on the Parish. The Board of Guardians complained and threatened again to expel me from Cornwall as D.H. Lawrence had been expelled in the first war. The Cornish are spy-mad in war time and trust nobody but themselves. I was arrested but not charged for drawing in the street and in a churchyard which was also HQ of the Local Defence and for 'signalling to a German submarine from the North Cliffs'.

CORMORANTS

91

The Angel of Darkness

I saw a winged and terrible thing
Hover in the evening sky:
Soon the sunset shells will sing
The Angel of Darkness make us die.

Nothing came of all this except that I was once more an outcast. We lived on potatoes, apples and broccoli from my patch. Then, for one week, entirely on eggs, which turned us green. One day Helga said, 'I can't go on. I'm pregnant.' The whole meaning of life immediately changed. I had painted *Man and Woman with a flower*: it was our point of precognition.

I walked to Camborne and by paying my butcher with a self portrait I got some meat. On the way home, passing the factory of the Milk Marketing Board, and remembering my time working as a heating engineer, I went in and asked for a job.

'Do you know anything about boilers?' the manager asked.

'Yes, I trained as a heating engineer.'

'Can you run a boiler house? We want a boilerman.'

I got the job.

When I got the meat home, which was an oxtail, it was a bit maggotty. I washed it clean under the tap and cooked it with cabbage and potatoes. We celebrated with an excellent meal.

The District Nurse Ferman, who was bossy as they usually are, was also a person of great friendliness and efficiency and we felt safer when she started to call. She was deeply excited by a painting I did of a young mother on one of the hessian sacks I had used as a cloak in my unlooked-for status as saint of the fields the winter before. Sadly it's now lost.

The experience in the factory was not unwelcome. Although I had not fired a boiler before I knew enough to take on a Cochran Vertical Boiler: an iron clad giant who became my friend. We got on well together. I found it exciting to feed his great mouth like a furnace in hell and loved the colours of the fire – emerald, gold, crimson, violet, black and pungent ochre, turquoise. Sometimes it would leap out at me like a playful tiger as I threw in shovels of Prussian blue coal upon which it pounced and teetered into a spark-needling death. I was proud to keep his brass clean and his water pump properly working. I even recalled the words of the old boilerman in London whom I scalped, 'Why burn the fuckin oll when yer got fuckin coll.' His apron was swept clean and at night I put him to bed, damping him down with wet ashes to dream till I came in next morning, with just enough steam up for the night shift.

After I had got up steam each day I had to go in to the platform at the front of the factory to unload the incoming churns from the lorries of local farms: a hard, rather brutal job, but I worked with other men and could contain the sight of a dead rat being taken from the great milk vat by the tail and squeezed of cream before being thrown away amid laughter and obscene comment, which makes it easier than if you are on your own. And the energy pool was greater. Yet I had the boilerhouse to retreat to and be on my own, read poetry or talk to the friendly live rats with whom I shared my sandwiches: they lived in the old mine workings over which the factory was built in 1929. I have written about this in *Pride of the Peacock*. The thing of importance here was the way the chains of security were knocked apart almost directly they were formed. It was as though a malignant force was intent on redirecting my life.

At first I knew no wrong. They looked upon me as a prince of work because I kept the steam pressure exactly right for the great butter churns and steam rollers on which the dried milk was made. I was sent to central Wales on a week's course which I spent drawing all day until the village policeman wanted to arrest me for drawing maps of the area. It was difficult to convince him I was not, it being wartime with Germans disguised as nuns dropping by parachute to blow up the ammunition dumps. I did not mind. I had a Welsh grandfather and the landlord's daughter was pretty. I enjoyed the break and came back knowing enough to take over the milk-drying plant as well as the boilerhouse. I have always had an instinctive knowledge of how things work and did not have to learn.

The day came when all workers were called to the manager's office to form a Local Defence Unit. Each man answered his name, each man said 'Yes, Sir!' until it came to me, 'No!' Dead silence. The man looked up. 'Why?'

'I am a pacifist!'

The man made a mark against my name and the meeting was dispersed without anything being said. Everything went on as usual until the next morning when the foreman came to the boilerhouse and asked me to attend a meeting in the canteen. I followed and walked into a concrete room with tables set down three sides. At the table under the window with their backs to the light, sat three men.

'If ee are found to ave guilt we will cast ee down the mine shaft outside!' I was on trial for my life.

'Guilt of what?' I asked the spokesman.

'Guilt of innocence!' I thought he said. Perhaps he said 'Guilt *or* innocence'. 'But that doesn't make sense.' He remained immobile. Perhaps he was too self-important or too ignorant to realise he was talking nonsense. This was madness. His voice was like an Old Testament God. This was the other face of the Cornish peasant I did not know, had not seen, never guessed at: the primitive Celt defending his land in time of war, bringing the invader to trial.

'Do ee believe in God?' said the inquisitor.

What I said I do not know. I have tried to simulate it but it explains nothing because, like the oracle, I spoke out of my deep self and I knew now there was an inner voice, the voice of the ancestor, the voice of the questing soul – perhaps the voice of God. I was not a vagrant animal wanting to take their territory, but a tiny point of light crossing an immense plain of darkness. This was beyond life and death and I was no longer afraid. When I had finished I heard some whispering and the man's voice said:

'Not guilty. Ee can go free!'

I don't know how long it lasted. The tension was terrible. When it was over I went back to the boilerhouse shaking and seeing myself in a fragment of mirror white as marble. I opened the fire door and a huge dragon of flame roared out to welcome me. I knew everything was all right.

As usual at the end of day the men came with pails full of slurry from the separators and drying machine and tipped it down the mineshaft.

'Good job they didn't cast ee down there today, my beauty,' said one.

'How come?'

'The swill is not what is belong to be – something the rats wait to feed on. Tonight it is laced with strychnine. The Old Man's orders. They would a bin eatin you instead, I shouldn't be frightened.'

That evening Helga went into labour and we got her to Redruth Hospital in the nurse's car. When we arrived there it stopped. I returned to the empty cottage late too tired to sleep, distraught, nervous, not knowing what to expect. I fell asleep, when there was a hammering at the cottage door. Thinking it was news from the hospital I opened up, but it was the manager I will call Pinochio and the under manager. It was midnight. They were shouting that the boiler was about to blow up. The pressure was up to danger point. No water was going in. The pump had jammed.

I ran to the factory which everyone had evacuated and went in to the boiler room to work the alternative to the pump, the steam injector, which meant hanging on the side of the boiler till the steam suction took the water and forced it up into the tank. I talked to my giant friend, coaxing him to respond, knowing that at any moment the village could blow up. Then there was a terrific hiss as though he heard me. I thought he was going to blow but instead there was a backward roar like a mating buck and the water leaped past my hand from one pipe's mouth to the other and sucked up into the boiler. She had taken. In ten minutes it was safe.

I had taken special care that afternoon to test the pump and damp the fire down which could not have got up to that temperature without the pump going into action. Slowly the workers came back into the factory as I climbed down the hill of coal and went into the drying room, knowing the boiler had been sabotaged. The little manager Pinochio came in and started raging at me. I threw him into the slurry and walked out.

On the way back to the cottage I phoned the hospital from the village kiosk. 'A son was born!' a voice said.

I danced under the stars, did an entrechat over the moon, pirouetted round Mars and ran into the valley. Turk was away. I hammered at the cottage door next to his. When it opened I told the man 'A son is born'. He nodded and closed the door firmly and slowly as upon a lunatic. 'That's all right, my 'ansom. I won't tell anyone. Now off ee go to bed before you wake mister Turk.'

I went home and drank some cocoa to celebrate and smoked stub ends of stale fags till dawn. Many years later Pinochio died of a liver disease carried by rats, but he had given me a new outlook on life. I was lord of the stars.

The advent of a son is a marvellous thing, perhaps because it extends oneself into the generations like firing a golden arrow at dawn which returns to you at sunset. In him is contained all past history, the ancestors' offering to the future. Their quest was for him and for the whole silver chain of life back to the beginning of time, the unspilled time of the future.

When I saw this strange little Japanese doll with red body and black hair laughing at me, I was convinced that manhood and motherhood were at the very source of creation. Youth now was over. The shoulder of time clicked back into joint with a loud crack.

As with all brave women Helga's life had been put at risk because she had been weakened by hardship. Thankfully she survived this time. Perhaps her long training as a dancer had given her a physical plus that others might have lacked. I had asked a lot of her. This she had given me.

Only a few hours before the birth of my son my own life had been put on the line: I had been faced with execution. Also I had been set a high premium saving the boiler. Both times I had won, but I could well have killed the manager when I flung him in the slurry if his nutty little head had hit the steel footing of the drying machine.

I had come to the factory on the impulse of need and fitted the job so well it meant that, because I was connected with agricultural work as the Judge had directed I should be, I would have been exempt from going to war for the duration and automatically be promoted to foreman and then manager of my department.

Just before the birth of my son I had thrown my job away: we were again penniless. We were rejected absolutely this time by the Board of Guardians before whom I had to state my case once more, and visiting the great Bastille building with its aged ghosts toiling in the sunlight I wondered when death would take them quietly by the arm. There was no work anyone would give me and to avoid going to prison as some did, I joined a pacifist community in Devon, at Ashburton from where I worked as a coal-heaver unloading 20 ton truck loads in the railway siding. A harsh enough job which tore my hands till they were bleeding, but which was thankfully terminated when I let slip a two and a half hundredweight sack of corn over some steps to a barn. It wrenched a muscle in my back: an old wound from the dancing years. I could not walk.

The community in which we found ourselves was run by a tall, silent and serious person named Bazelgette: a man of infinite patience, for when I was incapacitated I realised that nobody worked, save one or two, and that nearly everyone lived on the central kitty to which I was now unable to contribute as part of the collective organism. How it worked I never understood. But for them, while I was down, we would not have eaten or had sanctuary. Now there was a child that was unthinkable. The central responsibility was shared by an attractive woman novelist who later married Bazelgette. I, as best man, reluctantly gave her away. Sometimes the Goddess smiles and passes by. That evening I spent with Oswald Blakeston and Max Chapman, poet and painter at a pub in Buckfastleigh. Walking home was the only time I can remember a main road flying up and hitting me in the face as

Forbears: Christian Gissel Berlin (great grandfather), Max Axel Christian Berlin (grandfather), Sven Berlin (uncle) and Karl Gustav Berlin (father).

Sven Hedin, explorer.

Uncle Sven jumping with Hawaii at St Cyr.

Wells Park, Sydenham.

The Crystal Palace, childhood playground.

Crystal Palace, with (right) Brunel's South Tower on fire and (below) the interior c.1910.

Mary Louise Berlin (mother), with Sven, Alma and Jack in 1915.

Alma in 1932 and Jack in 1934.

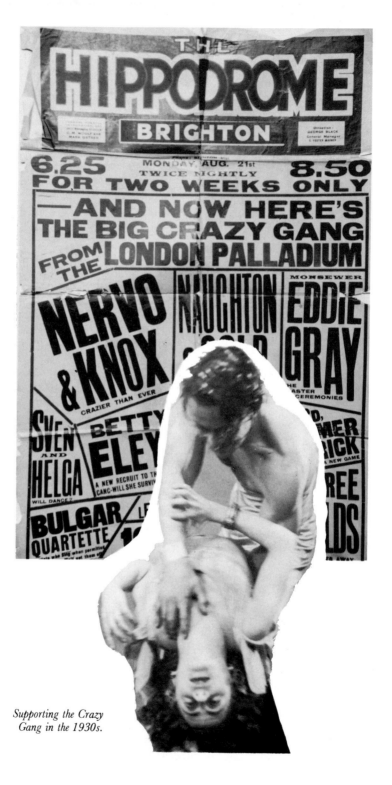

Supporting the Crazy Gang in the 1930s.

Adagio and bolero.

Adagio dancers *in bronze, 1966.*

Woman dancing, *bronze, 1966.*

Drawing for red dancer in alabaster, 1947
(photo: Dopita).

Drawing for weightlifter in marble, 1949
(Dopita).

Above *Flying angel and* left *ankle & thigh lifts (photos: Dopita).*

Arthur C. Hambly, 1960.

*Frank Turk, pencil & wash: Sven Berlin, 1940
(photo: John Polglaze).*

Jack Wilson, 1940.

Cottage, North Cliffs *watercolour 1939*.

Studio, *ink drawing 1939, and the author's first sculpture: sandstone head, 1938 (Dopita).*

First one-man show, Camborne Community Centre 1939. Looking at a portrait of Helga.

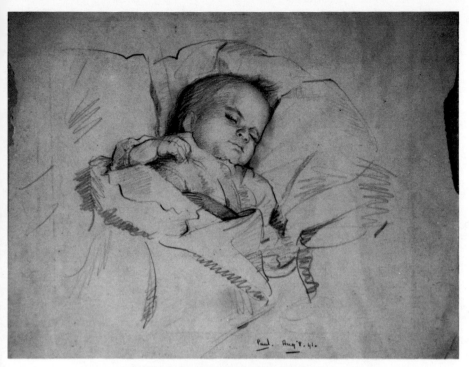

Paul sleeping, *pencil 1941 (Dopita)*.

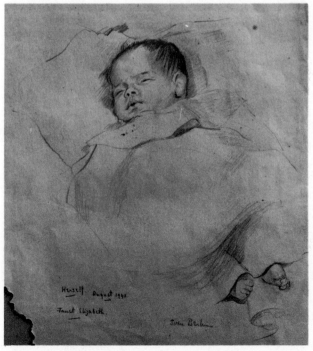

Janet sleeping, *pencil 1942 (Dopita)*.

Self portrait, *1941 (Dopita).*   Mother & Child, *1941 (Dopita).*

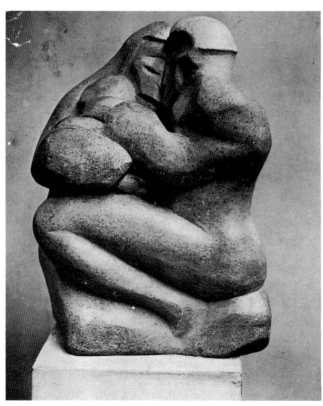

Man, woman and child *in polyphant stone.*

Man with a cat, *pencil 1941 (British Museum).*

*Naum Gabo and Adrian Stokes
(both Tate Archive).*

though I had stepped on a plank after 11 pints of rough cider. I did drawings of this genial pair. Most of the community was neurotic and quarrelsome, and it seemed to me, though its ideals were sincere, that only a half-truth was seen, which suggested a certain inner dishonesty, as though that cowl at birth had never been cut clean away exposing them to the tiger of reality. Perhaps that is why they gathered together.

I worked as a gardener in a girls' school and by reading the instructions on the seed packets planted a fine kitchen garden with even an asparagus trench. In between hours, or when it was raining, I sat in a bothy cutting and splitting wood and reading Thoreau and poetry, which has become a lifelong devotion. It was another haven. One day the head girl appeared at the door giving out all those vibrations a woman will when she wants a man to take her and I was sore put to it not to, for she was a fine creature. After several visits I found this very disturbing and knew that I would be vanquished if it went on. I went to the Dickensian but perceptive headmaster and gave in my notice. He looked at me over the top of his half glasses and said, after a pause,

'What a pity. You work so well. Is it er . . .'

'Yes!' I said.

'The German girl?'

'Yes. That is right.'

'Then I can easily correct that and you will stay.'

I refused his offer saying that it was also because I could not trust myself and I had a wife and young child. He finally let me go. But when I got back it had leaked out and I was accused by the community of fornication with a schoolgirl.

One day soon after another messenger of the Gods came in the form of a Miss Charles. She was a schoolmistress and a frequent visitor to the community. Miss Charles was a positive person with short hair cut like a man, a grey tweed suit, cut by a tailor, and brogue shoes with slit tongues. She was a nice honest woman and I got on well with her, for the unevenness of sex in others never worried me, as with Oswald and Max. It was their business if simply because the patterns which destiny present have to be worked to as they are and not as someone else wants them to be.

'Sven!' she said when she arrived one day. 'How would you like to go to Cornwall?' This was uncanny because it was just what my friend Jack Wilson had done, and just as unexpectedly.

'But I've just come from there!'

'How would you like to go back?'

'Yes, I would, but I can't see how it's possible.'

'I will tell you how it is possible. There is a school in Carbis Bay that wants a man to work in the kitchen garden and teach art in between. What about it? I am sure you will get the job.'

Helga was keen. We both realised the community was not for us, even though they had been so generous and patient. We decided to try it out.

That night I stood on the hills of Devon and watched Plymouth burning. Little did I realise till years later that Gabo the Russian was standing on the other side in Carbis Bay watching the same fire. The sky was lit up by flames from the city. Even the dull thud of bombs could be heard and the plonka-plonka-plonka of the anti-aircraft guns. The flak, the starshells, the explosions were exactly like the Crystal Palace firework shows I watched every Thursday evening as a boy. Perhaps this is what they meant. They were pointing a finger into history. History that was now exploding like the volcano described by Pliny the Younger. The forces of destruction had taken over and creation was no longer possible. The Dark Angel was among us.

The next morning I was out on the main road hitch-hiking to Cornwall. I walked through the still-smoking city, under twisted girders, a causeway of rock and concrete and death. The Old Testament God had vented his rage. Out of it came the horrifying beauty of broken houses like drunken women with pink, blue and golden skirts, their faces blackened. People crawled out of the dust. Here were the tracks of the tiger. The tigers of Wells Park, of Les Comberelles, and of my own self passing through a profound and intrinsic experience: that of becoming a complete human. A Composite Man strong enough to contain both good and evil.

As I got away from the city across that suicidal bridge of Brunel's over the Tamar, and the low hills of Cornwall started to close round me, I felt a sense of safety as though I was coming home; a great sense of uplift, because I knew I was on the right way to find an answer to my problem caused by standing against the cosmic forces of war when all the time they were active within me, tearing me apart. If I were not complete how could I become a complete artist speaking for my time?

An old Army man picked me up to give me a lift. He at once started to question me. Who was I? Why was I not in uniform? Was I on leave? When I told him I was a pacifist and my name was Berlin, he started to rage and threatened me with prison. But I stayed calm and told him I had already been on trial and allocated land work. That calmed him a little and I believe a natural sense of perception made him see I was not pretending. Eventually he put me off without taking me to the police station. After a further stretch, a beautiful woman in a fur coat driving a sports car gave me another lift, treated me to lunch at a pub, didn't care a damn that I was a pacifist although she had just seen her husband off to the front, but left me at her front gate when I refused going in for coffee. Until finally by evening I reached Carbis Bay and stood looking across to St Ives in the stillness of early summer. The little town that held the map of my life in its pocket for the time to come and the footprint of my searching soul.

This was my one attempt at teaching. I was wary. I found it boring and without reward to tell the laws of drawing and get people to master them. I expected them to know already, I had not the vital dedication of my own master. Helga hated it. Only up-to-sevens gave great joy and taught me by their innocent power of invention. But I am glad destiny diverted me from becoming a teacher. Later I saw friends, good artists and writers, go into the colleges or one of the great killing bottles of our time, like television, radio and the Royal Ordnance and Foreign Offices and the flame to be extinguished. The choice is theirs – however tough it is that is always there. They come out after doing a life sentence, knowing it all, but the candle has gone out, the shuttie is rusty and does not work any more. They have to go to the living artist to draw on his vitality and inspiration. What else can they do? Having all doors open they sometimes become famous for what is not theirs and the original creator is pushed out, which is a shame. When this happens they are like the fur-trappers: they don't want the rare animal for his own sake – they want his life and the gift that makes him beautiful, because the true self can only work from the original fountain head which is the only well of the living spirit and therefore of art. I therefore say that teaching is the Behemoth that drinks the rivers of creation dry. This does not apply to the great teachers like Turk and Hambly who are in line with Socrates or to dedicated teachers who are always everywhere as their vocation – thank God. But for me who cannot teach there were other compensations.

Many close friends are teachers who collect my work and for whom I have the highest respect. It is from them I have gathered the knowledge of the dilemma that sometimes faces them: but it is also they who enhance the vision of life for themselves and others.

The school was recently evacuated from Hampshire and settled in its new shell at Headlands Hotel, also overlooking the blue bay with tall pines, like a painting by Cézanne. I was kept waiting in the morning room where there was a single painting over the marble mantelpiece. It was of a ship coming into harbour, but the sea, the houses and harbour itself were turning round it like a wheel of which the ship was the axis. It was a new experience and I realised that this is how it must feel to be in a ship at the wheel steering it into harbour. It was painted in low tones of brown and green and white.

Someone said: 'Isn't it marvellous?' I swung round and faced a young attractive woman. A very vital person also, wearing dungarees. She spoke with a Scots accent. She told me her name was Wilhelmina Barns-Graham and that she was a painter. 'Moi aussi. Are you after the job?'

'Why yes. I've just been interviewed. He's all right but I don't think I'll get it! And you?'

'The same! But who did this marvellous painting? Did he do it?'

'No. It's by a local fisherman, called Alfred Wallis.'

At that moment a tall, bony, middle-aged, charming, etiolated man came in.

'I'm Rawson, the headmaster. Will you come this way? Excuse me Miss Barns-Graham.'

Although Willie had just come down from Edinburgh College with a diploma in painting, I could do the kitchen garden as well as teach art, though I had no references, except the incredible Miss Charles who acted as ambassador in this one instance and then disappeared. I got the job. And Helga could teach dancing, although I was never forgiven for including her in her absence, in a joint commitment that included work she hated. Also in that one interview was contained the strand that led to my knowing and even working with the leading artists of that time, with their revolutionary abstract painting and Constructivism. I was to be shared in my capacity as gardener with Adrian Stokes who had started a market garden at Little Park Owles a little further around the Bay. He had been responsible for getting Ben Nicholson, Barbara Hepworth and Naum Gabo from London and had set them up in houses also around the bay. Adrian was the doyen of all patrons, and in doing this he acted as bird claw upon which the seeds of contemporary art had been carried from war torn Russian, Europe and London to this one place where my own destiny, through a tortuous magnetism, had also drawn me and my little family.

It became all at once a source of revelation. My own physical prowess had enabled me to enter a closed community, an 'inner circle', as Ben called it later, of advanced artists, learn from them, listen to their ideas and discoveries and even become an intellectual of the time – at which I now shudder.

I fitted in well because Adrian was not only himself a good painter and had, till then, been part of the Euston Road School with Coldstream, Rogers, Graham Bell and Victor Pasmore, but was also an authority on the ballet, a friend of Ninette de Valois and other great ballerinas, and author of a book, *Russian Ballet*. It did not disturb him to find a young man with a dancer's physique digging his garden. He was excited that I had met Massine and keenly interested in my long experience as an adagio dancer. When I was digging he used to say, 'You look marvellous, Sven, just like Samson when you dig.' It became for me a kind of dance. His other books also were an influence, particularly *Colour and Form* which gave me a new understanding and consciousness in painting. He told me about Italy where he had been living, about Bernard Berenson, the great connoisseur, critic and collector. Also D.H. Lawrence for whom he corrected the proofs of *Lady Chatterley's Lover*, to take them to the printer the next day when Lawrence was ill in Florence. Each person I have met has given me something special to remember. With Adrian and Margaret, drinking tea on the loggia at Little Park Owles, it was many things I could not have heard in any other way, adding depth to my culture – and humour.

Abstract art was already beginning to affect my work when I went first to call on Ben and Barbara. It was quite breathtaking to be inside the new world: like being in the stratosphere. But I had gone there to see the Wallis paintings and they broke over me like a wave reaching deep in the caves of the mind, like hearing Beethoven for the first time.

Gabo, to whom I owed so much, was always for me the real genius in this group, and the most inspiring. I called him the Asian Bowman after a drawing by Pisanello. To go for a walk with Gabo was like passing through the invisible frames of existence when every tree, every flower, every stone and star was transformed into a beautiful construction. A man of intense energy, but subject to equally deep depressions.

'Humanity,' he said, 'eez zee protoplasm. Zee artist eez zee spermatozoa!' His gift to me was the awareness of invisibility in space.

Bernard Leach, on the hill, became a close friend because of my interests in Oriental art and Zen, first awakened in me by Turk.

John Wells was still working on the Scilly Isles as a doctor. It was to be 1945 before we met. But the central mandala which was to form this period of history was already pinned down and radiating its power. I had crossed a rubicon by returning to Cornwall, following the thin silver thread Miss Charles had carried to me. But it was only to set up base camp before a greater adventure on the dark side of the moon.

I was infected by the new religion: the liberation of form and colour, the discovery of space. Also the understanding of structure first learnt in my engineering days, finally growth and movement in space, awakened in the dancing years. I was painting and constructing in abstract forms. Even then there was a draught at my shoulder from the advancing holocaust which I must face before I could fully engage the unique experience of working at the centre of what John Wells later called the Disturbance in the West.

It was as though I was standing on the rim of a great wheel upon which I had to risk everything before I could be finally fitted to the act of creation: to ride upon it as part of an initiation to test my powers before manhood could be bestowed. At this point the slow beat of destiny could be heard again.

Helga had become pregnant again. Although the school was one of advanced Free Education based on the writings of A.S. Neill and Rudolph Steiner, devoted to the spirit and mind of the younger generation, there was no place for the yet unborn and we were told to go. Once more we trailed our few belongings out on to the Zennor Moors with horse and cart to a cottage lent to us by Robin Nance where I inadvertently burnt his secret supply of special wood collected from wrecks and stored there for cabinet making, for which he forgave me but I never forgave myself. We lived in terrible poverty near Zennor of which John Heath-Stubbs wrote his prophetic poem

> This is a hideous and wicked country
> Sloping to hateful sunsets and the end of time.

The hewn stones, the cromlechs and menhirs, quoits, Ogham stones, forts and foges of prehistory – and the merciless indifferent ocean are no place to be with no support at all.

My job with Adrian was no longer possible, my contacts with the artists cut off because I was too tired after working on the fields to go into town for any social reason but I did go among the old cottagers of St Ives getting stories and information about Alfred Wallis. Returning one night by bicycle across the moor to my cottage, where we now existed again at starvation level, out on the Atlantic I saw a British convoy being attacked by enemy planes. The flak, the bombs, the ships sinking as I had seen Plymouth burn. I knew then that this force was in me and would destroy my life and the lives of my family if I did not recognise it. Back in the cottage, late in the night, I silently tore an armchair to pieces. My daughter, Janet, was born at a friend's house, Frank Vibert, in time to enchant me with her marvellous eyes and feet. I joined up and went to war, as an Advanced Forward Observation Ack working between the two great armies. I was known as Bomb Berlin R.A.

Before I finally went away I got my family into a studio in St Ives where I was also able to complete my research on Wallis and start writing the text of a book after having published, with the help of Herbert Read, a pilot article in Cyril Connolly's *Horizon*. The impact of my initial reaction to Wallis had been strengthened even more by the knowledge of the conditions in which he painted his pictures, and lived and died. They took him away to the workhouse; this little old man who without realising it inspired the artists of the twentieth century. I realised that I must preserve his memory in a way that was never comprehended by the artists who had discovered him and collected his works for a few shillings: those unique paintings which came out of himself, unadulterated by any art fashion of the time.

Later on, when I came back on leave before the invasion of France, I started a collection for Wallis's gravestone. I wanted to carve it myself, but could not, Barbara Hepworth refused and in the end Bernard Leach produced the tall pottery lighthouse in large golden tiles with the inscription

INTO THY HANDS O LORD

Adrian Stokes bought the grave to save him from the paupers' corner – one with a sea view, as Barbara succinctly put it. I helped to arrange the funeral when Wallis's body was already on the train from Penzance to Little Park Owles, Adrian Stokes being the executor of the estate.

I finished my book on Wallis in the Army in a Quiet Room of the Methodists' Chapel at Hitchin after my initial training, and signed a contract for publication with the Sri Lankan poet Tambimuttu on D Day, then went on the Invasion in the barges from Gosport – the loneliest journey in the world – never expecting to see England again. Of this I have written in detail in my war book *I am Lazarus*.

But I will say here of the experience of war: it was the first time I knew myself to be on my own, though never alone for one minute among all those dying men.

> A sullen single bodied beast –
> and she waiting on the hill
> Pale as a feather . . .

save for the tiger at my side who occasionally roared, until after being terrified, I passed through the fear barrier and found fighting an ecstasy.

It must have been just before joining up and during my initial training that I made trips to London and discovered a tiny gallery in Charles II Street called the Modern Art Gallery, run by an outsize unique man, Jack Bilbo, with a black beard and an enormous energy for the work of unknown artists. We took to each other; he and his Swedish wife Owo were kind and enthused over the work I showed them: I even sold my first painting and a small sculpture in lead to go from a London gallery. After my isolation and indeed starvation on the North Cliffs, to find such people, free from the parsimonious habits of some dealers, was to recharge my beliefs as an artist at a time of massacre. Jack Bilbo was himself a powerful painter. What others called his flamboyancy has kept him out of the halls of fame until now: the museums are starting to collect him. Many famous artists owe a tribute to this fierce artist and most gentle person.

Gabo had told me about the fear barriers before I left. He told me that in the Russian Revolution they could tell who would die among the young soldiers when they came up to the front line, and who would live till the next day. If I kept my inner knowledge I would live and not be killed. I would be all right. I still see his inscrutable honest Tartar face saying this and his words went into my soul. Many of my companions died where I remained unscratched except when I was caught up in barbed wire in a shelling. Even then I flung myself free at the last moment. Until one afternoon I saw a low airburst shell against the sky. It was a ranging enemy round and I knew that at nightfall we would be shelled. The Angel of Darkness had said that I must die. But again I was spared though my closest friends were hit. After that I had to go forward and slept in a morass where the Maas had flooded, with rats crawling over me, and caught an illness that brought me home. It had been a massacre.

O lock up the stars, take down the sun
Earth is too violent for their ancient eyes,
Clear all furniture from the skies,
Put loveliness away till this is done.

They have seen Cain and Herod and Pontius Pilate
But no crime is equal to mine and yours:
Angels, stand fast at the Sacred Gate,
Stop the comet, close Heaven's doors.

It seems politic to put away the moon,
Fold your shame in the shadow of your brain;
None will disagree that Beauty dies too soon,
But it seems politic – the time will come again.

Until then I had made friends with death, with whom I had long
conversations, who taught me not to be afraid because, if life was
too terrible to endure there was always the safe haven of dying, not
to crawl maimed on the face of the earth or spit out my love as a
shattered lung. It was for this life, this death, first and last, that I
went to war. I returned with the Cretan look and a great sadness in
my heart which has never gone away, and which I did not see in
the face of my friends when I got home – only Gabo's. I was one
man unwritten by the Hun.

Helga did not want me to return. I set up in a concrete shack on
the rocks I called the Tower and there worked and lived as an artist
on my own. Like Brody Berlin, the Wandering Jew, I had crossed a
new frontier toward which I had long been skulking to be born. The
world had indeed changed.

I was on the threshold of a new experience which was not just a
personal change, but a seismic movement in the structure of history,
not before known to me. I was to be caught up in a profound
reorientation of the human psyche as the western world readjusted
itself to the exigencies of peace, of the change from the destructive
forces that had torn us apart to the creative processes that would
bring us a moderate Eden – 'at least Beveridge!' as Ben Nicholson
put it.

My Tower was to be my new fortress: my observation post from
which to defend my position against the enemy and formulate myself
as an artist.

It was here I knocked on the stone door of the unconscious to
enter the cavern of the Third Continuum and in the depth of the

Atlantic night, quite alone, I learned after several months and finally years to become a sculptor.

But before I went to the Tower and took up residence, I was in Penzance Hospital, expecting to go back to the front for the Rhine crossing, but the military report on my health ordered that I should go to see a psychiatrist before this happened. A sensitive MO in Holland had seen to this in his notes when I left. At the Penzance Hospital one of the nurses named Mary had worked on the Scilly Isles at the little hospital built by John Wells, the doctor incumbent there. This was the first thread between us and probably because of this he wrote to me when I was moved to a madhouse in Birmingham to be finally discharged.

So at this time I went about in 'hospital blues' like the soldiers I could remember after the First World War, in Wells Park at Sydenham. Because of the break at home I used to go to see my friends in my free time each afternoon: among them Adrian Stokes for whom I had been gardener, and his Scottish wife Margaret Mellis. They made me welcome and the atmosphere of space and culture and love of beautiful things did much to heal the mind after the senseless horrors of the battlefield. They were immediately so excited by my uniform of cobalt blue with a scarlet tie on a shirt of titanium white they simultaneously set about painting my portrait. This went on for some days. Margaret took on a full length reclining figure. Adrian ventured a portrait head and shoulders which he painted almost politely, apologising for, as he said, having 'forgotten to put in the mouth, Sven!' His son Telfer, then about four, had noticed it first and Adrian decided that was proof that the mistake was 'genuinely primitive' so the mouth was left out. These visits helped me to believe in painting again and to keep up a friendship which Adrian had nourished with letters to France in which he finally inspired me to write *I am Lazarus*. I met Gabo again and was guest at his bungalow 'Faerystone' where he showed me his spiral theme against the stars and Marion, Gabo's wife, gave hospitality. Ben Nicholson, Barbara Hepworth, Wilhelmina Barns-Graham, Bernard Leach, his son David, Patrick Heron also. All came and went to this tiny cell of culture and creation Adrian had kept alive during the war and I realised that there were other ways to minister against the dark angel than by murdering one's comrades and enemies. It was only that for me there had never been a way to compromise for long. All or nothing. It was usually all. Before the battleground had changed me I was content to dig for Adrian, and take a plant's eye view of passing genius. Ben in his white beret and red sports car. Stephen Spender with his beautiful woman Natasha who played Chopin by the open French windows. Gabo in two shirts – one ultramarine with short sleeves and one vermilion with long sleeves so that it looked as if his arms were bleeding. 'But you must keep on digging Sven,' Adrian told me in his humorous and kindly way. 'I know you are interested in my friends but I am frightened that awful agricultural inspector, Mr Rowe, will look over the hedge and see you idling. He could send you to prison!' 'Yes, Adrian!' I said and went on looking. When I came back from war and began to see the patterns forming I was more interested in what was happening behind the scenes, which might affect our lives. Such was a day when Adrian came hurrying towards me with the news that Rudolph Hess had dropped into Scotland in a parachute and his cleaning lady, who had told him before it was announced, declared that 'Hess carried a typewriter, Mr Stokes, my 'ansome, that typed out terrible diseases.' Adrian told me stories like this while he was painting my portrait without a mouth. He said that his own paintings, mostly of still life, were like a ballet by Mozart. A marvellous way to explain.

One day he looked up suddenly, hearing a voice. 'Gabo. Good heavens, Sven, what is wrong with him shouting like that? He looks quite mad.'

At the end of the drive was a tiny figure shouting and moving towards us with flayed vermilion arms, a linen hat on his Tartar face, linen trousers on his short legs: an Asian Bowman by Pisanello ready to do battle. I could not grasp what he said. Adrian could and was smothering a smile as he told me.

'Barra Barra, she 'ave stolen zee egg!'

'Who is Barra Barra? What does he mean?' I asked.

'Barbara Hepworth. He is still on about that. It is to do with one of his constructions in the shape of an egg. A perspex oval built on a curve with intersecting wires, like the spokes of a bike wheel.'

'And bloody beautiful!' put in Margaret from under her dark hair as she went on painting.

'He says Barbara took it off him and did a big one in wood with the inside scooped out and string instead of wire. I thought Gabo would be angry.'

'Who invented it in the first place?' I asked.

'Gabo I think.' They said this together and it was obviously true, but Adrian became cautious not wishing to offend anybody, especially Gabo who seemed to pass out of the sunlight, through the dark cypress trees into the room where I was being painted. 'What on earth's the matter, Gabo? You look quite white.'

'Barra Barra. She ave stolen zee egg!'

The quiet vibrations were gone. The place was electrified by this historic outburst against another sculptor who had taken his theme and interpreted it in in terms of carving rather than construction. It was something Henry Moore had already tried but neither of them in terms of invisibility like Gabo. This was his particular genius, that he made visible the invisibility of space without giving it opaque substance. It was the first time it had been done and was of great importance to Gabo, who was to have a show in London after my first show at Lefevre. What had triggered this scene was not only the dispute over the egg but he had heard that the month of his show had been switched with Barbara's who would now come first, following me. The egg would then be hers.

It was with the help of Ben Nicholson that my show had been fixed, after I had waylaid, with the help of Edward le Bas, the dealer MacDonald, and got him to come to my tower to see my work. I was but a pawn around which this huge drama pivoted. The outcome was that Gabo withdrew his show and went to America on the last leg of his journey into exile. There they recognised him in his own right, but it was about 20 years before the Tate finally gave a retrospective exhibition of this major artist, who though Russian, like myself was probably a Wandering Jew.

The memory has a way of squashing events together like toffees, so they can't later be separated. When exactly this or that happened is difficult to say. I came across a letter from Adrian recently which is concerned mainly about organising the subscription for Wallis's grave, saying 'you are the Field Marshal in all this' and giving a list of likely donors: 'Jim Ede should be good for £5. Then there is Watson's £10. That makes £20. Barbara should be good for £1 . . . I could not approach Barbara and Ben myself, as I am no longer on speaking terms and I shall sever relations and finally for a great deal too much more than excellent reasons.' I don't know if the break was to do with Gabo and the stolen egg, but I do recall Margaret being angry and Adrian feeling that he had been treated shoddily over some basic footing in their relations.

I know that about this time Ben sold Adrian one of his paintings and got them to alter the room to suit the picture by changing the whole decor and painting the walls white. But the decorator, not knowing the power of colour and light, chose a white on the yellow side of the spectrum rather than on the blue side. This brought out the qualities in the painting Ben had sold them but unfortunately exaggerated the yellows in both Adrian and Margaret's paintings, which were quite closely in sympathy with one another. It was about this Margaret was so angry. Soon after war was over they sold up, went back to London and I never saw them again. Two rare people for whom I had and still have so much to thank.

After my final discharge from the Army on VE Day I found myself in a demob suit in Manchester with the world spinning round my head amid Lowry-like streets and houses and matchstick people all as dancing drunk and bewildered as I.

During the war, as a lonely single-bodied beast, I had kept faith because it seemed to me that the dream of wholeness with the family in the midst of death and destruction was the only thing worth preserving. I wrote this for Helga.

> If I go down
> Remember how I loved this spinning world
> And loved my children's ways
> And all the tall brown trees
> That stand along the ridge at autumn time.
>
> Discard your rage –
> Crown of my death's triumph:
> Turn your eyes upon the sun, the sea
> And think how in our questing days
> We laughed . . .
>
> If I go down we may not roam again
> But O, remember how I loved this spinning world
> And listen in the silence of your home
> How I may move and I may spin
> Within your spinning brain.

What was to follow was the advance of the Eye of the Hurricane out of the ending of the war. It was in this centrifugal force of creation that we were all caught.

PART TWO

THE SONG OF THE TOWER

If one is as unfortunate as I have been, and become famous for things one has not done and words one has not uttered, one has to admit that legend is stronger than history, because history is truth which becomes false in the long run, and legend is falsehood which, in the long run, becomes truth.

Cocteau

Those words, classicism, romanticism, and so forth, are seen to answer to distinct attitudes of mind; and the transitions from one period to another show themselves as governed by laws of rhythmic change, the sway of which extends to moral happenings.

Cazamian

In all my deepsea orisons of stone
I carve you now my praise as then,
Simple as seaweed the wave chars.
Only in death is man alone – out there
Difficult and strange as the stars
When the seabell tolls its fist of prayer

Szaint Szven

The law of history is enantiodromic and changes into its opposite as the task closes, to save the life-force being totally spent: thus the destructive into the creative and vice versa.

Sven Berlin

Disturbance in the West

To be one in a tower is a rare and difficult thing: once it has happened, one is one in a tower for all time. There is no way out, no support, no rear echelon – nothing but an absolute belief in oneself as an entity progressing through the universe on a journey from nowhere to nowhere, casting a light for those who follow taking it from those who have gone before, never to let it be extinguished. This for me is the meaning of life on which all spiritual and physical progress, all growth of mind and soul depends, moving towards a superconsciousness as if God had created us to complete himself in this way. If the dedication is complete there is no room for personal salvation, which in the end is usually a parachute that does not open.

On my first night, my Tower was empty but for a packing case, a camp bed I had found there, a double-elephant drawing board from my days as an engineer and an old ship's stove in the corner. This was my new home for which I must pay £2.10/- a quarter in advance. I was looking across the Atlantic Ocean. Below me was the deep violet shadow of a fisherman's hut and beyond the curved sandy beach held in by rocks anchored to a black moon. A little way from the shore there rose a larger rock I called the Mermaid, because she looked like a reclining woman with the waves breaking round her, carved by time. Above all this was the gentle music of the sea and the stars in their courses. I say – alone, man alone, but there was a Presence that was tall like starlight and breathed the measure as the ocean. He who was always there during the five years that were to follow was myself – the moon glinted in my eye, the warm summer stung my lips with acicular salt wind. The voice within me was the voice of the sea-bird wheeling in the night. I had no candle so I went to sleep on the bed left there by the last occupant, who was a prostitute.

In the morning I was wakened by the fishermen coming in from the night-fishing to put their gear away in the tarred hut below my window. When I went outside to wash under the single tap on the wall they were at first silent, giving out that curious feeling of suspicion as the Cornish do, perhaps even a little scared. But when they recognised me it was all right. They knew me from when I worked with their fathers on the fields over North Cliffs and St Ives

– cutting broccoli, pulling turnips, picking sprouts and tilling the earth by hand with the long Cornish spade, planting potatoes. I had come in among them again and was no longer an outsider. Had it gone the other way I would have been thrown in the sea. This unconscious taking of my life into theirs saved me. 'Taz Svan!' they said. 'Ow are ee then?' One handed me a mug of cocoa, which burned the inside of my heart. I felt great joy as though I had come home. I had found a haven on a rock when I had nowhere else to go. They went on spreading their nets to dry, stacking their gear, mending their lobster pots, coiling their longlines. Short stocky men with clear blue eyes in dark jerseys and seamen's caps. They did not question what I was doing there.

They soon became quite friendly and when they changed the stove in their ship they gave me the old one to fit in upstairs instead of the one already there, which was cracked. The short metal stack was still alright. This meant that with driftwood collected from the beach, I could keep warm and cook a meal, even fish they gave me like a thick steak of conger they left on the wooden stair one day. I made cocoa and, like Gaudier-Brzeska, I got the things and had a *pot au feu* going, adding to it each day until one day I let the fire out and it went off.

I got candles.

On my packing case I placed the double-elephant drawing board in default of an easel, under the window on the Atlantic side. Now I was set up to live and work. A wild creature has its own survival kit built in: transport, heating system, defence mechanism, feeding and sleeping. Why should I need more? Once this footing had been made among these simple people, who adopted Alfred Wallis from Devon at the turn of the century, I had gained a tiny fortress I called the Tower. The Tower, The Island, St Ives. It was not a real Island but had been once in a bygone century, now joined to the mainland by a short neck being filled in just outside my door. When later I wrote *The Dark Monarch* I made the access tidal. Nor was it a real tower.

It was nothing like Yeats' Tower at Sligo, nor Jung's Tower at Bollingen, Hardy's Tower at Wimborne where I now live or one of Brunel's Crystal Palace Towers. Nor was it like Helen's topless tower at Illium, though one of such beauty did visit my shack and gave me her love. It was a simple upright square building set on the rocks in one of those backyards of the Atlantic that fringe the coast, built of concrete and reinforced with iron bedsteads against the ocean gales. It had an eaved slate roof with a galvanized iron stack. A single door painted red, upon which I placed a copper mask to keep away the evil spirits. Two tiny rooms. One upstairs for sleeping and painting, one downstairs I used for sculpture, where I fixed a bench with a vice and a turn-table made from the cast iron wheel of an old-fashioned clothes mangle. The rollers from the mangle were made from lingam vitae: out of these I carved some good sculptures. The larger work was done outside, often at night by lamplight, on a plat where I could set up a big stone like Jacob and come to it at dawn. Other materials were teak and mahogany from driftwood, sandstone, granite, diorite, quartz and blue elvin from the shore. When Guido Morris arrived soon after, he gave me handmade paper upon which to draw and if and when I sold something, which was surprisingly often, I gave most of it to the family who lived now in an expensive flat on the wharf and kept only enough for paints.

At first there was no income but the driving rain, the diurnal miracle of the sun and the universe at night, like a great mobile sculpture in the sky, to celebrate my existence. No time but the changing tides and no master but the maker of my hands, for whom work was my continuous and most ancient prayer.

This I understood to be the roots of Cornwall just as it was in 1938 when I worked on the fields at North Cliffs and on Zennor Moors in 1940. I knew the people from inside, working with them to survive as they had done for centuries. I learned their code of truth among themselves, always helping and trusting each other. They gave me this rough trust.

It was because of this that I was able to enter their cottages and listen to their stories by oil lamp and candle and firelight of Alfred Wallis, in those hard days before the war; of how they contained him with his suspicions of poisoning, his eccentricities and madness, outside away from the artists who came to see him and took away his work for a few shillings; who hadn't any idea of his real background and the stresses upon him. They gave me a picture of the secret life of a seaman and a country man outsiders did not know, because to keep it hidden has always been the fortress of the peasant people. I was inside the real Cornwall. It was from this centre that my own work emanated – not from any art society that might be founded on a false premise but from the deep ocean round the reclining sculpture that is the peninsula of Cornwall with its caves and tunnels and mines jutting under the sea, its wave-worn rocks and flashing granite cliffs that are themselves like giant sculptures watching over the oceans. The whole structure and psyche of this place with its endless orchestrations of sound and form and colour and light, is a symphony that can never end, to be heard by those who listen, seen by those who are watchful, from the meanest tinkle of a sea briton against the sunlight to the mighty thundering of waves and the blue and gold and violet melodies of creation, where once God split the rock with a falling star and death blackened the side of a hill. This was my shrine. A tower built on a rock that once housed a whore.

One of the first things I did when I moved into the Tower was to unpack an Army ammo box with my name and number on it which I had taken through all the battles in France to Holland, where I had to abandon it. But my Commanding Officer, Captain Harry Mainwaring, true to his word, returned it to me uncensored. I found in it many drawings of French peasants half eaten by rats, all my notes and journals from which I later wrote my war book, *I am Lazarus*. Also in a separate package I found a letter John Wells had sent to me when I was in the Military Hospital in Birmingham, no doubt reminded by Mary of Madron, Penzance to do so.

The hospital I had been in was horrifying, for it was a madhouse being used by the military for the purpose of rebuilding broken men, reconstructing them with new legs and arms, metal skulls, perspex eyes and plastic arteries – building the edifice of the invisible mind with searching labour and therapeutic art, psychotic analysis. Carving inelegant faces with plastic surgery and, as fallen statues discovered in a ruined city, set them up like clowns to laugh at themselves and learn to do good for others when so little good had been done unto them, and to forgive their trespassers. I listened to them howl in the night in padded cells and climb drunk through the windows at dawn. I saw them dying and go mad for their Kingdom Come. I saw them trained by nurses with endless patience to walk and face the unknown terrors of peace. It was here I received this letter from John Wells which was not only a private miracle, but an exact formula for healing a spirit that was like sunlight on a broken temple I had no way to rebuild. It was the start of a friendship that was to last a lifetime.

After skulking about the wharfs of St Ives and Penzance for a few days I decided to go and see him. I sent a message and on the spur of the moment in bright sunlight boarded the *Scillonian* at Penzance for St Mary's Island, running down the long peninsula that Alfred Wallis knew and painted so well: its rocks of granite, its tar black cottages, its cows chewing pungent green grass, until at the end of the land we headed for the pelagic seas toward Wolf lighthouse. Finally into the island waterways from where a motor torpedo boat came out to meet us, firing patterns of depth charges to celebrate Victory Day, the crew holding up great fish as an offering to life – the turning away from evil by which, like a Cain, so many of us were now marked. I leaned over the rail and saw a dolphin turning in the bow wave just missing cutwater, smiling with joy. He was like an image inside a greenstone. As the houses and the quay of the little island sailed towards us dressed overall with coloured flags, I saw a man waving. A broad red faced man with the blue eyes of a Celt. I knew it was John Wells, as he must have known it was me waving back, although we had never met before. His disordered hair and internal smile gave him a sense of indefinable madness.

Everywhere in the streets the islanders were dancing, looking larger than their cottages, dressed in bright garlands of flowers and coloured costumes with violins, accordions, brass euphonium, base drum and fife, sounding like the little town band Beethoven fitted into his 9th Symphony. It was, indeed, a great symphony being written and performed in the middle of an ocean the depth of the mind and spirit that inspired us. A victory carnival.

If John Wells and I had nothing else in common for destiny to bring us together, we both loved drinking and went straight to the pub, which was open till late. When they started to close John bought a sackful of drink and we went back to the house where we drank till dawn, with a beautiful Swedish woman and Tambimuttu the Sri Lankan poet and publisher who was down from London. John put on a record of Stravinsky's *Le Sacre du Printemps* and we danced, Tambi and I and the Swede, through the whole work, his dark figure and long black hair contrasting with her gold: a perfect conjunction with me weaving between them. The *duende* rose through our bare feet. I was in a natural heaven. The Ice Queen had followed me from the arctic circle that contained my ancestors, as though she were a goddess sent to heal me after the war. I fell away from her at dawn, extinguished.

This is what John called 'Living in all directions, my beauty!'

My friend took the revelry quite calmly and seemed quite unaffected. He took a cold bath. We had breakfast served by his housekeeper, the motherly Mrs Edwards. He went into his morning surgery and then took me on his rounds, not from house to house, but from island to island (Les Iles, as he called them) in his small boat driven by an outboard motor.

We landed for a time on the uninhabited island of Samson. It was so washed by the Atlantic tides, the light of sun and moon over the centuries, it seemed brighter than anywhere I had ever been. It was as though the circular sky acted as a giant searchlight reflector, making a polished form of almost celestial beauty enclosed in endless silence, except for the murmur of the sea: clear green, serene blue, suzerain purple, platinum gold; the call of the sea birds; the skull of a dolphin bleached white and worn smooth as though its creator had been too well pleased to take it further, leaving it as a colophon that he had been there. There were spiral shells about my feet, starfish and crabs. A shark fin passed in the deep to remind us of death, the eternal divider who made possible the coming together and the great battle for survival that went on below the surface. After having helped to split the skull of Europe I now saw the laws of creation converge to make a whole new image as though at the beginning of Time. Everywhere we saw that this was true – the more so because we knew it to be true.

John threw a stone into the sea, and shouted, 'Disturbance in the West! That's what we'll call it!'

We had been composing a ballet together as we chugged between the islands in his little boat to visit his patients. A ballet of the ocean which would include a galliard for the pelagic fishes, a mazurka for the crabs and lobsters, a pas de deux for the dolphins, a pavan for the octopus and an andantino for the dancing dead. Somehow the music would be written when we were out of our skulls with vision or some passing God had come to lend his mind, while we got on with the decor which would echo the architecture of the oceans, structure of rocks, colours of fishes – lung pink of gurnards, iridescent blue of coelacanth, nurse shark grey, putrid green and ochre of moray eel, scarlet of sudden death, violet of the unconscious, and the silver syzygy of conjunction – all painted by ourselves.

The vision was never to be completed, but it was unique and showed me how right I had been to follow the law that seemed to have guided me here and find another person who saw behind the facade of harsh realism the workings of the creator from which we were extended to ourselves create new images out of the experience. There seemed to be no crick in the way we felt about this and perhaps because it was shared it sparked in me the flash of consciousness I needed to see what was happening. There was a disturbance in the deep ocean of the mind, like a volcano to whose mountain range we were joined – deep answering unto deep.

Although John Wells had been exposed to the war as the only doctor on the islands, rescuing and attending at all hours to ships' crews that had been mined and to pilots who had been shot down, and made abstract constructions out of perspex gun turrets they gave him, I don't think he or I knew what violence the forces behind our vision would bring about as part of the slip-stream left over from the war. The stronger the movement of a natural force becomes the stronger its opposite will be. Pliny the Younger wrote, after the eruption of Vesuvius that destroyed Pompeii: 'My soul shudders at recalling the memory!' I feel much the same when I come to record how the beauty of our little volcano was to cast hot ash and molten lava on the forms of those who were working about its feet, painting and sculpting. The poets saw it coming. The Cornish stood and watched in silence with the ancient insight of racial memory. Lanyon fell from the sky and broke his back. Hepworth, like Joan of Arc, was burned to death.

> blackfaced the villagers
> Remember burnings by the hewn stones . . . .

Earlier, at the root of it all, Christopher Wood, who so influenced Ben Nicholson, threw himself under a train at Salisbury. Bryan Wynter died needlessly of heart failure in his prime. David Haughton's place caught fire and destroyed years of work. Roger Hilton held the hand of the golden lady too long and died of alcoholic excess. Augustus John's son, Elffin, was drowned off Sennen. Lord Russell's daughter burnt herself to death. Bernard Leach's pottery was bombed by a single land mine and my own cottage was set on fire at Cripplesease. Alfred Wallis died in the workhouse.

There is a force in Cornwall which, like the radium locked in its native pitchblende, unless it is transmuted by the spirit in man, will destroy who handles it.

When John Wells threw a stone into the sea and made his utterance, a jet of energy was released inside us and in the world around the uninhabited island on which we stood – signed by a dolphin's skull. The slow pavan of the octopus had begun and the andantino of the dancing dead.

It was the inherent goodness of the situation that made our vision so positive. I remember picking up a shell on the fringe of the sea and, holding it to my ear, thought I heard the first premonitions of eternity as its spiral shape entered my soul and I was at peace at last in this huge dream into which I had been imagined. The war was over. The dream atmosphere was everywhere a new reality. Even when John took me to the little hospital he told me he had built on the island of St Mary's, and showed me my own hand

under an x-ray as we searched for a bullet. We found the bullet and
watched the skeleton of the hand articulate freely. It was an
unconscious reminder that we were to help create a Renaissance.
We called on the young keeper of the airport named Nightingale
and carved fish on bones we had picked up on the beach for his
children. We joined the French crabbers to drink wine. We painted
together. We wrote to our friends about our work and theirs, as
John had written to me. Lanyon among them. I returned to the
mainland feeling like Odysseus again, having escaped the magic of
the island and done all I could to encourage this splendid painter to
come back to the mainland, which he did soon after. We have not
seen each other much since because we have each been searching for
the secret of life in our own way.

John Wells is the son of a bacteriological research worker of St
Mary's Hospital, Paddington, some of whose fellow workers in this
laboratory of Alexander Fleming's went on to discover sulphona-
mide drugs and penicillin. In 1909 his father died of a horse disease
called glanders on which he was working. John was then only two.
His mother was a Cornish woman and lived in Newlyn.

In those early years when we first met and worked together he
said this:

> One's training has given one some contact with other
> branches of knowledge – chemistry, physics, botany,
> biology, physiologic, psychology and their application to
> pathology, giving one a feeling for physical structures and
> a deep concern for truth – a meticulousness in painting
> such as is ingrained in the operating theatre also practical
> medicine has given one a humanity one would otherwise
> be without.

John Wells was later taught by Stanhope Forbes of Newlyn, an
academic approach far removed from his paintings as we know
them. But this training surely fed in at the roots of his being and his
vision the deeper understanding and love of his surroundings in a
more human and traditional sense which might well have been
overlaid when he first met Ben Nicholson who, through Malevich
and Mondrian, had already struck a gong for the future when he
and John met with each other, Kit Wood, and Winifred Nicholson
in Feock in 1928. He wrote 'This was my first contact with living
art. I remember a grey painting of the sea. Ben's seriousness made
me focus my attention on it and I began to see.'

Nicholson seems to have made a far deeper impression on John Wells than Kit Wood, who was caught up in his own personal dream.

> He was drawing all the time, Kit not so much. We all used to swim and go on fishing trips to Falmouth and across the bay to Helford. Once we went to St Mawes Regatta which was very gay, the harbour lit up with bunting. This and a girl's face in a crowd absorbed Kit very much. Kit was charming and lively. He had a bad leg but this did not stop him swimming. He told me that Van Gogh was his favourite painter.

> Ben said you must paint every aspect of an object before you can paint it. When I remarked how persistently he worked he said, "It is the only way!"

From these notes one gets a feeling of the creative centre in John Wells suddenly becoming aware of art as a living organic process closely related to the life around him, outside the principles of an equivalent reproduction. This was one of Ben's exclusive gifts – to bring about an awakening and set colour and form free in the mind.

1928 was an important year. Kit Wood and Ben Nicholson motored to St Ives in a T-Model Ford and after dividing to paint and draw met up in Back Street West where they discovered Alfred Wallis painting in his cottage. 'Looking just like Cézanne,' as Adrian Stokes said later. This had a great effect on Christopher Wood and the sudden jolt seemed to give his vision a twist that led him back to his own innate innocence preserved somewhere under the sweet dream of opium. He wrote:

> I am more and more influenced by Alfred Wallis – not a bad master though – he and Picasso both mix their colours on box lids! I see him each day for a second and he is bright and cheery. I'm not surprised no one likes Wallis's paintings. No one liked Van Gogh's for a time, did they?

I have never asked him but I should imagine John Wells was one of those people who saw the Wallis paintings Ben and Kit showed to their friends with such fervour, on that day when they returned from St Ives after buying from the old man himself.

121

Kit met Mary Jewels in Newlyn. These two artists were the twin factors that set his creative course so few years before his death. Through this experience, John Wells saw how the real artist in a man was discovered and operated within its own orbit, gathering light and fire from neighbouring planets. It also led him to himself and his own truthful ingenuousness which shows in all he paints. But full time painting was still a good way off.

John Wells qualified as a doctor in 1930. He was 23. After working for six years in provincial hospitals he bought the practice on St Mary's Island, Scilly, and became the only doctor on the islands, intending to stay for only three years, but the war came and he stayed for nine. His reasons for doing this were to find a living, to get an intimate contact with the sea and to get an opportunity to paint.

The islands became his point of focus. In them he found everything he could grow to love and understand, whether it was the slow journey of the moon across a month of heavens or the flight of birds over the surface of the ocean. So permeated is he by this handful of stones some forgotten giant once threw into the sea that he paints as a man who has found an alkahest to the nature of the universe in one fragment of it. It makes him a kind of alchemist.

As a doctor John became the biological nerve-centre to that small community. In their eyes he was a kind of magician, for in primitive people the practice of medicine is closely but unconsciously linked to magic, and for his loyalty and skill they loved him – and still do.

This life with its continuity was almost esoteric and was probably why, when he came to the mainland, he was inaccessible to all but his close friends. Even then it was difficult to see him sometimes.

I remember being stranded in Penzance quite late one Sunday evening. I had been to visit someone in a nursing home and, because it was private, had stayed talking till the last bus had gone. It was pouring with rain with that abandon which seems to happen when you are utterly exposed. St Ives was too far away across the peninsula, the streets were deserted. I decided to walk to Newlyn and see Johnny and ask him to take me in as often I took in a fellow artist to my Tower, if in distress. But I had not reckoned on his being out – away for the weekend at his sister's home. This only dawned on me when I had climbed the first steep of the Trewarneth hill and turned down the lane between the cottages by the school that brought me under the great dark wooden structure among a few trees that was his studio. In complete darkness, I tried the lower door. Locked. I climbed up the wooden steps and tried the upper door. The same. I walked round and round the place looking for an opening. Part of the building was raised on piers to correct the ground level. Remembering he had been converting the lower part himself and putting in a bathroom, I thought there might be a loose floorboard and crept under the building to see. But as I went in the gap got smaller as the ground level changed until I got to a point where I was jammed underneath the building unable to turn to get out. I was very cold and wet and after about an hour began to shake. Finally by some trick of Zen I found myself free and crawled back. My watch said one in the morning. There was a tiny window by the lower door and I broke the pane by the latch and slid silently, gratefully inside.

Upstairs, when I switched on the powerful fluorescent strip lights, the place jumped to attention. I was anxious John would return and find me intruding. There were many paintings, a marble mantle-piece covered with letters. A record player and benches of tools, well kept, chisels, mallets, pots of brushes and all the paraphernalia of a painter's shop. Also there were shells, beautiful stones, coral formations and the skull of a dolphin. And a brass plate with JOHN WELLS MD. upon it. It all came together and I saw his life, visiting and healing the people as he went from island to island across the open sea, becoming intimate as few landsmen can with the sea's many moods, rhythms, colours, smells, textures, the flight of birds, the action of the islands plunging in the mists like porpoises; with the action of small craft, their engines, habits, vibrations; with the nature of rock structures; with the shapes of objects from every aspect; and with the intensity of colour from all distances from the eye under all conditions.

Being here in this most secret place – familiar but secret because I was unbidden – I had entered into John's mind – a mind that had itself entered into the structure of the islands and into the islanders. In his art he had made a meticulous examination of all he loved and transmuted it into new forms. I thought of his words in his first letter to me:

Each stone when you consider it is shaped by elemental forces acting over countless ages on the inherent structure which was perhaps laid down when the earth was first crystalized from flaming gases. So I do not despise the smallest stone. No wonder Miro said, "Each speck of dust has its own marvellous soul!"

123

I laid down on the couch and fell asleep till morning.

When I awoke I thought perhaps John might appear, but he did not. I tried to light the primus stove with what I thought was colourless meths, but it might have been pure alcohol because a blue flame shot to the wooden roof, terrifying me. I dared not try again so I wrote a little note asking forgiveness for my intrusion and went away. He need never have known otherwise – except for the broken window by the lower door. Some weeks later I saw him in a pub in Penzance called the 'Globe' which was then still old-fashioned. I was talking to an ex-boxer with a broken nose and a cauliflower ear named Tiger who was a keeper on the Bishop Light: John knew him also. But John was morose and strange for a little while and then laughed and clapped me on the shoulder.

'I'm sorry, Johnny!' I said.

'That's all right my beauty, but don't do it again!'

After that we met the painter Julian Trevelyan and got drunk with him and some Spanish sailors.

At heart John was and is an ascetic who lives alone much as a hermit. It is his way of meditation and not breaking inner contact with the universe. Even if I call on him unbidden after ten years he sends me away at first. Dealers he hates to call: a seldom seen, aggressive, even violent side of him leaps out. But like myself and many artists, if he finds the inner life too intense, he gets drunk to preserve his sanity – even to throwing something through the canvas before he can get into work on a new painting: a way of breaking down the barriers of the mind.

I had broken into the esoteric shrine which every artist must build for himself as his place of protection and in it the world where the things happen that no one else at first can understand. Like shaping a stone inducing the *duende*.

In shaping a stone for himself or wearing a painting to a beautiful surface he likes to feel he is repeating in his own working time the process of those 'elemental forces acting over countless ages,' giving himself and his work the full mystical sense of complete reality. It is indeed that mystical quality in his painting which brings greatness to his work in a field where abstraction can so often be an emptiness efficently executed by less profound painters posturing on the carnival float to win the prizes and rosettes of our time. And it is surely these whom all ministers of grace and beauty would wish to keep out.

Tambimuttu, who came to the Islands before John left and gave to everything a touch of poetic madness, was still publishing my

Wallis book at this time and indeed had given me a contract for the very book I write now. The two Roberts – MacBryde and Colquhoun – had been down to stay with Sydney Graham, John Minton, also. The Moors Poets had arrived in Cornwall: George Barker, David Lewis, David Wright, Heath-Stubbs, John Fairfax, so conversely there was much to influence us from London and John used to travel up there with me to see the latest developments with Tambi, go to a party with Roy Campbell, drink with Stewart Scott, see Dylan Thomas at a distance holding forth in a night club called the Gargoyle.

It was a disappointment that I did not meet Dylan. Several times Tambi arranged that I should but it always fell through. I found later that Dylan hated Tambi and that was probably why on one occasion it had failed to happen at the Gargoyle where from Tambi's table I watched Dylans spouting. About two in the morning I went to rid myself of the huge transfusion of alcohol and had settled for a long quiet pee against the cascade when the door crashed open and Dylan, very drunk, appeared at my side. He was much smaller than I thought with tawny hair and bulbous eyes and a Socratic nose. He grunted, undid his flies and settled, as men do, to pee anonymously. After a time he swayed my way, squinted again, looked up and said 'Hallo, you alright?' 'Yes, fine,' I said. 'And you?' 'OK'.

Then by some extraordinary but mutual impulse we turned towards each other and crossed swords. 'Pleased to meet you,' he said. 'Me too!' I replied. And then, as the supply ran out he shook himself, did up his flies and stumbled out. That was the only meeting I had with Dylan Thomas.

Lucian Freud and John Craxton performed their cloak and dagger humour in a Greek Street restaurant and, most wonderful, there was a chance meeting with Kathleen Raine in Tambi's office. She was very attractive, still with a touch of Girton about her in a blue Melton overcoat and her hair a little shorter than the fashion making her very slightly butch, but with those beautiful blue eyes which were lit by the spirit as well as by the light of day. John Wells, who was normally very nervous with women, immediately fell for her, and the drawings Hepworth had done for her volume of poems, *The Stone and Flower*, made retreat for him almost impossible. It was not only her presence but she had that same mystical link with nature that was colophon to his own vision. I was diverted by Wyndham Lewis rattling on about the wartime price of eggs and trying to find his lost spectacles which were still on his nose that I did not know what happened. But I know the meeting had a deep impression on John.

We would go along with these visits to Tambi for about a week and then suddenly get up from the floor of his flat and catch the early morning train back to Cornwall, driven by a mutual need for purgation in the brilliant quartz air while we were still safe. The 24–hour rounds of drinking took their toll on the gates of the mind and trailing through the labyrinths of London with Tambi, that exotic flower who drew the strange and often the rare lepidoptera of society around him, lost its excitement after seeing knife-fights and punch-ups in the streets of Soho. He was the one person to bring that generation of poets to the light in the pages of *Poetry London*. He *was Poetry London*. When I heard of Tambi's death I realised he wrote only one poem and that was his life: a thread he spun secretly for us all who are strong enough to keep the need of poetry alive and which no one noticed until he *was* dead.

Death of a Poet

(For Tambi)

I recall him dark, in red and brown,
Shouting poems to the stars,
Conducting Sibelius through Camden Town,
Dodging the drunken cars.

Or on an island, dance a wilder dance
With Stravinsky in a high.
Disturbing seas from there to France
Under a circular sky.

He was always up the Whisky Tree
Or some slim blonde in Soho Square,
Pouring poetry everywhere
From 0100 hours to 03.

He published poets then unknown,
Walked to the moon with worn out socks,
His reckless spirit's substance thrown
Among the stars and island rocks,

The rubbish tip for poets' souls
To rot with Rimbaud and Verlaine,

But not to pilfer their discarded jewels
Hung on branches while insane.

Then he died – a liver duct complaint.
They gave an obituary in the *Times*,
A memorial service said, no saint –
But forgave his early crimes.

No one knew he made one lasting line,
Of secret thread on deeper looms inside,
So well none saw it as a poet's sign –
He never wrote it down before he died.

I heard him shout out once in ancient tongue,
Crazed at night by vision near at hand –
'No song by living poet ever sung
Has he found listening ear to understand!'

Throughout each day he slowly wove his man
In red and gold and silver thread,
A drunken poet written out of scan,
Only completed when they found him dead.

The pubs and alleys of Soho were part of it, and it was through his press the pages of my book on Wallis emerged. As always, it was the measure of the experience that mattered. We went when we had had enough.

Drinking in Cornwall was not so fierce and was regulated by our own discipline of work. I had a rule not to drink and work at the same time in case the two habits became bound together. It was my fear that if I took opium, which I was once offered, like Kit Wood I might come to depend on it. But I do remember doing my best drawing when we had been at it in St Ives. There was a meeting with that fragile refined young painter, David Haughton, at the Crypt Show and somehow with John we had spent an evening together talking and drinking beer until the pub closed. I asked them back to my Tower for some strong tea, but we lost David on the way. David who lived in St Just and painted beautiful lonely, domino cottages in which nobody lived, had vanished like the spirit Ariel. Later someone said he was in the sea.

We went down to the beach where great breakers were coming in and showering the sand with phosphorescent light. David was out there towards the Rock, they said, and knowing how strong the currents were I plunged in to get him before he was swept away.

But the great waves coming in picked me up and threw me back on the beach. John, being a man of sea more than I, told me to wait and look across the moonlit surface until we could see where he was. This we did and soon saw a dark form in the glowing surface. It was David. This time I waited for the big breaker to approach and when it was near enough before it broke, dived straight through it like a wall of glass and came out the other side where it was quite calm and swam toward David. He was very drunk and sang happily, just keeping himself afloat and not going anywhere. I told him it was dangerous there and he simply fell in with my effort to bring him back, which I did while he kept on singing the song which I have now forgotten. We took him to the Tower and flung him naked on the little camp bed in the candle light. While someone made the strong tea I had promised I did a direct pen drawing of the sleeping man, my hand guided by a ghost of the moon.

The next day David returned to his cottage at St Just where his curiously patient and quietly beautiful woman waited for him. He went home, John went with him, I was left alone. I sat on the rocks:

> So all around the morning air and the sea's blue light
> with pints of diamond and the gorse incandescent beyond
> the trees – countless rocks, round and jagged and of every
> colour – birds nesting and flying and a sense of a
> multitude of creatures living out their minute lives.

The memory of John's letter again came upon me and I found myself after the inferno of London back at the centre of things that were the real structural support to one's life and the vision that emerged from it. As he had said:

> All of this is part of one's life and I desperately want to
> express it, not just what I see but what I feel about it and
> beyond it . . . but how can one paint the warmth of the
> sun, the journey of a beetle across a rock, and thoughts of
> one's own whence and whither? That's an argument for
> abstraction. If one absorbs all these feelings and ideas and
> if one is lucky they undergo the alchemistic transformation
> into gold and that is the creative work.

It shows the intensity and with what seriousness John Wells lived on the islands and how he realised in himself the need to find a point of fusion between an idea born out of such experience and the materials available – paint, wood, flax, coal or whatever you like . . .

> These things have their own qualities and reach out to their own forms and shapes and colours and combinations. I cannot and do not want to make copies of nature. But everywhere watching and studying natural rhythms and processes (within and without) till very humbly one begins to create entirely new things as nature does – when the idea and the material are in dynamic sympathy, growing together toward the same end.

John Wells, by devotion to both the sources within and outside himself and to the means he invents and borrows to create, has charged the abstract world with a sudden vitality which came straight from the life-force being redirected after the destruction of war, and linked it to the energy already inherent in him and in the islands.

He not only gained an original impetus from Nicholson at Feock in 1928 and later when Nicholson and Hepworth returned during the war, but from Naum Gabo, the inspired Russian, who brought with him his miraculous powers of construction. These three artists were of major importance to Wells and his own work completed a quartern in what they set out to achieve.

His intention to paint while still a doctor worked best, he said, in 1941–42 when the war gave more time and more stimulus. He made friends with several fighter pilots who were stationed on the islands. They stimulated his imagination and understood his painting, which is not surprising when you watch a dogfight in the blue sky, for all you can see and particularly what you can't see is abstract – forms in flight, flight paths, volume in space. I have often thought how right the Greeks were when they named Daedalus the 'first artist' because he not only invented the saw, the axe and the gimlet, designed and built the Cretan Labyrinth for the Minotaur, but was to invent the sail and finally the wings with which he and his son Icarus were able to fly. Airmen and aeronautical engineers would have most certainly have understood abstract art in Ancient Greece. Gabo and John Wells would have been as well or better placed than they are today. They would have invented *Concorde*.

If swallows could talk they too would understand abstract art – and Euclid would. There seems to have been a certain amount of action and the threat of invasion was always present. When a plane crashed John was called out to attend the wounded. They gave him blood-stained sections of smashed gun turrets out of which he made constructions in space. Nothing could have been a more direct transmutation of what was happening around him. When I went over I remember the Sunderland seaplane was flying out for the last time. In the bright sunlight of that magical day for me it was smooth and white like a giant bone bleached by the centuries' tides, and when it took off I thought a prehistoric bird had falteringly tried its wings again. It was moving and beautiful to see. The highest and the primitive converged.

Another source of 'endless encouragement' was the 'Vicar of the Islands, now an engineer RN'. This was a boon to a man so isolated dealing with such a unique and difficult problem as had been set for him, and with which he had consciously engaged. In a letter of this time, from which my notes are generated, he says how he enjoyed my visit and how thankful he was to find someone speaking his own language. We talked many times of religion. In fact he was one of the few people with whom I found myself able to discuss these matters because of a natural secrecy I have always had about them, so that I cannot remember in chunky words what was said – only an overtone of what was felt and perhaps experienced by us both. So I have only an idea rather than the knowledge that he was a believer in the existence of God, the holiness of nature and the profound sacredness in the highest purpose of man. Otherwise I left these matters as private for him as he did for me and did not probe for the sake of it, accepting only what came through friendship. If he has turned to an orthodox religion my guess is that it would be Catholic.

These beliefs would fit in with all I have said about this unusual man, even to the constructions he made from the blood-stained gun turrets of crashed fighter planes in 1942, which would have been flung off from the Battle of Britain being fought over the English Channel and in which I would have been engaged had I not rejected the offer of rear-gunner from an arrogant wing-commander in Oxford.

'Construction,' he says, 'is the basis of all good painting and sculpture. The four basic elements of a good work of art are:

COLOUR
FORM   Metaphysical   SCALE: Physical and
RHYTHM   Spiritual'

His approach to colour is searching, with the scrupulous aseptic technique learnt in the operating theatre, but is based on the close observation of nature and a study of the Byzantine Primitives – their purity. Also in earlier days he constructed a loom and made a study of vegetable dyes. His colour is biological, mineral, vegetable, aquatic and atmospheric. He works in neutral against which he places arterial reds, choleric yellows, crystalline violets, stratospheric blues, seaweed browns and purples, pungent greens, intestinal and brain greys, arranging them till the greatest power is awakened at every point of the canvas. He spends many hours, for his processes are slow, with coloured papers as a basis for a painting. The purpose of this is 'to explore colour in three dimensions to the point where the crystalline and the protoplasmic meet.'

Although his medical training and his experience as a practising doctor permeated his art successfully, one scarcely noticed the doctor in him once he had given it up. Indeed it was forgotten unless some chance happening brought it forward. Early one November evening we were waiting to be served with our beer in the 'Sloop' at St Ives and I noticed that Miss Gibbons, the manageress and Lady of the Bar, had not had time to light the fire. I offered to do it for her. There was some dry wood there and while I was breaking it up I made a jagged cut in my left hand with a sharp end. It was bleeding quite well and I said to John: 'Do you think it's all right?' But he didn't look at the cut. He immediately picked up the piece of wood which was from a fruit box and had the word Tangiers printed on it. He asked Miss Gibbons for a piece of paper and wrote out my name and a prescription for 'Prophylactic dose of A.T.S.' signed it and gave it to me. I was taken to a friend's house where a doctor came and injected me right away. For a moment John Wells had changed places with himself.

The only other time the need for a doctor came was while I was with John Wells on the Scilly Isles. Victory Night and we were going to sea in a boat with the Swedish mermaid watching, to join the French crabbers anchored outside the harbour, but something went wrong and we started to sink. The sea must at all times be respected even when it is calm and also shallow, so we got out and somehow hauled the boat toward the shore. John fell over and, thinking him injured, I gave him a fireman's lift up the beach with his seaboots waving against the moon and set him down on an old launching slip, steadied him on his feet and took my hands away. He stood there for a moment in the moonlight and then fell to the rocks underneath. When I helped him up again his face was a map of blood. We had a car, driven by whom I don't know, it may have been the mermaid, and we took him to the surgery in the middle of the night, run by the doctor who had taken over the practice from him. I watched the skin on his face stretch and relax as it was stitched up round the right eye and John remained impassive without flinching. Then they covered him up and let him sleep. Where I slept I don't know, with the mermaid I hope. I have no doubt that this short intense period of 'living flat out, in all directions at once', as he put it, was a necessary part of the deep changes that were taking place from one who healed to one who was able to create, as were the silent conflicts which he must have sometimes endured.

I have often wondered if this fall was a preliminary factor in his losing the sight of one eye after a later fall which caused a weakened optical nerve to fail. And if losing the eye impaired his binocular vision. 'Heavens no, I can see better now!' he said when I asked him, which was probably a more profound remark than either of us realised. The truth is that the mysteries of art are not, and cannot be, capsulated separately in an intellectual concept, but are often triggered off by some chance happening which permeates all the corridors of the mind, opening doors that would otherwise be locked and revealing as in a hidden tomb the treasures there hidden. Even if it is only one artifact or one crystal, one golden beetle, one new star, it adds to the experience and understanding of the universe in which we live. What then if it is a new form created for the first time with the stereoscopic vision of the mind, the duende of the spirit?

The form which is familiar to us in John Wells' painting is the ellipse rather like an egg. (Barra Barra, she ave stolen zee egg!) Well, it was all going on, but in Wells' case it happened to be the stone shape of Scilly, of the islands themselves, of fish, water-worn pebbles, rocks, waves, leaves, drops of water. Also the shape of testicles, kidneys and lungs. He has used it with every imaginative variation. Because it was a fish, a stone, an island, a face in the first place as well as an ellipse it meant so much more. And the spiked forms of icicles in *Clear North*, the articulation of triangles in *Flight Forms*.

His rhythm was and is musical.

The scale of his painting is large, though small in size – and four dimensional.

Colour, form, rhythm, scale all have a close affinity with music – in his case Bach, Mozart, Stravinsky and Sibelius.

We listened to music a great deal together in his tall wooden studio, while he wrote a letter on the marble mantlepiece or made tea on the Primus stove.

'We learn so much from that for painting,' he said suddenly of Bach. 'I want to do a painting like Bach one day. It goes on and on. You never get to the bottom of it. It's a source of infinite knowledge.'

Of wisdom also, perhaps.

Bernard Leach pointed out that close affinities with certain Chinese paintings are not mere technical influences, but parallel attitudes John Wells attained through his own contemplation of life around him. He has arrived at similar conclusions to those of the painter Ryu-San-Jin, the Dragon Mountain Man. His fishlike islands floating in the mist grow deep into the sea. His monolithic rocks pierce the sky, his edges of land are wing tips of huge unseen birds flying away over an eternal ocean. Where Ryu-San-Jin describes minute human beings awe-inspired by the magnificence of nature, John Wells has none, as though not wishing to admit his own singular existence and aloneness. And everywhere a sense of unfathomable and clean space that sends the mind hurtling to eternity.

> One lives to make a work which gives oneself a sense of wonder, as if in part another hand had formed it – that is full of tension of light, yet alive perfectly within its own boundaries and which radiates and is nourished by goodness.

It is wonderful that this word goodness should appear so natural and unexpectedly in this context. I do not and cannot take it as the slightly soiled raincoat of ethical behaviour in which we parade each day, but a rare sense of its being part of the diadem of eternal values, Beauty, Truth and Goodness, over which all great artists have kept vigil.

That is what I mean when I say John Wells gave up medicine to become a Doctor of Magic, seeking the secret of life. What happened to the tiny active volcano of creation we discovered together on the Islands and the truth that sometimes slithered near the surface of the ocean, I don't know. I believe they were absorbed into what we came to know as the Disturbance in the West and transmuted into our work. Now it is over the galliard of the pelagic fishes and the slow pavan of the octopus will never be completed, but will continue forever in the secret stadiums of the sea.

When I returned to the Tower from the Scilly Isles the loneliness was almost more than I could bear. It was as I had left eight days before save for a few letters on the stairs, the door open. But no one there. No one at all. I was One in a Tower once more.

Thankfully the chance of a show in London was there and worth working for. This would be my centre. Gradually over the weeks the patterns started to form and spread out like fingers on a hand as the various people started to return from the war or else from some occupation to which they had been directed. They were the younger ones; that fitted the shape that Adrian Stokes had already laid down as early as 1940 with the older generation: they fitted onto it as exactly as a glove fits on to a hand, each finger pointing to its own direction. I had thought and believed this new structure would fit into the old traditional sleeve that was still used by Leonard Fuller's School of Painting and the Art Society, incumbent for years in the Mariners' Chapel, which it did for a time. I and a few of the others like Nicholson and Barns-Graham, Stokes had already joined us at the invitation of that ebullient and honest person, Borlase Smart. We were gathered round the Font and were called the Font Group. Peter Lanyon, being a local, had been in this for much longer: he was taught by Borlase and Leonard Fuller, later by Ben and Gabo. He came back from serving in the RAF in Italy, frustrated and quarrelsome, friendly but angry about something I was never able to divine. Alternately kind and aggressive. He seemed to need that to crack the shell that held his full talent for inventive and meta-morphic painting.

One great pleasure was when Terry Frost turned up from a German Stalag where he had been prisoner since action in Greece. His enthusiasm was unbounded, painting like Vuillard in crimsons, yellows, veridians, blues beyond the power of the tube and I was early to realise that he was more in love with the colour itself than the image, especially later when the abstract vision took over and he was able to paint a picture entirely in black. 'If I was rich,' he exclaimed, 'I would buy a Persian carpet, throw tubes of vermilion all over it and squelch 'em out under my feet. COR!' A frank, astute, lively person whom I call my first student and he 'my old friend and master'. He found his way without me but perhaps I made him a map. One thing is certain: he had the secret spark and the volcano had already singed his beard.

Terry Frost attended St Ives School of Painting run by Fuller but was not on the scene much after that because he went to Camber-well School of Art, partly under my encouragement, where Victor

Pasmore was teaching. In 1949 he brought Pasmore to St Ives and introduced him to Ben Nicholson which act functioned as a flux to weld them both irrevocably on to the abstract movement. I left the Tower in 1950 and Cornwall in 1953, during which time Terry stepped forward as a more mature abstract painter. I remember spending all one night in a room in London lent me by William Brooker, trying to enter an early abstract by Terry. I was locked out by some mechanism I did not recognise or understand and left it at that, which is the reason I mention only a life long friendship and not his work. I do not know enough. Terry was one of those who remained an artist first and was tough enough to take on teaching as an aid to creation. As an artist he plucked flowers from a field I had not seen until then – that of his own inventive genius.

Another almost esoteric and unique vision to appear was Tom Early, about whom I will say more later.

The Boat of Fire

Sydney Graham, who was not one of the Moors Poets, was already living at Marazion with Nessie Dunsmuir like Scottish tinkers in a waggon on a strip of ground in which they grew violets. Barbara Hepworth first told me about them and I went to Pengersick Lane to see them. This was an exact opposite to my experience in meeting John Wells. Here the poetry fountain burst out of the ground instead of the sea, out of this rough man from Greenock and his woman, sweet as a mountain flower. The draught Bass and the songs at once began to flow and when they came to my Tower they blessed it with their poetry from the kingdoms of the sea, and later, the great poem he wrote especially at my request for my book on Alfred Wallis.

I quote the entire poem later.

> World-hauled he's grounded on God's great bank
> Keelheaved to heaven, waved into boatfilled arms,
> Falls his homecoming . . .
> He's that stone sailor towering out of the cupboarding sea
> To watch the black boats rigged by a question quietly
> Ghost home and ask right out in jackets of oil
> The standing white of the crew 'What hellward harbour
> Bows down her seawalls to arriving home at last?'

In my opinion it will remain one of the great poems in the English language, and I am proud to have asked him to write it for me. In London Tambimuttu, who was the publisher, introduced me to the Cornish-born poet Ronald Bottrall who looked just like Hans Andersen. He said to me right away, 'I understand you want me to write a poem for your Wallis book!' which surprised me.

'Heavens no! I already have someone – Sydney Graham. The poem is written – Tambi knows that!' Bottrall took it well and wrote his own poem anyway, which was another experience. He was friendly enough to ask me to join him on a trip to Sweden and Denmark, but I declined. I have always been glad I stayed with Sydney over this, although the poem has been disconnected from its original home so many times since the world had forgotten where it truly belonged, until a new edition of my book was published in 1992.

I don't think Graham liked the Wallis book anyway, and he dismembered it to examine it and hung parts of it on his wall for several days then sellotaped it back in place. He didn't think much of it, but always stood by its authenticity and understanding of the man himself. He thought I should have written about the paintings as formal organisms, which in so many ways Graham's poems also were, 'working and sustaining themselves as a life, not at all depending on the literary value of the subject they are symbols of . . . the Seayness or whatever the subject is.' We were into all this as soon as we met and much later when the book came out he wrote to me from Mevagissey reminding me of my early visits and to 'remember our sudden descent on St Ives from the caravans.' It all seems to me now one thing – my visits to Pengersick Lane where I met the painters Colquhoun and MacBryde looking into a sprouting ivy bush which they said was like a city and made little drawings of its streets and houses. And John Minton with his sad face and satirical humour, who showed me in the Tower how to do monotypes. There was no intrusion of the homosexual element and I did not realise till much later it was so, perhaps because it was balanced so sweetly by Nessie who fed us with medieval-sized salads and fish, and poetry surging from Sydney in his rough male quartz voice, or both singing songs of the Western Isles.

It worked in this way: whoever had money from the sale of work – a poem or book of poems, a painting or a carving – a message was sent across the peninsula by telegram and they (or else I) travelled. Sometimes it went wrong because I was out and returning to my Tower on the rocks over the curved lunar beach, I would find on my desk a strip of drawing paper with the line of a new poem upon it:

THE PACING WHITEHAIRED KINGDOMS OF THE SEA

It was left to pin among others on the wooden windscreen at the top of the stair. My Berlin Wall. I knew that Joke Grim had called. Doing this instead of leaving a conventional note gave him an extra dimension. He was no longer 'poorrr putty nosed Scots cloon,' but a man with an ocean on his back, a star in his pocket and a sunset folded in his hand. The search would begin for a wandering poet who had come to see my carvings and drawings: to walk with Nessie on the starlit sand and wade into silence.

When I found him eventually in a pub he would strike the counter with his fist and shout,

'SZVEN BEARLIN WE'LL BE DRUNK THIS NIGHT!'

The process began along with announcing some new discovery
like the *White Goddess*, which Robert Graves, whom I was to meet in
later life and become friends with, had just published, and reciting
parts of the *Song of Amergin*. These particular discoveries and our
active investigation of them, more than anything else, released in me
the inspiration for my sculpture *Mermaid and Angel* in which an air
figure and sea figure meet, resolving a collision of opposites by
piercing a stone. This same excitement took me when I first read
Lorca through Tambimutti who introduced Lorca's translator, J.L.
Gili, to me and I had already met, at Adrian Stokes', Stephen
Spender who collaborated with Gili. John Wells also took this
excitement, especially when we read the *Theory and Function of the
DUENDE* by Lorca and translated by Gili. I always felt a great
madness come upon me when I read Lorca or quoted him from
memory. He had a tongue of gold and a stable of poetry in his
throat that drenched me with the magic of life and death. One night
drinking in the Sloop I wrote the 'Casida of the Clean Death' on
the toilet wall. The fishermen chanted it as they pissed on the same
wall.

> Many times have I lost myself in the sea
> With my ears full of freshly cut flowers
> My tongue full of love and agony:
> As I lose myself in the hearts of some children
> Many times have I lost myself in the sea.

What a way to be drunk, when the mind floods, the dykes are
broken, are as though drowned. I ran out and plunged into the
green waters of the harbour.

> Green, green. I love you green.
> Green wind, green branches . . .

I was covered with branches of green blossom: green foam.
The walking into the sea had first happened spontaneously when
I had returned from war in a very highly-tuned condition, as were
most other people and St Ives itself seemed to carry an electric
charge that held us at that pitch. Restrictions were still on and beer
was short. In order to be sure of a pint we carried our own glass
mugs with us and went about the town drinking from them, joining

the nearest queue when they were empty. On VJ Day I was on such a mission with a young man named Alister, whom we called The Saint, walking along the wharf toward the Sloop. It was a beautiful day with a neap tide just spilling over the edge of the harbour wall: clear green translucent water, with the boats rocking gently upon it. 'I've always wanted to dive into that with all my clothes on!' I said to the Saint. 'Why don't you?' he replied. I handed him my pint mug half full of beer. 'Hold that,' I exclaimed and, fully clothed, took a running dive over the railings into the harbour, swam under a fishing boat then surfaced and swam in a kind of slow karezza to Smeaton's Pier. The effect of this spontaneous act was to put my whole life back into joint as though a charge of energy had entered me. I was no longer afraid, no longer hesitant or doubtful about my destiny, no longer did I suddenly black out in the street for no reason. The Gods had touched me with a magic that enabled me to work and survive through the next five years and I knew how to do it. No one knew my secret and I was a golden haired lion.

> I am the wind that breathes upon the sea,
> I am the wave on the ocean
> I am the point of the lance in battle
> I am the God who creates the fire in the head . . .

We were unlocking the doors of the mind till all levels were open and we could speak with the tongues of devils and angels. That indeed was the meaning of the drink. We were not helpless alcoholics looking for any excuse to get stoned out of our skulls, but men and women wading deep till the tide took us, what Nessie has called 'the fierce joy and love of everything around us.' We did not do this often. It was not possible. Sydney wrote to me one day in March from Mevagissey:

> It's a long time since I've seen you, Sven, there seems to be so much happening to me. It should be good to talk and have a few walks round on the drink. I've had about three drunky nights since Christmas. At the moment things are at their lowest and it is rather a hopeless horizon. I'm never out at the pubs and I don't mind at all. But I would want to be on the drink coming to St Ives, so I think I shall wait a little. Sometimes something turns up unexpectedly. I'm impatient to see your

drawings and carvings. Everything you've done for a long time will be new to me. You've mentioned writing. What's it about?

Drinking was a device controlled by our lack of income and the different domestic burden each of us might have to carry, and of course the austere self-discipline of work, which for a sculptor, anyway, was not helped by excess.

In spite of the isolation, the poverty, the ulcerated stomach of this man – who was surprisingly thin and fragile under his too large clothes – he remained a vital unit on his own. Even his connection with the abstract artists, whose influence on his work visually, as with Guido Morris, was considerable at a time when they were extending their own discovery into wider consciousness, did not spoil this tenacious independence. Nor did the bow wave of Yeats, the slip-stream of Dylan Thomas, both affecting him as they passed by, make him of their school – or any school. He was like a wild bird always trying to build his own fragile place hanging from a cliff to write his poetry, and never seemed to find anywhere for long; but what he wrote, tore from the rock, was his own.

The Constructivists who influenced the form and structure of his poems did not have the same in-built mystical qualities that Graham, as a Celt, saw and expressed in his Cornish experience.

After I had left Cornwall he wrote asking to borrow a cottage I was trying to rent furnished. He said he had a quarrel with Nessie and had decided to forgive her but they had nowhere to go. I thought their need was great. They took up residence at Cripples-ease.

Yes, what a lifesaving device you have turned out to be at this time. It is strange thing that although my position as a serious poet becomes consolidated every day and although I wait patiently for signs that the fight is easing, it has never been more difficult than it is now. And the sad thing is that I need a sense of at least an ephemeral security stretching ahead for at least a month or two because I am working on a long poem which (let us hope Sven) will knock them into a half-cocked hat. I mean I don't just want to write occasional poems at the moment but complete good big long poems that will cover the experience of whatever technical field was uncovered by the last poem.

This letter was written at the Castle Inn at St Ives. Jock had earlier written a poem 'For the Castle wall' which the landlord had framed and hung on the wall as an exhibit after Guido Morris had printed in on Barcham Green handmade paper. The landlord was that sensitive, kind Welshman who had known Dylan Thomas and was sympathetic to poets and painters, for which his name, Endell Mitchell, known as Michael, and brother to sculptor Denis, shall be always alive. The letter goes on:

> Sven, Nessie is sitting here in Michael's Castle beside a rucksack filled with candles, flour, monkfish, tripe, potatoes (the rucksack not Ness) and this is my first day up since getting into Penderleath.

They seemed to have spent a hard winter working and being there. The Zennor Moors were no place to be without money to live, as I knew. They left the following Easter. Sydney Graham came from Greenock on the Firth of Clyde. The sea and rock formation must have been a close reminder in Cornwall, and the magic of the place for creative people, so well described in Denys Val Baker's *The Timeless Land*. I will not attempt it myself. My little island must have been close to *Gigha*, a poem he wrote for my wall. From Mevagissey, he wrote: 'I've just had a walk out to the quay-heads. The sea's rough and noisy tonight. This coast has not the same mystic feeling as the coast from Penzance round Lands End to St Ives. I must get down there sometime again to stay awhile. Though I've been thinking a lot of the Western Isles recently. You would like them, Sven. They would without doubt, send you daft.

> The Kyle of Lochalsh
> The Pass of Brander
> Rannock Moor
> The Sands of Morar.'

Sydney went to America for a while lecturing and reading his poems. I don't know how it was there. He returned with new clothes instead of his ragged tweed jacket and jersey, smelt sweeter, was more aggressive and policed by a powerful American lady who kept him behind an invisible barrier. But it did not last. The difficult, aggressive, jealous, argumentative, humorous poet returned to his own way of life with his Lady Ariel from Blantyre, Nessie

Dunsmuir. I in my turn went away to live an even harder life on the road and in the Forest and our friendship seemed like falling snow that faded into Time's darkness. Yet years later I was recovering from a serious illness. The experience of Cornwall brought from Nessie the *Ten Poems of Nessie Dunsmuir* which are profound and moving, making her a poet in her own depth. Even the direction of the land and water is the same in Scotland both places pointing south west from a western coast. I don't know anything about Graham's early life but have often thought that sea-behaviour, boat-forms, mariners' ways, launch and landfall must have been part of his mind's furniture from the beginning, and re-awakened by those who

> . . .ask right out in jackets of oil
> The standing white of the crew, 'what hellward harbour
> Bows down her seawalls to arriving home at last?'

He had found in Wallis's painting and in Cornwall what he had at last come home to, even among granite and Celt, though, as he wrote in a letter 'taking care to shoo the twilicht awa!'

It was perhaps only instinct that made me ask for the poem, bringing the two things together in his deep sea mind, for I felt as strongly as he did about poetry and Cornwall and Alfred Wallis.

It is not surprising that a man from humble origins should finally evoke great poetry out of the most rigorous conditions, if only because he had the unknown face of truth distilled from the Cornish mirror into his poetic image.

It is not surprising that he stood up at a literary dinner in America, looked at the audience and roared, 'You bloody lot a boors!'

It is not surprising that when Harold Macmillan, then Prime Minister, offered him a literary award he said he did not know if he would accept it. 'After all, I ha ma Scottish pride to think of!'

It is not surprising that he lunched with T.S. Eliot when he went to Faber about his poems – or that Legouis and Cazamain just manage to squeeze him in to their History of English Literature but Palgrave's Treasury (Book V) leaves him out, to the shame of John Press.

What is surprising is that he continued working under the incessant bellring of poverty long enough to write the first of his long poems – 'The Nightfishing'.

He was living at Mevagissey at that time, waiting for his collection

The White Thresholds to come from Faber, when the large poem overtook him like an ocean and he had to go with it, though always with perfect control: sometimes agonizing.

> moving on near-stillness enough
> To keep the rudder live and gripped in the keel-wash.

When *The White Thresholds* came out I wrote this.

In writing poetry the poet has only words to unlock his vision: a vision in this case of poetic power coming from the suddenly appearing fountainhead of the real vital world of imagination, hammered into an organic whole. Behind this there is an almost abstract severity of construction. His powers of invention grow from his own images rather than words – words fence in what he means and sees and feels. His music grows from language strongly Celtic (Cornwall and Scotland). Meanings and sensations are experienced by a way of displacing, re-arranging and even reversing images and their behaviour: the land sails by, the boat stands still, the crew remain still on motion:

> Watching the restless land sail rigged alongside
> Townfull of shallows, gulls on the sailing roofs.

His poetry takes us through the 'black branches of the brain' to the world he has made through rich sometimes brutal language from earth, sea, heart and brain as though working in hot iron, revealing a land and an ocean outside geometric reason – even mystically so. His poetry has not the haunting despair of the more socially conscious poets, but a pristine belief in Creation.

> . . . there in front of God to lie down sweet.

In this house he is building sound and meaning, image and speech, symbol and experience interpenetrate in miracle and there is no question of the work being an organic construction on its own without content, as he had perhaps hoped, if only because his passion, like the sea, has welded the whole experience together into a

143

mystical whole which is the mark and stamp of great
poetry – has been from the beginning of time.

> Winter strikes bright on Christ's walls and glass
> Stain'd into saints and lantern'd all disciples
> Acting the bible ghosts gone wild into fire
> At blind dust. I'll be a struck silence
> Fix'd as the bell strikes the midnight dead still.

Even Yeats is melted down in the intense heat of this
poem and transmuted into new gold.

Graham's obscurity is sometimes due to his sculptural
vision – a need to get behind images and words seeing
them all round and through to the other side – which is
unusual in a poet and is the result of living near visual
artists and stone cutters.

The White Thresholds is a moving force like the sea, which
permeates all he writes with a peculiar preoccupation with
death by drowning, the mull of the moors and coves, the
ghosts of West Penwith.

> Only one faint waif, the whipend moon,
> Makes a poor might of light to swim
> The petrel-treaded gale of the landtrawled drowned.

Through his sea-passion he merges his dominions of land
to make an austere shorescape equal to Sibelius, but less
grandeur. Out of the ruggedness a sweet innocence before
God – rare in a poet of a Godless time. His growth will
bring simplicity by his withering away

> . . .an ambitious dust
> Through native pain endured and through my earliest
> Gesture towards the first fires of my past.

I don't know what he thought of my writing this. He would not
even care or even read it if he was absorbed in progress of work:
and the only validity such writing has is the attempt by another
artist, not as critic, to understand what is happening: *not* to help

him. He was beyond 'The White Thresholds' even while he was correcting the proofs.

> It seems like my childhood poetry now. Now at a long poem. For me the most exciting thing I've worked at called – 'The Nightfishing'. Meant at the start, to be 300 lines and now half finished at the 600th line. See – first two stanzas of second section:

> I, in Time's grace, the grace of change, sail surely
> Moved off the sided land, and the moon-trawl sails
> The sea-strange nightfaring natured on my life.
> Landvoices, lights and dogbarking ebb away
> Laying the darkness down. Made up as my words,
> My changing motive pays me slowly out.
> The sea sails in. The quay opens wide its arms
> And waves us loose.

> So I would have it, waved from home, to further
> Out after that silence, the continual offer
> Of intellect singing in a garment of innocence.
> So this made-formal sea maintains all seas
> Thoroughfared by their movers into an intricate
> Moment. Yet on dead stillness, fathers itself,
> The common sea. And, here, see how this boat
> Rides in its fires.

At the time of writing these two stanzas he was at The Green Steps, Mevagissey. There were long times when neither he nor Nessie could get over to the Tower, nor I to Mevagissey, but letters flowed, sometimes two or more on the heels of each other: since I love letter-writing I kept this going all I could and found it to be a companionship that blessed my loneliness. He alternated from excitement over his new poem to talk of the Wallis book when it came out. He cut out the photos to pin on his wall among his drawings and towers of words.

'I love Susan Agland (Wallis's wife) and the Schooner at Night is a fine one. I am cutting them out one at a time and having them on the wall for a few days, then sticking them back neatly with tape – the best way to get to know them.'

But then he sends only one of the 'Nightfishing' and no more, as though he is tired or used up, and complains that his wee putty nose is sore from trying to work the inhaler up it. I knew his state and surely there was the outright asking at the end of the letter. 'Important to me . . . try and round up a good team of whites!'

This meant, could I send him some benzedrine tablets, which I had introduced to him during this time, and of course he loved them. They were such a help in his state of poverty and the accompanying despair. I had a prescription from a doctor who treated me for depression after the war and I was able to get a new supply every week. After I had sent him some he was elated and wrote well, as indeed Coleridge and Poe and Baudelaire and many others had done.

He wrote 'Thanks for the white friends, certainly a Godsend or St Svensend. Here's 10/- for anything you can do further in the matter. They go quickly. I've watched, as you advise, and haven't rushed them too much. They are a great help in putting in a really long stretch of time on the work – when it is specially needed.'

Benzedrine tablets give a certain elation and release of vital energy, but for the writer, and indeed the bomber pilot, their great virtue was in wakefulness and lack of tiredness. Over five years I found no ill effects. Their main danger seemed to me that you could drink all night without getting drunk and use up too much life-force. But phenobarbitone were lethal with alcohol. Inasmuch as benzedrine was a sweet refuge from depression after the daily procession of death in France, so phenobarbitone was a blessed release from the deeper agonies of living. That's as far as it went with me – a blessing after the ghosts of war. There therefore was enough for my friends. Redirected to Graham they released his fountains to the full.

The drinking problem – if it was a problem beyond affording it – came about by isolation, insecurity and the magnetic attraction some artists have with tragic circumstance. Otherwise most poets and painters drink a lot because they work with the whole mind, and whatever acreage of spirit might lie behind invisibility. Not so much with sculptors because of the physical implications of stone and the need to have unimpaired manipulative powers. Alcohol is oil to operate these difficult machineries. We work too hard to be drunks: but it helps, till it gets boring. It is the failures who become alcoholics.

Sometimes Jock was gentle about life, even tender: at others he was almost arrogant and argumentative and difficult, as though he was jealous about something or angry. I often blessed the songs he and Nessie sang to me until I wept. They released love and lessened tension. Otherwise there would have been more disaster, when Colquhoun and MacBryde were about particularly, for they seemed to carry a violence. I was once nearly kicked to death in Soho when with them and Bernard Denvir's beautiful wife: somehow it was avoided and another man got the boots squelching in his face. But they never did anything. On a summer day they all came over from Pengersick Lane to St Ives and the drink was raging high. At night we found ourselves with nowhere to go until Willie Barns-Graham, the Scottish painter from the Edinburgh élite, gave us her studio as sanctuary, where we got down to snoring with the long sea outside. I woke later to find Colquhoun's head wreathed with fire where he lay on the long bench under the window. His pillow was alight and his eagle face pale with sleep. I leapt across to put it out. MacBryde leapt after me thinking I was after Colquhoun, who was his lover. There was no time to explain I was not gay, but I hung on till the fire was out. The studio was all wood – we would have all been burnt to death, Joke Grim and Nessie included.

I often think that kind of sudden violence is likely to activate where people of strong creative power are gathered together – as if it is an explosion of waste gases at the volcano's very heart and each poet gives shape to the burning larva. Wyndham Lewis wrote of Colquhoun's paintings: 'A grave has been dug behind each of his canvases of a certain kind.' It is because of the mission we have at a certain time in history that lives are often in danger. For each artist it is a new problem.

Another traumatic incident was when Jock was living in St Ives – or perhaps was staying the night – at a house in the back of town. It was probably the one Barbara Hepworth bought later at the top of a walled garden in a hill: the house was built in a hollow at the side, its roof level with the top of the wall. Graham had a room here. Returning late on Saturday night from the pub, or too late to go through the wall gate having forgotten his keys, he climbed the wall on to the roof in an attempt to reach his window. But the roof was slippery and he was oiled: what worse combination could be? He slithered down the roof and fell into the courtyard 40 feet below.

I first heard of this early on Sunday morning when I was walking on the quay where I used to go and talk with the fishermen waiting for the boats to return from the night fishing. The little town was like a white bone washed clean by the sunlight and the salt wind. I met the Canadian writer, Norman Levine.

'Have you heard about Jock?' he asked eagerly.

'No – is he all right?'

'I think he's dead!' What a shock – it was like shellfire!

'DEAD! How can he be dead?'

'I don't know for certain. But he fell from his roof early this morning and was rushed off to hospital. They didn't think he would live! I'm trying to get there now, but there are no buses and I must phone first.'

'Jock DEAD. He CAN'T be!' That was unbelievable in the cold light as the boats came chugging through the harbour mouth. Not DEAD.

I have forgotten how long it was before he came round and we got an official report. It was an anxious time. In the end he had only smashed a kneecap and was otherwise all right, proving the story of Chuang Tzu that the drunken man falling from the cart does not die, because he is in harmony with natural laws.

I visited him with a pad of paper to write his poems and some volumes of poetry to read until he came out, and there were many comic references to the silver patella they put in his knee. And there in another bed was Harry Rowntree, dying. I shook hands with him. He died.

It was the love that Jock and Nessie gave out through their courage, their poetry, their humour and their being about that I valued and so missed. They made me realise that after all life was an adventure to be lived and an experience to create from a puzzle to be solved – not a quest for power and fame. I only bless the Gods that he was tenacious enough to survive the American syndrome, as he did that fall from the roof to the stone courtyard of the house where later Barbara Hepworth was to be burnt to death by the flame from a whisky bottle and not, like Dylan Thomas, be discharged toward England in a casket.

I left the magic peninsula – or, more rightly, the peninsula of magic – in 1953 to travel by horse and waggon to the New Forest, leaving also many dear friends, among them Joke Grim and his Lady Ariel from Greenock and Blantyre. I went to live an even harder life for a time than had he when I found him hoeing his violets in Pengersick Lane. Apart from corresponding over the cottage I had lent him the friendship seemed like falling snow to float away in Time's darkness. When I heard of his death, as though the words and feelings had been trawled like fishes into a net over the years, I wrote this letter, addressed to the deep ocean.

Joke Grim

A letter to Sydney Graham
Gull Cry – Deep Ocean

Dear Joke Grim,

Deep ocean to my shore.
To hear you are dead is a terrible thing –
A ship gone down in the heart
Anchored absolute
By God the Octopus,
On the profound floor
Of the seal-furred sea
Green with Leviathan ointment
Which you have stirred
Only a wavefall before me.

It is no use talking –
Not Talking Talk
Because you were a Man of Talk
And you can no longer hear
Now you are invisible
Where you walk
Under the water.
Only the silence of the written word
Might reach your ear.

There is no way at heartbeat
That I could anvil my words
Into the forge of your listening ear,
Or tongue to tell
The celcius sorrow
Of a burning tear
And a lone seabell.

You wrote me words of miracle my dear,
In the SONG OF THE TOWER:

> 'Vain Merlin
> Lonely stone
> Sven Berlin.'

As though you knew the secret link,
Outside and in,

149

Between the stone and me,
Welded by your words.
No talk is needed, you see.
But it makes me think.

When we were about the drink
And waves of poetry crashed
Their dominions through my Tower,
You sang of the Western Isles, with Ness
Sweet as a mountain flower,
And I wept with love that was joy –
Now a fierce sorrow and distress
At your absence
Walking kneedeep in starlight.
Only an olam ago
We leapt the fires on a flaming shore:
Now you are burnt for a few pence.

When you grew violets in Pengersick Lane
We drank the Two Roberts daft –
Eaglehead Colquhoun was wreathed in fire
And Great Art, the Assassin, laughed.

Later, when the Night Man came
Did you know? He who
Took you in his boat
For the Nightfishing:–
The longlines, the idiot eel
With ultramarine eye
Barking at death in the moonlight
Like a longdog at the sky –
And you struck the bell with your fist:
Did you know him?
How the mystical language
Would enter you –
Make tryst?
Did you know the Night Man
When he came in his boat?

Now you are in the granite rock,
The seabell and the storm,
Now you answer the waves
With a trawl of visions
Out of God's houses of fierce salt

I shall listen from my emptiness
For those words to form – halt
As they speak a ministry of fish
Down fathoms of each tall dark
Shark haunted hall
Till you steer for landfall
In your boat of fire painted by gull cry:

JOKE GRIM PZ

So you signed your letters to me
Addressed to me

SZAINT SZVEN, THE TOWER
UNDER THE SEA

Thus I to you, now you are dead.

The women lie
All in your bower
With the songs of the heath:
Only words from your pen
Have slipped the fierce nets of death.

Families of fishermen will carry you.
One woman will weep by the shore
And brush the sand from your eyes
Closed by the north wind
Lifting your tawny hair
And sing the Western Isles once more
Under storm-written skies.

Your death was a poem that was not written
Only whispered by the phosphorus waves
And the fishtailed maids of the sea
Who slithered under your dreams
Under wonderhand in moonlight
Where the gannet screams.

But wait for a moment. Once again
'Wash the front of your face'
And listen now! the bell tongue speaks

A lighthouse honoured by octopus
Points its tentacled white beam
At that tall man of glass

Who died a sorrow ago.
JOKE GRIM. See him
Shining on the sea's horizon – pass
To where the eternal go,
Beyond poverty and pride that craze
The vagabondage of inspired men
Who speak with the voice of oceans.

In all my deepsea orisons of stone
I carve you now my praise as then,
Simple as seaweed the wind chars:
Only in death is man alone – out there
Difficult and strange as the stars
When the seabell tolls its fist of prayer.

      Love

          SZAINT SZVEN

      Envoi

You were the flame
That bent the iron font
And wrote its transfusion
In branches of fire
Till you moved England –
Now the ancient level
Of her language
Has paused a century to cool.

'Joke Grim' was Graham's nickname for himself. 'Szaint Sven' was his nickname for me. The manuscript of the 'Song of the Tower' is now in the National Library of Scotland along with a drawing of Sydney Graham I did at the time.

The last time I heard his voice read poetry I was trying to listen to his broadcast of the 'Nightfishing' on the Third Programme. I was in the deep forest living rough, in a waggon much like his at Pengersick Lane. The battery on my wireless had almost gone. I could just hear his Scots voice saying the last lines of his poem:

      . . . and has
The iron sea engraved to our faintest breath,
The spray fretted and fixed at a higher temper,
A script of light. . .

THE BOAT OF FIRE

It was just loud enough to know him there:

contrary and rare as sand.

and Nessie standing in starlight. Then it faded and I switched off, leaving him to sail his boat of fire.

Lonely Stone

Life in the Tower had the great value of being free. That is one of the gifts of poverty and the quest of the inner man who wishes to become complete through intrinsic experience and not at the dictates of conforming to a prefabricated pattern of society. As Sydney Graham altered the form of the English language in order that he should say what he had to say in his own fashion, so I altered the form of the stones around me.

Starvation, I have said, is a woman with one blind eye who will not open her mouth or her legs and who can utter but one word: NO – eternally echoing down the halls of death. Watch her and learn to cut stone. The face of a stone is also totally blind like a shut door and offers no way in. The implacable male face of granite, the gentle female gown of alabaster. In each case it is closed in one dimension. In each case it can only be entered by an act of constant and patient penetration. The neophyte carves the face on the outside of the stone because his mind cannot see inside or know the way to penetrate the secret shrine where all images of creation are housed. He thinks and acts on a flat surface as though he lived in a wall painting. He paints himself on the outer wall in several planes all round the stone and thinks he has victory in hand, but in the end that is only a series of drawings fitted together round the stone which is already itself a form in space, still holding its secret. There is one magic word as ancient as time. OG. Find the Og stone standing in space.

> Find the Og Stone
> Standing in space:
> Pierce the Og Stone
> And find your face.
> Then you have space
> In form alone – and grace.

That is a magic chant I have invented – it should ignite the sudden spark that will illuminate the stone and the mind simultaneously. Drawings for sculpture also are simply that. Diagrams to find the right key that will unlock the stone, as with a woman. Once a stone has been pierced so that suddenly the light roars through like a white tiger, the first act of sculpture had been made and the image can be released as a new object existing in the world. And if it is stirred by the deep groundswell of feeling and emotion I experienced in Cornwall, by being part of the landscape and the people and the mystic feeling which my poet friend found in St Just, then there is a chance of profound work emerging. This is the act of creation that comes from nowhere and is to nowhere going. It takes a life to achieve.

These were the problems I wrestled with in the Tower, quite alone. At one point I was asked to go and work with Barbara Hepworth along with Terry Frost, John Wells and Denis Mitchell, and would have learnt a deal more, I knew. But I did not want the Medusa touch. I wanted to find out for myself, keep my vision intact. I refused.

The work for my show in London through the summer of 1946 was painting entirely. I established myself as a painter in the contemporary scene of that time and was invited by the Arts Council, UNESCO and the British Council for exhibitions all over the UK and the Western World. I did not *want* stone. I was a painter.

It was this first winter in the Tower, 1945–46, that was memorable for its hardship, for indeed I did not know what it meant to face the Atlantic gale alone. Hear it roaring toward the Tower like a train and hit it with the impact of a rhinoceros, feel the building shudder but not move, for it was built upon rock, of concrete reinforced with cast iron bedsteads. I had the family in a luxury flat on the wharf and they were safe and with friends. I was also being helped by a grant from Dartington Hall arranged by Bernard Leach and by the Artists' Benevolent Fund since my Army pay of £3.10/- a week family allowance and 10/- for me as an ordinary soldier was cut off. This help went on throughout and extended to help with the children's education later. I had no pension or dole for myself. In fact nothing, which for those who don't know, *means nothing*. In later years when my books were published the Royal Literary Fund helped generously, during my 30 years exile.

I think it was the last winter the Commando Unit was there, for which I was thankful because they and the U.S. troops were responsible for the undoing of the marital structures while St Ives men were away at war and a wave of suicide was going through the town as the husbands returned. That little town by the sea whose every cobblestone was monument to a broken heart. Somehow it was plenty and nothing that Christmas. For me, nothing – or nearly nothing. I had shut the door to settle to work and be alone when a knock came. I opened it to find a fisherman standing there with expressionless face. 'Appy Crastmas!' he said and held out a green pound note. 'Thank you Richard!' I said and took it for I had nothing and it was Christmas Day. My novel, *The Dark Monarch*, will elucidate further anguish endured over the next five years. I still thought of myself as a painter and still do.

But this was not to continue. The dull beat of destiny was heard again and with it was being announced in tendrils of thought and dream and event a new theme: SCULPTURA: FROM THE LATIN WORD TO CARVE. That is the toughest definition of sculpture I know – especially if it is in stone, of which I speak because I am a man of stone.

> Unclench thy teeth, Stone Man white!
> Hammer darkness with thy black brain,
> Cutting through to yesterday again,
> And let thy woman hold the fragile light.
> Cut form free to turn about in space -
> Time, length, width, weight and depth,
> Gravity of azimuth and breadth -
> Dimensions of the everlasting face.
> True to the wind, obedient to the sun,
> Hold gentle balance on the fingertip,
> And moon and tide and stars till Time is done,
> As though guiding God's Titanic Ship
> Beyond that last horizon's polished bone:
> Master thy agony – Man of Stone.

If I raise an ithyphallic pillar against the sky, as Jacob did to communicate his vision of angels, in so doing I isolate a form. If I pierce that form by tunnelling through it with a hammer and chisel, as in some Ogham stones, I have made space within form and form within space: it is these two elements and their interaction on the mind of man, that creates a sculpture in its purest sense. To these the sculptor is bound by the law of his art. In poetry there are words, which are really sounds, which in turn are invisible, so you can approach an explanation through the invisible world. But because sculpture is hard and factual it can only be approached from the visible world, although like poetry it has the same invisible sources of energy and imagination.

The ancient Chinese, because their minds work in the opposite direction to ours – from within outwards – start with the Uncarved Block containing the 'ten thousand things'. In the *Tao Te Ching* the Uncarved Block, Arthur Waley tells us in the introduction to his translation, is 'the symbol of the primal undifferentiated unity underlying the complexity of the universe.' In the West we work away from this by cutting into the block, and try to arrive at unity in the things we carve, so that they have wholeness. The East starts with the symbol of unity, which contains all things: we start by destroying the symbol in order to seek and find unity. I speak and see through western eyes. Each image in the stone becomes the microcosm of the universe and therefore arrives at the same thing. It also becomes a newly created syzygy of space and form, from which arises mass, form, volume, growth, rhythm, harmony, weight, gravity and magnitude. It is out of these elements the beautiful symphonies of the centuries have been created in stone. They compose the structure within which emotion is enclosed, and it is the emotion in man that makes for greatness and drama, as distinct from beauty in his work – beauty is something else: I don't know what it is, I only know it exists and I sometimes capture it. Thus stone is the sculptor's man.

The sources of sculpture, as with poetry, are from the original fountainhead in the dark places of the unconscious where the Violet Man moves and has his being, but they are also in the world about us because sculpture needs a stone: the Uncarved Block. Poetry can be loaded into a song and thrown into the air. Into this stone, and within it, the sculptor works to release his image: it is not an image that is within sound or word or gesture or even flat surface, but an imago-vision which sees form in space from every possible direction. This is the unique nature of his mind, but not unique in nature. Nature does this all the time but cannot observe it or be conscious of it, only through man, who is able to turn the form about in his mind and alter it by motion and also emotion.

To help in this he must be able to draw, for drawing is a visual root to sculpture and painting, apart from being an activity which can be used for its own sake. In sculpture the drawing extends from the flat surface into actual form in space: in painting it extends into colour and light on a flat area. So drawing is like a crocodile bird: it can pick at the teeth of the mind and of the landscape to see what is going on and what it can find – a fragment of bone, a gristly shape, a growth of sinew or structure of mountain. What is drawn for sculpture is a diagram on a flat surface for an idea in space, often from many angles, even superimposed. These can be extended into wax or plaster as maquettes. But the transformation and tightening of vision comes immediately the chisel is set against stone in one of the great adventures known to man: the first hammer blow is made, the surface is broken and another dimension is invaded. From then on it is between the mind of man and the stone to create an image in space, which Henry Moore said to me was so difficult a task. In this case there is the physical power, the direction of the hand, the ache of thew and unity of mind and spirit which only a man of stone can know. He is tough as a miner, sensitive as a mayfly. The feeling is the same as early man knew, digging his fogou or his stone bed at Chysauster. The sound is the same as rang through Ancient Egypt, where the great arm of Rameses, like the arm of God, was carved in porphyry or pink granite: and the black granite princesses of everlastingness who smile so sweetly. Beauty indeed is not only a structure, but a spirit that pervades a sculpture, shines from it, around it, and through it. Behind this there is the stone, always the stone, whether the image is already within it or not. Michaelangelo believed that it was:

> The best of artists has no thought to show
> Which the rough stone in its superfluous shell
> Doth not include; to break the marble spell
> Is all the hand that serves the brain can do.

Nietzsche also referred to 'the image that slumbers in the stone'. This arrives at the universal, the Uncarved Block that contains the ten thousand things. But the image is also in the unconscious mind, and the unconscious mind is awakened by trees and shells, bones and mountains, elegant women, and the coelacanth: in fact by all forms of nature. The hand of the man drawing these things is like the divining hand of the fisherman who knows where unseen fish move. There is magnetic force between the mind and the things which emerge from it and from the landscape so that they come together, even from vibrations out of the future, so that there are new things created in the imagination that also grow and merge into natural forms from past experience, fired by what Michaelangelo called 'the fierce desires that from the passions flow'. Perhaps spirit and matter are the same after all!

From another sculptor's point of view, speaking as the workman in his *Notes on Sculpture*, Henry Moore says this:

The sculptor gets the solid shape, as it were, inside his head – he thinks of it, whatever its size, as if he were holding it completely enclosed in the hollow of his hand. He mentally visualizes a complex of form from all round itself; he knows, while he looks at one side, what the other side is like; he identifies himself with the centre of gravity, its mass, weight; he realises its volume as the space that the shape displaces in the air.

So it is true that this quest into stone, as distinct from flat intaglio, is largely unknown. What we bring to it and project into it helps to light our way and alter the original image we think or believe is already there, so that a human back in grief might heave with a sea-force, a head split by a sword of thunder and lightning become a cloven fruit, a hand become etiolated by roots and the main form from which these are grown become a woman born of a mountain that contains a hollow tarn. All at the point of a single chisel that covers the work with a net of cuts and hauls the form out of the block of stone, until the main excavations are concluded.

As in a gold mine, the vein is reached. Or like meeting a stranger in the darkness, the main form is felt for the first time, made known for the first time, by cutting away the last layers of stone – they come off like peeling an orange and the form can be seen as it reveals its own levels and directions. For me there is always a feeling of discovery before this happens as though that third person were near and guiding my hand and eye with unerring skill; and a feeling of miracle when it does happen. The excitement, the ecstasy, even! The quiet pleasure, as when light comes through after piercing the first tunnel in the centre of the stone. These things are the real gold by which the sculptor is paid: the reward for taking the journey into the unknown: that cannot be shared. But with him who has made an image of the inner and outer landscape within the law of the stone – that can be shared. 'There it is!' he will say. 'That is IT!' He still does not know if it slumbered in the stone or if he projected it there or if he was guided to it: he has created something new that has never been seen before: like going in search of the North Pole and finding it – inside you. On these discoveries and on these themes, endless variations can be made, because, as with nature, there is no end to the possibilities of creation.

This is why the sculptor remains with his chisels and with his naked hands. He is a workman and these guide him at all times, enable him to have direct contact with the mind and with the stone

– and whatever mysteries are there contained. Chisels have not altered over thousands of years. You can see the scars of the point on the granite sarcophagus of an Egyptian Pharaoh, and the claw on the Baboli Slaves of Michaelangelo. And they ground the surfaces by hand. Power tools are alright, but only for rough grinding: the journey into the stone and all round and in through the image must still be by hand – the man with five legs. For some years I have used a power tool to grind and when I decided upon this I taught myself first to draw with it so that I could follow the forms truthfully and the tensions were retained. For some reason the ultimate form will only leave you and go outside finally to exist in its own right as a new image, if it is completed by hand. It won't do so from the power tool and to force it will take its life. This is my experience.

There are also many new man-made materials and many new angles of vision included in the act of sculpture today. I tell myself it is a good anchor that remains in the original seabed rock until these new and possibly unenduring aspects have been tested by the groundswell of history, to which all things have succumbed except the stones and bronzes of shipwrecked civilisations. For me poxyresin fibre glass polyurethane does not hold the elemental qualities for true sculpture. And it is a poor man that no longer cares about volume, weight and structure.

Speak of stone with gentleness and respect. Speak of it with undertones of prayer, for stone is the container of great cities and storehouse of man's passions down the ages. Stone is washed into forms by the sea, so smooth that they are like insects and flowers, caves in the side of the earth, quiet thoughts in the mind of man. Stone is harsh, brutal and male with cut of granite, shape of quartz, scratch of felspar, fingernail-split of mica. It is smooth and obstinate like a woman, takes you and flows into you, fills with light, is translucent in alabaster, offers its darkness, bruises if struck too hard. In Portland it is prehistoric with pungent Jurassic smells like pike, semen or snow; it is gritty, sparkles, plucks, bites, flakes, cracks, splinters, flies, remains whole – is obtuse, holy and truthful. Stone is beautiful and stark, calls back only with its tongues of silence and echoes of creation. It is empty – a tomb stored with images of the past, for discovery and use in the long dynasties of the future. It is a smile from a blind girl, a tear from a tired king whose name is Man. Tread softly when you tread near stone, in case you wake the sleeping forms of its inhabitants.

The sculptor is inspired either by the things made by God or the

Anerley Hill, *oil 1938. The Engineering School is on the right.*

Bernard and David Leach conferring with staff at the Pottery; Bernard Leach with Naum Gabo, and his memorial to Alfred Wallis.

Deep Seasaint: Alfred Wallis and a characteristic painting.
Below: Christopher Wood who, with Ben Nicholson, 'discovered' the reclusive artist.

The Wandering Jew, *oil 1988 (Dopita).*

First self portrait, oil 1938 (Dopita).

David Philips, *oil 1941 (Hamill)*.

Clown, *oil (Dopita)*.

Shah of Persia, *oil 1938*.

In the fields: Dung cart, *1939.*

Broccoli planters, *1938.*

Man in sackcloth, *1938 (all Dopita).*

At croust, *1939*.

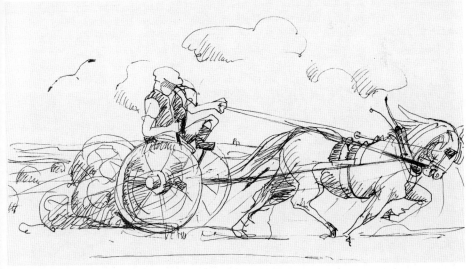

Horse rake, *1939*.

Packing broccoli, *watercolour 1942 (Dopita).*

Orchard, Treswithian, *oil 1941 (Dopita).*

Nancemellin, *watercolour 1934 (Dopita)*.

Nancemellin, *oil 1939 (Dopita)*.

Barbara Hepworth (Tate Archive).

Berlin's wrought iron mask,
1948 (Studio St. Ives).

Ben Nicholson (Tate Archive).

Pregnant Mother, *Berlin's sculpture in*
teak, 1948 (Studio St. Ives).

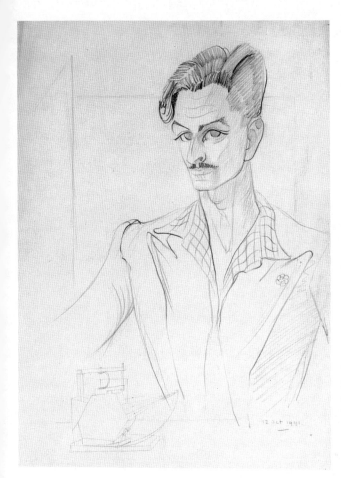

Self Portrait with a
construction: *1941
(Dopita)*.

Construction by the Sea,
1941.

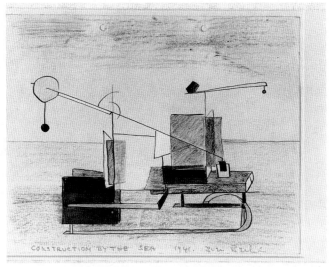

Man and woman with a flower, *oil 1940 (David Brown).*

Construction by the Sea, *gouache 1941 (V & A Museum).*

The artist at war; Norman peasant *and* Dead German soldier, *from* I am Lazarus, *1944.*

Animals, *watercolour 1946*.

Cornish village, *watercolour 1939*.

Mousehole, *gouache 1947*.

Self portrait in a
Lapp hat, *oil 1988*.

things made by Man. The tendency in the last two decades has been to follow the latter because the exigencies of early materials do not suit the newly emasculated man bred from our colleges and universities – usually half teacher: he is not fitted to the sheer work with the hammer, as hard as any coal-face worker, or the tenacity of mind needed to hold a form in its entirety until it is released, with the result that he turns to more incestuous forms of inspiration and easier materials.

After the London show which was concurrent with the first Crypt show I lived and worked for a time quite dangerously: it seemed that I had arrived and I wondered what was to happen next. A woman critic asked me at the end of an interview, 'And what will you do next, Mr Berlin?' I replied, 'Go back to Cornwall and cut stone!' Hearing myself say it rather than knowing I had said it and not knowing why. It was only much later I realised this extension of my work into space had been pushing me for some time and had to happen.

The Flight of Icarus

That show in London made things easier both before and afterwards, because I was in the light, but I also had my family. I saw my own children once a week. They came to my Tower – Paul in his Great Man's Coat and sweet truculence, Janet with her blue eyes and gentle defiance, both in that paradise of life which is a garden built round a volcano.

Guido Morris appeared like a ghost from nowhere and like a phantom I housed him in my Tower till I found him a place to work and live. This with the help of Bryan Wynter, who had taken over the lonely cottage on Zennor Carn. And Peter Lanyon who was immediately busy getting the idea of the Crypt Group together as though he were gathering the strands which were to be woven into the eye of the storm that would burst later. I was painting for London and without my knowing the oils were already pushing their way out of the first dimension from thick gesso deeply carved while it was wet. Fish. Shells. Skulls. Bones. Weed. Fishermen. Boats. These paintings were interpenetrating with a dream world of the imagination which was quite personal and released by the dramatic landscape and inner magic of Cornwall with its structure of mines and foges, hills, cromlechs and cliffs. I was still drawing. Arthur Hambly came to see.

As winter came on, things got harder and my own survival as well as Guido's was due to Mr and Mrs Keeley who ran a *pension* in the Back Street called St. Christopher's. They gave us an open invitation to breakfast, which extended later to other meals if we wished. I paid by leaving a small sculpture among the cornflakes every now and then. Guido, with a present of printing in beautiful Bembo on Barcham Green Pink handmade paper.

I was introduced to Peter Lanyon one afternoon outside the Lifeboat House by John Wells. We had written to him previously from a pub when I was staying in the Scillies. He was a good-looking man with grey-blue eyes and large hands with a strong grip, a mouth that turned down at the corners when he smiled and toward blonde hair. The meeting was short but friendly and enthusiastic. He was still in uniform of an RAF Corporal. I don't know if he had been on flying duties. I was once offered rear gunner but refused and later volunteered for Air OP in those little

Ostercraft that worked the front line and was turned down. So there it was. He was an ex-Corporal. I, a Bombardier. Known as BOMB BERLIN. We got on. He was simply intent on getting discharged and into painting. But the meeting seemed to have upset him. When he got back to his unit in Italy he wrote me a withering letter telling me in harsh terms how he intended things should be. I had not realised I had trodden so far into his territory and was bewildered after our cordial meeting. I was in the Tower absorbing the shock when Bryan Wynter dropped in for some benzedrine. He saw I was upset. I read him the letter. I did not know at that time that he did not like Lanyon. His deep voice full of humour filled my Tower.

'My advice is, don't answer it. He's talking rubbish. Leave it. Just drop a card saying: "I see what you mean, Peter, but I think it's a lot of balls!"'

I exploded with laughter and did exactly what Bryan had said. It was a great relief. My way had been hard but not fraught with politics because I did not think that way. Recently I found a letter I had written in reply but did not send after Bryan's advice. It is well that I did not.

This was a pattern that followed, alternating between complete charm and sudden aggravation both of which I seemed to trigger in Peter but could never tell quite which it would be. Having had a tough life I could not help seeing there was still a strata of spoilt schoolboy aggression in him. I liked him and that has always seemed for me the best basis for friendship, and like a boat rocking gently at its mooring that friendship started to develop. He called often at the Tower and I climbed the hill over St Ives to his home from which you could survey the town and the whole of the Atlantic Ocean. His mother I remember as a kind, white-haired, sensitive lady who poured me tea from a silver teapot, as my mother had done, in a room of Edwardian homeliness, talking interestedly about everything in a middle class well-to-do world: or that is how it seemed to a poverty-laden painter back from the war. I got on with his sister Mary, a lively, attractive and married woman of about my age. It was a haven in my lonely life. In 1945 Peter was seriously ill with a streptococcus infection. I telephoned him every day to see how he was. After his recovery when I met him in the street, I mentioned that I had telephoned. 'Yes,' he said, 'I know. From now on I shall distrust you!'

His father had died earlier − a reputable photographer and musician. His studio, he told me, was the one his father had used for his photographic work − an unlikely setting otherwise for a painter who was to break through to a unique vision once he had shaken off the fragments we all had to shake off after knowing Gabo and Ben Nicholson, to both of whom he was pupil after Borlase Smart and Fuller had given him a traditional grounding. The action time for breaking through the screen was exactly right. Even smashing it like a bombed city. In the process of doing this he broke through the shell that held his personal view of the world, and Cornwall in particular, looking out and over it from an abstract proscenium suspended between earth, sea and sky, as he might well have stood on the Suspension Bridge at Clifton over the River Avon when he was a boy at Clifton College – a beautiful construction created by Brunel a century before. Like the Crystal Palace it was pure Gabo.

St Ives at that time was still quite a sleepy little town, not yet covered by rubber ducks and beach gear in summer, sold to the roar of rock music. It smelt of fish, not the frying of fish and chips. It twinkled under the lights from the houses and boats at night under an orange moon. There seemed always to be a Presence over the town and the dark hills behind, the boats negatives of themselves in the strange light. The granite houses gave one a sense of an ancient coliseum where historic happenings were performed. By dawn the little town was washed clean as a bone and every day a new beauty was born. The harbour held the boats in its claws for safety.

The Cornish wisely and thankfully gather their harvest from others since the fishing has gone, knowing their little town will be returned to them in winter. Now it is being gradually consumed by the invaders. But the fishermen are still the guardians and the spirits of their ancestors scream on the wind to keep the devils away. Nothing will change their Cornishness.

I lived a lot of my life at night, for it was then the moon created its negative beauty and the goddess walked at starlight, holding my hand and the arm of darkness was gentle to the touch, in spite of the agonies by day. When the town got busy again about its life, the crustacean granite of the houses sparkled, vans, fish carts with horses, lame Matthew with his fruit and vegetable flat, Ben Nicholson in his red sports car and white cap, me in my 1924 Morris threading through the crowds. Jimmy Limpots, John Craze, Akkie Beard, Johnny Lookup, Edward Mouse, Willie Wilde, Richard Care in Japanese armour, Petrouchska the Toymaker, Bernard Leach, Guido Morris making up the crowds and John Park painting the sea as though he had thrown down a handful of jewels he was forever trying to recover. All crunching the sunlight. And Peter Lanyon in

164

his green drophead coupé driving towards the Tower where so often he came to see me.

On one such a day when the sun was working that strange miracle which mesmerised the soul into painting without knowing why or from what, as though a hidden hand was guiding what happened, I was working on a painting I had been wanting to complete for sometime – of the bay sweeping away from my window beyond the town, Carbis Bay and Hayle Towans to Godrevy Light and that stretch of the Atlantic known as Seaman's Grave. The painting started to go on its own, colour flowing over its rocky surfaces. I had seen a semi-circular burning glass of the sea with the eye of an unknown man looking through it. The magenta and greens of floating weed turned to kelps of violet hair, blue brains, nacreous teeth: a fish-infiltrated head. I was at work looking down on the table like a primitive man, which suited me, and I turned the panel sideways, upside-down, longways to see what would happen and was happening. The marine features became the face of a head looking out from a seascape and surrounding land, the sweep of the bay his cloak, the lighthouse a brooch on his shoulder. A man-into-coast-scape, as though the land and sea had entered into me.

I was just at the end of this dynamic painting experience when I heard a motor car engine switch off, a door slam, a voice call. It was Peter asking if he could come up. He climbed the wooden stair enclosed by the windscreen where Sydney Graham often pinned poems when I was out. He looked clean and neat but ridiculous in knickerbockers that were like too-small plus fours and a service beret straight on his head. What on the professional stage we called OWRIC. I wanted to scream but I was too excited and said wildly: 'Look, Peter. COMPOSITE MAN! What do you think of it? Out of nothing it came. Yes, I've finished it so be careful. It's still wet.'

It was one of those moments between two painters which held complete understanding of what had happened. I had made a painting. Peter was also very excited: 'Amazing. Quite amazing!' he kept saying.

The Tower was a strange place and when anything happened it was electrifying, especially on those days of magical sunlight when the brilliant reflector of the sea intensified the light to an almost unbearable brightness and gave to events a dreamlike everlastingness that was stamped on the mind for all time.

We talked about the painting for a long time as though someone else had done it. Then he drove away. But when I went out for my midday drink, I met him in the pub talking to people, which was not usual for him. He was asking if anyone had seen the amazing painting Sven had done of the Composite Man. I had not known anything like this before and felt curiously embarrassed. But always when I had done a good painting it seemed it was nothing to do with me, so I shrugged my shoulders and stayed silent. I was secretly pleased. When it came to my show in London I made it the centre-piece and had it reproduced on the cover of a manifesto printed by Guido Morris. Sadly the painting has been lost sight of.

Inasmuch as Peter's genuine enthusiasm and remarks had made me realise that I had taken a step forward in painting, the Composite Man did the same for him in his subsequent self portrait and the metamorphic paintings that were to follow. But I could not tell if it was the same for him. In some ways the Composite Man was a self portrait as indeed everything one paints is a self portrait: my image permeated into and locked into his landscape was fatal, for as always his territorial instinct was stronger than expected: especially in this instance.

We went on working together with John Wells, Bryan Wynter and Guido in forming the Crypt Group, which was Peter's idea, and the first Crypt Show in 1946 fell simultaneously with my show at Lefevre, so I had quite a lot going – all watercolours, oil paintings and drawings in London – but a few small early sculptures in the Crypt, among them my first sandstone carving of 1938 and a construction in wood and glass, 1944. Sculpture was awakening. The Third Continuum was announcing itself like a theme in a symphony. I probably talked about it.

One day in November of that year when all had again gone quiet, Peter took me in his little green car to Polyphant Mine near Launceston to get some stone. This was one of those acts of kindness which had no pomp about it, but was quite clearly objective and genuine. In fact he was not in anyway an ungenuine man, only difficult, not even that on this day. It was intensely cold. The day before I had taken a strip out of my left thumb, cutting a mount in the Tower with a sharp boot-knife. The bone was exposed and I had to have hospital attention with several very painful injections in the joints before stitching. So on the long journey across Bodmin Moor, under Cornwall's one mountain Brown Wille and past the radio station that looked like a painting by Paul Klee, I must have been silent and seemed very morose for I was in great pain and had not eaten. We loaded some blocks of steatite and returned. I almost fainted when he left me alone in the Tower. I have always found silence best so said nothing. I don't know what was said on that journey: it is blank: my straight through memory cuts out. I only know that the stones he had bought for me were the ones from which I did my first larger sculptures and stopped painting. The switch was uncanny and unexpected, as it was complete, as though it had been done for me without my consultation. I had taken on the stone forgetting my responsibility to painting. It was as though the hot stream of lava that poured from me up to that time in hundreds of paintings was diverted. All colour was gone: until I left Cornwall and got to the Forest several years later. History had changed the points. Whether it used Peter to do it I don't know, and don't know if he knew. The extraordinary thing was that I didn't want it. I was an established painter as I had set out to be and the rest was a matter of growing and improving in that way. It was put about that I could not paint. Painting is my first love and the colour of the coat in which I grew up.

I was faced with stone and with it I was faced with 'the hardest task a man can set himself,' as Henry Moore told me later, 'to make a sculpture in space.' It is the entrance into the Third Continuum where ordinary folk do not journey. Yet the poet knew when he wrote later:

> Vain Merlin
> Lonely Stone
> Sven Berlin

I did not even know the chisels I should use to start. The only thing I had was an immense physique from a decade of dancing and lifting and swinging another human in space, and an abnormal power of endurance from my ancestor Sven Hedin, the explorer, about whom Bryan Wynter was never tired of chiding me. Also, of course, an extraordinary arrogance which would not admit failure. From this point I cut out some large primitive images which had great volume and presence. Moore came to a show of these in London and explained to me that they had no necks, were a series of flat surfaces and praised any kind of tunnel I had instinctively made. 'It is one of the greatest adventures when you get through your first tunnel to pierce the stone and see the light come through,' he said. 'But you must see the image from every possible point of view, to do it. Be aware of what it looks like at the other side all the time.' It was his dynamic intrusion into my work and insistence on my cutting deep that gave me the impetus to go on and finally one day know that I had made a sculpture, as when I did my first self portrait and knew I had done a painting. There *is* a guiding force which comes into play when you are tired enough and the doors of the unconscious mind slide silently back and let it through. SIMPLIFY SIMPLIFY SIMPLIFY I wrote on my wall. I worked at night by candlelight because the deep shadows gave me the sense of another deeper form than the flat surface of paper and worked out an hieroglyphic by marking in broad paint that only I could read or understand in the morning, and was led in this way to the other side of this side and the nether side of that side of the stone by going through it. Then the image started to reveal itself and even cast off great chunks of stone as if they fell away from the exact contours for which I was searching and which had slumbered there for centuries waiting to be found. That was the miracle. The mystical company of body and mind and spirit were in perfect harmony with the stone. I was simply an agent for letting the stone sculpt itself. All this made me terribly humble and awe-inspired and I worked at night so that I should be there none seeing me.

> Blest night of wandering
> In secret, when by none might I be spied,
> Nor I see anything;
> Without a light to guide
> Save that which in my heart burnt in my side.

So Peter Lanyon brought me toward one of the greatest experiences of my life by buying the stone I was to carve and at whose face I was to work for 50 years.

St Ives was a strange place in its pristine state, but during a war, just before and just after, with a heavy contingent of American, British and Canadian troops it was even more so in and around the artists' colony.

In the early part, Alfred Wallis was KNOCKED DOWN BY A MOTER CAR IN THE STREET which he never got over and recorded it in his honest script.

One day in 1942 I stood in St Peter Square when a German plane strafed the Back Roads bringing the fisherwomen out of their cottages wailing with terror, until the pilot dropped his last bomb on the Gasworks, which did not go off, while he flew into the distance leaving a continuing wave of destructive force in his wake.

Bernard Leach's house was hit by a land mine, and after I returned from the invasion of France, I was threatened by a madman with a knife in my Tower. Later my house was burned down.

This is a simple record of a powerful force working in conjunction with an abnormal creative power that rose in us as the war ended. A tidal wave of energy that carried us on, overcoming and transforming the destruction that got in our way, and sometimes passed through us. For me as a Forward Observer it was a change from having your best mate blown apart before your eyes and be expected not to say anything – even when I was nearly run over.

It was not only the surface geography of Cornwall: its low cromlech-crowned and storm-cut hills, its cliffs like Amenhotep sculptures, its terraced undulations and sea-frontiers that brought about a pinnacle vision in some artists. There was also the body, the solid land of Cornwall with its mine-shafts and foges, pierced stones, setts, caves, caverns, tunnels, holes and undercliffs, that gave the opposite experience to mass and volume that I found enriching.

It was with some excitement I heard that Lanyon had fixed up to go down Geevor Tin Mine with John Wells and myself. The mine is at St Just, a little town on the western coast 'built into the landscape in the best Cézanne tradition,' as Adrian Ryan succinctly put it. It was a day of wonderful sunlight and we were driven by Peter in his little green car across those mysterious moors with the Atlantic flashing its vast glass signals at the sky, sending messages to an unknown planet, leaving the mind an empty palimpsest to record a miracle. It was a day of happiness spent with two painters who were truly Cornish, each with a unique vision of Cornwall. For some reason I had always wanted to go down Lelant Mine but it was closed. Geevor was next door north. Its workings go for over a mile under the sea at a depth of 3,000 feet. Just as exciting a place to fire a dream that would punch me into the womb of Cornwall like a human bullet.

The mine boss greeted us. We were each given a miner's hat with Davy lamp and put into a cage which immediately and silently became a falling stone with ourselves inside, dropping into Hell's mouth from the sky to the unknown. Instant death to the senses. Stopping was suddenly to awaken. After that we were taken in trucks along tunnels, like those at Rouffinac in France where the mammoths thunder into war, to where men were working underground under the sea, as if we had come to an earlier notch in evolution. They were helmeted and half-naked, cutting the rock with huge drills that had diamond heads and were driven by compressed power air, gnawing into the rock with tremendous power. The man drilling upwards was drilling an overhand stope and the man drilling downwards was drilling an underhand stope. I made drawings of both these operations, and of a miner with a great belly, using the orange mud from the walls for a wash. Water was dripping everywhere with green and blue dyoptase from the copper deposits. The noise was tremendous. I don't know if Lanyon did any drawing, but I think he got a painting out of it later. Johnny did not draw. It was a matter of being there that counted. I was so excited by this concentrated experience of being under the seabed – a million years compressed into an hour and a half – that I was not aware of my companions until we surfaced into the bright sunlight, like creatures returning to land after having lived in an inverted vertigo that now held the soul hovering over the ocean.

The whole experience had pushed my vision forward as a sculptor in one stroke and I became aware of Cornwall, and its landscape, not only a combination of strange forms, but one also containing a network of spatial areas which honeycomb its whole being, making a complete sculpture.

1946 was a very full year. The mind becomes once more a tin of worms and I can't tell which event followed which, but somewhere at this point Lanyon married Sheila who came from Woking. I did not get an invitation to the ceremony but only to the reception, which John Park and I attended by walking up the hill to the sunlit garden where it was all going on. After six drinks we found them to be non-alcoholic, so we walked down the hill again to the Sloop where the immortal Miss Gibbons served us on tick with pints of glittering English beer and I listened to the humour and unartistic, simple, slow, wisdom of this most lyrical of traditional painters, who, with his angular face under a bony Trilby hat, a dark suit upon his narrow back, looked like an Irish poet of the twenties with a northern accent. From his long sensitive hands he could spin webs of fragile colour, and make of a common tree a cathedral of light.

It was on this day when John Park and I were talking in a magical shaft of light coming through the window that a woman visitor came into the otherwise empty bar, except of course for Miss Gibbons.

The woman ordered her drink and started talking to John who hung on the bar like an old but very friendly parrot, answering a few ordinary questions, like: are you an artist? She then turned to me and said: 'What about you, have you been in St Ives long?'

John looked up from under his Trilby hat and said 'Madam, Sven *is* St Ives!'

'You are like me,' he used to say. 'You drive a lone vorrow. That's the best way. Then no one interferes with you!'

In spite of this remark by John Park, which was true, especially concerning my work, I became involved with Lanyon in his Crypt Group and thus learned my first and last horrendous lesson in art politics, from which my innocence had so far protected me.

Except for a spiteful cartoon of myself sent as a boyish joke, I did not see much of him otherwise until we banged into each other outside Sue Wynter's toy shop in the Digey – a completely unique creator of images amongst us. I was hawking a portfolio of drawings round town. 'A pound each, Sir!' 'But haven't you got any in colour?' asked a Naval Commander. It was not an easy earner. But Lanyon took it quite seriously, without pity, so I was not embarrassed. He looked carefully through the portfolio in the street until he came to two drawings of a bull. He chose one and gave me the pound note.

'Fancy,' I said. 'I thought you would have chosen the other – it's better!'

'It's too like a bull!' he replied and went.

It was a penetrating remark that pierced directly at the difference in vision between me and him. Still true today.

The first exhibition of the Crypt Group was held in the Crypt of the Mariners' Chapel in September 1946. The Chapel above was the St Ives Society of Artists' Gallery of which I was already a member on the invitation of that embullient personality Borlase Smart, who, like myself, believed in regeneration rather than demolition; in this we both had our trust. So the Font Group was formed which injected new sap directly into the old tree. But I did not know what a Guy Fawkes job the Crypt was going to be underneath.

We cleaned and decorated the place ourselves. It was spacious and with its windows set back in Gothic recesses there was good light. Although I was able, and did a certain amount, I was enough of a frontline squaddie to let the rookies do most of the heavy work of limewashing the walls. Besides I had my show in London to attend, so I did most of the curating, which was more interesting because of the people coming and going. A small band of writers I called the Moors Poets had come from London – George Barker, David Lewis, David Wright, John Heath-Stubbs – and they would all call in to look at things and talk, exchange methadrine for benzedrine, offer alternatives perhaps. Some of the finest minds who formed a much needed literary injection into an arm that knew little of poetry, except Sydney Graham and Nessie Dunsmuir. They were all painfully poor, as was I and Guido and some others, although I believe the Royal Literary Fund helped them as much as possible, as it did me in later years. Otherwise we were the tattered outlaws of the earth, which label the Chief, George Barker, thought a rather coney bit of prose when I published it somewhere. Poems and images for sale – nothing for a song.

It is risking a charge of being snobbish when I say that the one thing I noticed in the St Ives movement was a marked absence of learning – by which I mean that natural culture of the mind that had absorbed the philosophies and literatures of the world, not as dry learning, but as vehicles for understanding and enriching life, as I had found with Wilson and Turk during my younger years, later with Robert Graves. Only with Stokes in music and painting, in Leach in Eastern Religion. Even among the poets there was a paucity of understanding save with Graham, who was largely uneducated but had a natural intelligence in life.

SVEN BERLIN
JOHN WELLS
PETER LANYON
BRYAN WYNTER
GUIDO MORRIS

This was the first order of exhibitors at the first Crypt Show in 1946, for which Guido Morris printed the now famous CATALO – so titled because he could not fit the whole word into the width of the narrow booklet he made from the limited number of paper offcuts he had to do the job – printed in 'beautiful Bembo'.

The first Crypt show was a success, was repeated for three years and was enhanced when the second show with Kit Barker included Willie Barns-Graham. The magic still held. In the third year others came in, and for unknown reasons the original spell had gone. It was no longer a unique experience but just another art show and not a very good one at that. The sweet balance we had achieved and the magic had vanished.

A little after this I got a testy letter from Peter ending his own creation, because, he said, there was no longer any co-operation from the group and that he had achieved his objective in forming it in the first place, but did not say what that purpose was. I was glad to be free of the frustration. But it had done a lot of good in showing the awakening in St Ives of a creative happening after the holocaust of a world war. But indeed it was the eye of the hurricane that approached and would cause an explosion. One of the good things was for each of us to see what was happening to our work in relation to each other and to Cornwall. And perhaps for the first time I could see how Guido's printing fitted into the abstract idiom, as did Sydney Graham's poems through their internal structure.

Then in the winter of 1949 came the silent explosion. That deadly night when the St Ives Society of Artists was forced to call an Extraordinary General Meeting in the Galley upstairs and the whole thing fell about our ears. Being a non-political fish it seemed to me like a pike pool. I was appalled. Barbara Hepworth was surrounded by younger artists whom she urged to heckle and shout for a vote of no confidence in the chairman. When she called me I swore at her and refused to join in. Only Ben Nicholson was silent, standing there in his ARP overcoat, his face like a white falcon, the vault of the chapel towering over him, casting a shaft of light. The vote was cast, there were almost fisticuffs to follow. The life work of Borlase Smart and Leonard Fuller was smashed.

It has always seemed to me that the continued dedication of Borlase Smart and Leonard Fuller to the traditional structure of art was an honest and valuable contribution to preserve the setting wherein art might grow and absorb the new life force with each generation. That it became hidebound was inevitable but this, like dead limbs in a tree, can be dealt with by an honest surgeon. It was not necessary to fell the tree and replace it with a sapling with square roots. It is a tribute to these two men that the old society did survive and the school also, under Roy Ray who was later appointed Principal by Fuller's wife after his death. Smart had died in 1947.

I came out in the moonlight afterwards feeling bewildered by what had happened. Feeling as I had felt in Holland when my gun crew had been blown up, I walked back to my Tower. How could this have been designed? I thought to myself. It is so disastrous and there is no need.

The next morning was Sunday and I was walking through the empty town when I met Bernard Leach cycling towards me on his tall bicycle looking like the man in Dali's *Chien d'Andaluse*. He dismounted, looking as Bernard so often looked – very anxious.

'Have you heard what happened?' he asked.

'Yes, I was there.'

'What are we going to do?'

'Form a new society. What else can we do?' I said.

Bernard seldom, if ever, drank. But on this occasion he came into the Queen's Hotel with me and had a half of bitter. Denis and Endell Mitchell were there and we discussed the problem. I think they had already heard. Sure to have done because Endell ran the Castle Inn in Fore Street and all news went through there as though it were telexed, especially about the artists, of whom Endell was a patron. Denis at that time was an assistant to Barbara Hepworth. The outcome was that Endell offered his lounge at the Castle free for the first meeting the following Tuesday. The news went round and many turned up. We sat around talking and I was astounded to hear Peter telling how it had all been pre-arranged, like a battle in which there were many casualties. They got Harry Rowntree ginned up and so stirred his hatred of the Moderns that he called an Extraordinary General Meeting, quite unaware of the plot to overthrow the Society when they were gathered together. The chairman Leonard Fuller, the secretary David Cox, Shearer Armstrong, Hyman Segal and Peter Lanyon as members of the committee and the entire Modern Section (the Font Group) resigned and were present at what turned out to be the first meeting of the Penwith Society. That is how it was born. Segal with his insight into humans – the *isness of him or her* in each drawing – was fortunately there to save for us the passing images of all concerned, just as Marie Antoinette was recorded by David from a window on her way to the guillotine in a tumbril: though none of these was destined to take such a journey, there were some equally sad endings. Subsequent meetings were held at St Christopher's under the patronage of the Keeleys and the rules and intricacies were worked out over long arduous hours – and weeks. I was voted secretary and David Cox chairman, but this was before minutes were kept and my patience with the Machiavellian nature of the proposals ran out. Then Peter Lanyon was voted, in his absence, as a publicity liaison officer, having been proposed by Ben who was an old hand at this business. Peter appeared suddenly and equally suddenly made a personal attack on me which stirred the rage of the ancestors. Bernard Leach went white. But for him I would have thrown Peter through the windows to the beach below. How I controlled the situation I don't know for lights were flashing in my head, but part of it was to shake his hand until I nearly broke it in a sculptor's grip. That was the only time I acted in anger. Bernard commended me for my self-control – of which I was not in the least proud – regretted, even.

My eventual resignation from the Penwith Society was nothing to do with Lanyon's behaviour to me, or mine to him, but for quite other reasons of disagreeing with the machinery for selecting artists' work, which I thought prejudiced and unfair. I still do. I think what decided me was the first practical example of the selection committee in action for the first Penwith Exhibition in which my sculpture (*Mermaid and Angel*) was rejected along with a painting I had submitted and I was represented solely by two drawings, because I was not abstract. By these rules abstract art became a form of apartheid, leading to the exclusion of all who produced work outside the abstract idiom and its adjacent forms, so bending history. It also led to insincerities among the artists themselves which, in the book kept by the keepers of truth, is a sin that is not redeemable. Abstract art and all it stands for, like climbing Everest, is one of the special achievements of Modern Man but was diminished by this act.

Peter Lanyon's resignation came after mine and I think was partly due to the long and bitter quarrels he had with Hepworth and Nicholson over these matters, which were largely territorial in origin. As he said: he was King Penguin. I suppose for a time he was. In the end they took over. The sad thing is that none of this was to do with one's work which is why we were there as part of a Creative Disturbance. It led to all manner of distortions of judgement, division of loyalties, considerable human suffering. It is as well to say that it was spiritually, socially, and artistically destructive. I can only think the force of which we had become warden was too strong to control. Otherwise it was a slip-stream from the war. It had become an inverse octopus which, instead of spreading and creating as it grew, started to draw all into itself and devour the lives that gave it birth. Otherwise it was calculated sabotage. The last ironic unction was to dedicate the Penwith Society of Arts in Cornwall 'To the memory of Borlase Smart' whose life's work had been destroyed after his death.

I left it and went away to follow my own star.

I saw Peter again when I returned in 1954 to help my daughter out of some difficulty. When I got off the little dream train that ran round the bay from St Erth, I walked along the Wharf to the Sloop and there, sitting in the window of the lounge waiting to greet me, were Peter and Sheila, having heard on the grapevine I was coming. This was my last meeting with this artist whom I so respected as a painter and this man with whom I found it so difficult to be friends. It was exactly a decade later in a pub in the New Forest, that I read of his death in a gliding accident. Like Icarus he had fallen to his death after flying too near the sun. Later I wrote this:

The spirals of your life off-centre rose.
They did not pivot on the axis joint
But always like a lonely tercel chose
To use a thermal tilt for counterpoint.
You spread across the sea your gliding wings
Like Icarus made, soared and cut the foam,
Sought invisibility of things
You fought to paint, and built a metronome
To time the surging edges of the years –
The brown moor, the milky sun, death's rage
Across the moonscape of your unshed tears,
Turning the revolution of an age:
Then the enantiodromic falling stone
Gave you the endless blue – the vast unknown.

Somewhere in the back of my head I heard a distant wave breaking on the rocks.

As a Cornishman said more simply, 'E was all right. Just Dicky Opposite! One of the wreckers, you!'

Now as I look back over the years I realise none of us was greater than the force which moved each to do his own work in this creative emergence, and that force was never more than the aggregate of what we had all achieved. The Legend has become Truth.

If it had not been for that trip with Peter to Launceston to Polyphant Mine I don't think I would have been faced with the lonely stone in the night when I most liked to carve it. And it was only that Guido came and took up residence on the opposite promontory of rock to mine and lit his candle in the window at night to signal me to break work for tea that my integrity held long enough to get those early sculptures released from the stone. It was the hardest task a man could set himself – what Henry Moore had said was right.

Magic Mask

One of the difficulties of writing this book is to attend to Time, which has so many different levels. The great movements of history are going on, but so are the daily slipstreams that seem to move at different speeds and those indeed that are acted out in our dreams. Living in a place like the Tower alone – meaning that I was the lone centre around which my work, my love life and my dream revolved – was to find certain events and comings and goings, like the waves slithering in gently on the sand below, some breaking early, some late and others returning through those just dying and being born, formed an endless chain of design that wove a tapestry to make up my days and nights and seasons, running into years. And when an event happened it was nearly always a surprise because I had forgotten it might happen.

By the break up of my marriage after the war the whole shoulder of my life was wrenched out of joint. Things, events and affections were balanced by being displaced. There was a constant pain but, like a wounded animal, one did not know what it was. The terminal of this was seeing my children only once a week for a whole day, a sacrifice which finally expressed itself in cutting my devotions out of stone to transfer what was otherwise a deep bruise in the heart.

One such other and happier event was when Denis Mitchell came to my Tower once a year, usually in the Spring, pushing a handcart, a great smile on his face, with all the gear to decorate my rooms. We packed everything moveable downstairs and whitewashed the upper room, scrubbed it clean, filled it with light. Then, when we had reset it, we hauled all the bottom room out in the open and painted those walls, set back the turn-table I had made from an old cast iron clothes mangle from the rubbish dump. We then cleared the bench, cleaned the tools, stacked the stone, leaving all in readiness for work. On one occasion we even snowcemmed the rough outer walls so they shone bright in the sun and kept out the damp. Painted the door red. Fixed the copper mask back to keep out the devils. The only sweet visitor was the light. This was an act of friendship which I could only repay by being grateful. Denis was at that time painting and I think had started to work with Barbara Hepworth, about which he had mixed feelings, but he realised, as I did not, that the know-how and craftsmanship he would obtain was priceless.

Well, I went my way and it was not only tough but finally neglected. But this did not interfere with friendship. As with Terry Frost, Denis matured 'out of sync' with me because he was working for Barbara during those years and did not seem to step forward as a sculptor in his own right till after I had gone and he later moved to Newlyn to share the Old School House with John Wells. By this time he had evolved his own unique place-images from the Cornish landscape, with the highest craftsmanship and stability of physical sensation. In the early days he painted small landscapes and portraits that were incised in pale colours on to board and drawn with an almost primitive simplicity: his portrait of Tom Early and one of his wife Jane are little masterpieces. In a way I was a maverick down there and am not the person to assess. As I said to an art official later of the St Ives movement, 'I was *with* them but not *of* them.' It remains true today. That is why I think it is worth writing about, but not extending myself as critic of another artist's vision.

But I will venture to say that Denis Mitchell's sculpture done in Newlyn with the co-operation of his assistant Tommy Rowe and John Wells finally reached a perfection and splendour that makes him a master of our time, unequalled by his Domina, Hepworth – or any of us who worked on the stone face.

Denis and his brother Endell, with whom I was also close friends, had both known Dylan Thomas, when their extraordinary kind mother was alive. I knew Blanche and remember her straight-forward insight and direct humour. Endell befriended the artists and his pub, The Castle, became a haven for them. He arranged early exhibitions of the young modern avant garde before anyone else had thought of it and the first Penwith Society meeting was held in his lounge bar, where Peter Lanyon amused us all by baiting Barbara. He knew I was carving a pale green stone at that time.

'What will you drink, Barbara?' he asked her, when she came in.

'I really don't know!'

'I tell you what. Have a Pernod!' The drink came up and as he poured the water in, it turned to a pale green.

'There you are. You'll like that. It's just the same colour as the Egyptian green stone Sven is carving!' Smiling of course to us. But Barbara's face remained immobile, like white marble. She was not pleased.

Endell was understanding and tolerant, also generous and trusting with the artists. One day when Arthur Caddick insulted me, I hit him on the jaw and laid him full length on the floor of the bar and

went on drinking after we had heard his teeth hitting the glassed
pictures like hail. Later I myself got hit in the mouth and lost my
own front teeth, because a young petty officer had removed a
painting of mine and turned it to the wall. When it was over Endell
said to me.

'I don't know, Sven, what's the matter with you. You're always in
trouble!'

'Sorry,' I said, mopping the blood from my mouth. 'He insulted
my work, but I didn't reckon on his father hitting me from behind
at the same time as his son hit me in the face.' Endell paused. I
thought he was going to throw me out.

'Well don't do it again, or I'll have to bar you. What are you
going to drink? You look a bit white. You'd better have a brandy.'

Such was the viscosity of life: never too thick to get bogged down
in rules and regulations, never too thin to run riot and go to seed.
Being in the pub was my domestic life. Endell helped me to do it. If
I went to London with Johnny Wells, as I did sometimes, to stay
with Tambimuttu who was publishing my Wallis book, when I
returned, instead of going to the empty Tower I went to the pub
and there found kindness, friendship and, fortunately for me, a rare
love.

So many things happened which at the time seemed slight but at
a distance assume an historic or even legendary nature. A letter
from Denis Mitchell reminds me again of the demonic humour with
which Lanyon tormented even his friends. Particularly Barbara.

> After you came back from seeing Epstein, you said to me
> [that] when you told him you knew Barbara, Epstein said:
> "O, the person who carves lollipops!" Just afterwards I
> went up to see Peter Lanyon and I repeated this to him.
> He immediately picked up the phone and rang Barbara
> and said, "Do you know what Epstein said to Sven about
> you? That you carved lollipops." I couldn't believe it as at
> that time I thought he was her friend.

Denis also gave an account of the Caddick affair:

> He had driven you mad by saying you had left him in St
> Ives, when you had waited a hell of a long time with your
> car. Without getting off your stool you clouted him one
> under the chin. The letter that followed was a marvel of
> legality, to wit, two broken dentures, and then you

179

counter claimed for indecent assault for him pinching Juanita, and it was all settled for a goat.

The goat was worth £4.

Among others coming from London now the war was over was Patrick Heron, who used to call at the Tower after having travelled down on the milk train, so it was an early visitor for me to receive and I never had more than a mug of tea to offer, but it was an enjoyable meeting always and as often as not I was already getting down to work. For me the early hours have always been the most creative. Patrick was a tall, slender young man with Prussian blue hair which was fine and grew from a high forehead and sensitive face, had clear bone structure and an almost permanent smile, behind which you could not always tell what was going on. We talked enthusiastically about painting and I usually showed him my new work. I had known him at the Leach Pottery and had stayed with him in London after the war, where we would walk round the Tate together. The fog, having entered the building like an invisible crowd, swirled gently round us, revealing the pictures one by one.

'But where are WE!' I exclaimed.

'They have left out a whole generation, Sven. It is our turn now,' he replied, and gave his enigmatic smile.

His painting was about in his home at that time. The Braque-like interiors and still-lifes were all part of my knowing him and his family. His own special train did not seem to have come in at his station at that time. His work seemed suddenly to expand in vision later, after the bubbling of the lava had died down and I had left Cornwall. I got on particularly well with his father, Tom Heron, who was one of 'the world's first huge whitebearded kings' and genial with it. He came to the Tower and bought a little early ivory of mine and got his friend to buy one in alabaster. They were small sculptures for the hand but had a secret magic of their own one cannot get later, even for the ridiculous prices we are expected to charge now. Tom Heron was connected with St Ives in the twenties where he was managing a factory, Cryséde that produced ladies' silk fabrics and scarves. Encouraged by Dufy and Zadkine it was founded by that much ignored master of design, Alec Walker and his wife Kay, at Newlyn in 1920 and later moved to the Island, St Ives. Tom Heron left later and founded his own firm 'Cresta Silks'. It has always seemed to me that the translucent, and even ephemeral quality of Patrick's colour comes from the influence of working in this idiom as a young man, as Renoir's did from painting pottery at Limoges: his amazing window a metamorphic scarf in the sky.

This seems a natural sequence of evolution for someone who had led a sheltered life growing up in Welwyn Garden City and educated at a respectable private school and not exposed to hardship except as a pacifist labourer during the war. The fierce images of Picasso or Van Gogh would not have emerged from that background.

The great creative force that was upon us in those days and would spill over into tensions, arguments and much more enjoyable expression, happened spontaneously. There were parties at the Tower when I had sold something at Endell's pub, the Castle Inn. I immediately announced a party at the Tower after closing time and based it with a quart bottle of beer. Everyone in the bar was invited to bring the same. Endell would turn up with two crates of beer and bottles of spirits and glasses. Thus 50 guests were entertained in a room ten foot square and were carried down the stairs if they passed out, to be laid among my stones in the moonlight. Music came and the *duende* rose through our feet to a thunderous dance in the Atlantic night. When all was over I insisted on clearing up the bottles and broken glass before I went to bed – Denis helping me, sometimes my girl, Jacqué.

Sooner or later everybody called at the Tower and I am sure its walls still ring with their voices: Jock Graham roaring his poetic madness like a falling wave, Nessie singing as the stars plunged into silence. John Minton quietly professional, directing me how to make a monotype. The Salvation Army major talking about Wallis's funeral. The enigmatic and fragile Tom Early. John Craze splitting the stone while he told me how he split a cliff face from jaw to cranium. The Scottish painters Colquhoun and MacBryde silently looking at sculpture. Ben in his ARP coat talking of the Inner Circle and Hepworth looking at the stone and not at the sculpture. The Moors Poets. A little Cornish mermaid who pierced my ears. The voices of my own children. But of all the ghosts that now abound in that 'lone cave's stillicide' it is those of the children, who thought I was the Devil.

One day I nailed a mask to the door to stop them throwing stones. It worked by magic. They stopped throwing stones and stared at the face on the door.

'Did you make that, Mister?'

'Yes. Of course I did!'

'You reely are the Devil than. COR!'

'I'm the Devil all right. That's why I wear thick black hair – so you can't see my horns.' They gazed in awe and wonder.

'And the gold earrings. What's they for?'

'To keep away the Evil Eye.'

'But you are the Devil.'

'Yes. But the Evil One is so strong that if he looked in the mirror and saw his own face it would kill him. I wear the gold earring to stop him looking at me: the light distracts him when I move my head, see. Even I need to be protected.'

They held the lobes of their ears looking incredulous at being addressed by the Satanic Presence himself.

'What else do you make, Cap'n?' asked a tiny Cornishman as big as my thumb.

'Mermaids. Gods. Spirits.'

'What wiv?' they asked in unison.

'Anything. Stone, wood, iron, paint, metal like that mask on the door.'

'Can we see?' said a playful little girl with the straight pewter hair. I stood aside and let the Little People in to bless my Tower.

'Can WE do some?' the little girl asked. A minute red headed boy with a fat heavy eyed girl joined in and finally the others in chorus, so I could not say no. It would have broken the spell. I was hard put to it for paints but I found some powder colours in the old ammunition box I had in the war and they were just right for the job. We fixed up a platform for them to work on, from a couple of chairs and some planks and after a long silence strange images started to appear on the walls. The Evil One with ibex horns looking like me. John Craze with one eye and a body like Quasimodo. A fairy with beauty beyond dreams. A gorgeous mermaid with a young man like Edward Mouse. The Gods of Joy and Sorrow dancing in from of the others. Johnny Lookup on a white horse and an old prophet like Jimmy Limpots. All the fantasy and the reality of back street fisherfolk in wedded rhythmic movement, clear colour, fluid forms like the sea, containing the most wonderful distortions. At the end of the afternoon there was a handful of happy children who never threw a stone again. They were my friends.

Walking through the Back Streets 40 years later when I had come to lecture and open a show, very early in the morning as I had always done as a young man, I came upon some fishermen who were spreading their nets to dry on the road in St Peter's Square. It was where I had stood on the day the cottages were strafed by a German plane. When they saw me approaching they stopped work.

They came towards me from nowhere as though I was a Messiah. 'Sven Berlin!' they said. 'Taz Svan!'

'But you can't know me, like that,' I said. 'You are too young to have been on the boats when I was here and lived in the Tower. Your faces are familiar but I don't know who you are!'

'But we remember you, my ansom. We threw stones at ee. It was our fathers on the boats in them days. Ow are ee, Svan, after all these years?' They shook me by the hand. This was the unexpected memory of the Gods rewarding me for my work in those far gone days.

'But what have they done to your little town?' I asked.

'Tarrable,' they said. 'Taz tarrable!' and for a moment I was an old man being young again – or a young man pretending I was old.

Everything emanated from the Tower in those days: my life and indeed my art, and it became the centrepoint of forces working round me, where my voice has not been forgotten. The magic and goodness the children's paintings generated protected me from the Evil One, who was often abroad. When I went away I left them like murals in a deserted temple to keep their spell of innocence in one place.

Architypographus

But the first memorable visitor to the Tower arrived one morning in full sunshine in the autumn of 1945. I was standing in the top room looking out at the Atlantic beyond the half-moon beach and the Mermaid Rock, thinking of the winter ahead and wondered how difficult it would be with the summer gone and with it the visitors on whom I depended for any sales I made. I had no income. Nor had the Keeleys yet offered their lifeline of breakfast every morning. There was nothing. But I was comforted by the thought that I was doing what I wanted to do in the way I wanted to do it at the time I had chosen myself. As NEED was my only watchword, I dispelled the anxiety and went on drawing a dolphin's skull I had found on Scilly and hummed a little lullaby I had learned there when listening to music with John Wells. It was by Mozart.

> Guter Mond du gehst so stille
> durch die Abendwolken hin,
> gehst so ruhig ich fühle
> dass ich ohne Ruhe bin.

It was the only tune I could remember and then only when I was happy. Otherwise I am tone deaf and cannot get a tune right owing to a bash on the head by a music master when I was at boarding school as a boy.

An unfamiliar high-pitched voice shouted up the stairs and broke the spell.

'Hallo, there! Is anyone at home?'

'Yes. Come up,' I answered absently. 'Who is it?'

'Me!' The voice climbed the stairs. 'Who is ME?'

Immediately a small man of about 35 leaped from behind the wooden screen, to present himself at my side like a spirit.

He had fair hair which was long and fell toward his shoulders. He had a way of throwing his long head back so that he looked hunched, which showed his pale face and blue eyes unguardedly. He wore no hat but a shabbily loose raincoat. High under his right armpit were pushed some books and papers. He was excited. He gave out intense energy, and something more that I have always found in unusual people but have never been able to define. He sounded eager.

'Are you Sven Berlin?'

'I am!'

'My name is Guido Morris: Printer and Writer. I want somewhere to live and work!'

I looked out at the Atlantic again.

'Survival for the artist is very difficult,' I said slowly. 'Why do you come to me? Why do you think I am able to help?'

'Because I was told that you would. That you were the one person who would help me.'

There was an urgency about this man, a truthfulness of need. I looked at his raincoat, worn shoes, then at his face. I realised he was starving. The bright light was in his eyes, the skin stretched over his face – no one can fake that – only the starving know about it. Prolonged want had given his face the look of being too big for his body. There was a nobility about his face. I respected him. He had long parted friends with pity – especially for himself.

'How can I help you. I have nothing myself. Who sent you?'

'The cartoonist. Harry Rowntree.'

'Him. The Ronouk Rat!'

'He says he sends all the strange ones to you.'

'Does he? I didn't know that. He hates us really. Perhaps he is afraid of privation and loneliness, or frightened there is a spark of genius locked up in one of these scarecrows like you and I have become. It is possible. Someone has to do the great work in each generation and be a serious artist. He is not even good at what he does, when you think of great cartoonists like Gillray, Rowlandson and Giles. He says he never had time for *real art* and that we just clown with it.' I was feeling particularly vicious because of the state of this man before me. But Guido was of finer steel than I and even defended him.

'I am sure he is not as bad as all that. Don't you think you are being unfair? He has taken such immense trouble on my behalf.'

'I expect I am,' I admitted. 'Only those who have starved know about the dryness of the heart. I think you know because you are as kind as I once was. In the end it will make you as ruthless as I now am. Have you had a meal?'

'No, but I have my pockets full of buns!' he shouted. 'Hundreds of heavenly buns!'

'Good. I'll make some tea!' I said, thinking how ridiculous we are at our best.

185

Another, more familiar voice called up the stairs. 'You at home, Sven?'

'Bryan!' I shouted back. 'Come up. How are you? How did you get on in London?' Bryan Wynter appeared at the top of the stairs dressed in his old tweed jacket and cord trousers. I was delighted to see him. There had always been a natural harmony between us: I can never remember a cross word. 'Have some tea!'

'No, truly. I've just had coffee with Lanyon at St Christopher's. Awful bore really don't you think? But thanks terribly. Have you any ben, Sven?' he asked with a satirical smile as he stumbled on the rhyme. I passed over the question by introducing him to Guido. They knew each other.

'You know, we were both working for Solly Zuckerman in Oxford during the war on his research into the menstrual cycle in monkeys and apes!' Guido was obviously pleased to find someone who had worked with Zuckerman and remembered him as secretary and assistant at London Zoo also, as well as the Department of Human Anatomy at Oxford. He bowed like a wizened courtier of Louis Quatorze, looking distinguished before the tall elegant and unique person of Bryan Wynter, who had charm beyond price. A Prince of our Vagabond Race.

'Tell me,' said Bryan turning to me. 'Who has that ten shillings – you or me?' This referred to a ten shilling note that floated between us – an emblem of trust for which the other asked if he had no money.

'With me!' I said and having a pound on me I gave him ten shillings of it.

'Thanks frightfully,' said Bryan, as though · he was imitating someone else better educated. I think he went to Bryanston. 'I've been in London trying to squeeze some blood out of the Redfern stone – with not much success I'm afraid. What about the ben?'

I gave some tablets to Bryan from the prescription given me after the war. It was a kindness I did for one of two of my close companions on the basis that if war made you depressed the exigencies of peace were more lowering and a reasonable way out was to use the same aids as did the bomber crews going into Europe. As an OP crew member I was never given them, though I was expected to stay awake for over 48 hours on any mission. Now it was a harmless help. I gave some to Sydney Graham while he was writing the 'Nightfishing', with great results. 'Send more of the little white devils!' he wrote from Mevagissey. It was one of the menial jobs on my part as Szaint Szven, as Sydney called me. I was not a 'pusher' though, ever.

Bryan took one of the tablets and in ten minutes he was already excited. His large, bony, loosely-skinned face broke into a huge smile as he described the sensation in his beautifully sonorous voice, looking like Rembrandt's pupil, Fabritius.

'Do you know, Sven, I can already feel those little white corpuscles elbowing their way through the capillaries of my heart.' I smiled back at his abandoned delight, believing as he did that if the choice was possible it was wrong to become a manic depressive.

'Guido wants a workshop. Do you know of anywhere?' He replied at once.

'What about the Crowsnest?'

'Of course, what an idiot I am!'

'Where is it?' Guido asked, his face lighting up. I pointed through the window.

'Over there on top of that great wall of rock, beyond the Linoleum City.' Guido seemed awestruck. As if to soften the shock he said,

'Linoleum City?'

'That's Bryan's name for it. I will tell you later. Let's go and look.'

'Splendid!' said Bryan. 'Let's do that thing!'

We left the Tower, crossing to where the tide was starting to come up by the rubbish dump, explaining to Guido about the quicksands, climbed the rocky path to the top where three geese were guarding the Linoleum City, which was a collection of fishermen's huts put roughly together and repaired over the years with sail-cloth, corrugated iron and strips of linoleum.

'There it is, Guido – the Linoleum City!'

'O I see,' said Guido. 'How simple. But of course. . .'

'What you really have to be careful of is the quicksands. They will swallow you quick as a mermaid.' Bryan loped away toward the Crowsnest like a cheetah. Guido pranced nervously about with a spring step.

'What a marvellous thought. I'd simply love to be swallowed by a mermaid. My dear fellow, I've never heard of such a thing.'

'I hope you will never know such a thing!' I shouted to him. 'But it is rather a nice idea.'

Bryan, still with his hands in his jacket pockets, was staring into the dusty window of the granite loft. 'There you are. One huge, empty, bare room with windows all round. What could be better?'

Guido was wildly excited.

'How wonderful. How do we get in?' He danced dementedly on

the great rock with a bun in each hand tearing at them alternately with discoloured teeth. I tried the door. It was locked.

'We will have to find the landlord,' I said. 'Meanwhile you take over my Tower if you have nowhere to sleep.'

'And you come to Carn with me,' Bryan put in.

'I was hoping you would say that, Bryan. Thanks.'

Bryan's cottage at Zennor Carn was a place I loved. I had done a painting from there some years ago for Turk who drove me over in the heat of summer, and several drawings. Ever since it had haunted me. Nowhere ever before had I got the feeling for prehistory that I had among the rocks worn by centuries of wind and rain and from being under the sea before that. It awakened a coelacanth in my bone.

'I must go,' Bryan suddenly announced. 'Thanks for the ben, Sven. I'll be leaving Town in about an hour. See you.' He cantered away.

Guido and I stood against the Atlantic which in turn stood against my Tower like a blue giant. Over the roof of the Tower we could see a black stallion grazing near the Breton Chapel. The sea was coming in fast.

Guido looked frightened, as though he had suddenly understood an inexorable law. Then he smiled, realising he had found what he was looking for: a place to house his press – his Iron Soul, as I was to call it later.

Within the next few days we found the landlord, a Mr Gilbert, and a ceremony took place in the Tower in which a document was signed by Guido to rent Carncrows Studio. I called it the Treaty of Versailles. How the advance was raised I can't remember. I think I borrowed it for him and he paid back later. The place on the tall rock became the home of the Latin Press for the next eight years.

This was at a time when the creative renaissance after the war was just beginning to stir. I was back from the Invasion of France and Holland. Lanyon was back from his duties with the RAF in Italy. John Wells had sold his medical doctor's practice on the Scillies and returned to the mainland to paint full time. Gabo, Nicholson and Hepworth were working in Carbis Bay. Bryan Wynter had taken over his bleak cottage on Zennor Carn. Leach had rebuilt his pottery on the hill after being hit by a German landmine. Terry Frost was out of Stalag, Denis Mitchell working on the land, Barns-Graham incumbent at St Ives. Adrian Ryan painting his haunting land and seascapes or a skate hooked on a chair in Mousehole, taking no notice of the Abstract Priesthood.

Joke Grim (Jock Graham) was in Pengersick Lane. Wallis was dead. The pattern was already set for the lock to spring back and open the magic box, though none of us knew. It was this sense of adventure, of timing, of creative impulse and need, the magnetic force that Cornwall exerted, that Guido Morris had obeyed. He had come down on the train from London, having bought a one way ticket with his last money as a kind of guess which direction destiny would take.

Tom Early was another painter whom I have mentioned, but I cannot write further into my document of time past without recording that in him I met possibly the most fragile and sensitive but gifted person I have come upon in this strange journey. A young doctor who had been forced to give up his practice, because of the falling sickness, to find he had that rare double vision that looks through the window of the eye both ways and records the poetic image of the thing seen, empowered with the emotion and imagination coming from his lonely vision of the universe and clothing it with a strange beauty – yet seeming not to be conscious of what he had done.

We all loved his work and I am convinced the paintings he left on the walls of the Castle Inn and the Penwith Society had a profound influence on both Peter Lanyon and Bryan Wynter, showing them what they should do with their Cornwall, as he had done with his.

> As with Dante in Hell
> With his one love, he reached and rang
> The Poetry Bell, till the angels sang:
> Took his offering alone
> To the altar stone
> Where Beauty bowed:
> I found him there!

Then he disappeared.

There is no doubt in my mind that they were all needed to detonate the charge of energy of which John Wells and I had become conscious on Samson Island. And there was also now that dark chthonic force in Cornwall which drew men and women towards it, impelling them to create or be destroyed – sometimes both – which in the next generation Max Barrett has transmuted so beautifully. This has been written about so well by Denys Val Baker, the most searching observer on the creative emergence in Cornwall, and recorded in his remarkable little book *The Timeless*

189

Land, that instead of taking the risk of trying to follow him (for that is not the reason for writing this book) I will quote from my article in *Facet* in 1948 which was part of my original 'Notes for Disturbance in the West'.

> The open coliseum of each little cove of sand and rock may be the theatre for any natural or supernatural or unnatural event. The unending presence of the sea breathing ceaselessly over the shoulder of each hill, the rock charged with a thousand sunsets and carved by a hundred years of rain. The little trees loaded with berries growing away from the prevailing wind, offering crimson to green. The mind's incessant vertigo at the cliff edge and the slow constructional flight of the seagull. These events in some way act as the chanting of magicians to open the deeper rooms of experience in man, make him aware of his origins, of being part of nature and the universe at the head of a great unseen procession of Gods, Devils, Spectres and Dragons, of being a channel for unknown and undefined forces, of facing the mystery of life, awakening powers of perception which search beyond the frontiers of normal events, stimulating painters like Bryan Wynter, John Wells, Barns-Graham, Peter Lanyon, Alfred Wallis, Nicholson, Gabo, Frost . . .

This was a recurring feature of the Cornwall I knew. Its primitive nature could not be ignored by those who came here and to whom in so many cases it spelt death or else spiritual anguish of the most devilish kind. It could not be ignored, nor dominated, nor brought to computed order because it has its own law buried deep in its heart and administered by mermaids and angels.

And this from my *Dark Monarch*, 1962.

> I stood upon the Hill of Cuckoos, looking west, to the sunset, a fierce wound in the sky cut by the jagged edge of the darkening moor with its carns, few lonely cottages and a twisted roadway, like the nerve drawn from a tooth. Far beyond these were the Islands of the Dead.
> This stretch of land, jutting out into the sea, seemed as though it was the backbone of some giant coelacanth thrown up by the waves thousands of years ago, there to ossify in the sharp, salt air which sparkled with uncanny

brightness. On one side it was scorched black by the breath of the Devil; it was cut and scarred by the hands of an angry God; tunnelled and twisted by the generations of strange quartz-boned men who lived there – progenitors of the wandering ghosts who cried in the night when the wind came from the west. This strip of land, ending in nothing, slanting to the end of time, the rock-infested sea to the Islands and the vast unbroken wilderness of the Atlantic beyond.

This was a terrible landscape where the paramours of evil walked on the bare hills, lichen-haired, hands twisted like old thorn trees and the smouldering dull red of dead fern burning in their hearts: hearts that had known the bombardment of radium for centuries. Here the Mermaid had risen from the sea in the first dawn of love and experience – she who is called the Fish-tailed Queen of Heaven and brings men through anguish and torment to death, who touches the poet's tongue with song and the painter's heart with vision, would also bring down the angels.

Everywhere there was a brooding Presence over the hills, like Saul, emanating desolation, loneliness and destruction: the Dark Monarch who wrecked men's lives, smashing their ships on the rocks and cut off terror-stricken fingers to snatch at the jewels of eternal life.

This volcano was psychic as well as somatic.

I won't go into the history thing. It has been done well by David Brown and Tom Cross with accurate dating. Turner was first in 1811 and since his mind was an ocean in itself he was probably apprehensive of the strange shores that presented themselves, sensing danger more than would have Sickert and Whistler who came later. Newlyn had an art gallery in 1885 and painters like Lamorna Birch, who looked like a trout fly, and Norman Garstin were soon working. In 1927 the St Ives Society of Artists was formed with Borlase Smart, Julius Olsson who was the only man ever to paint a phosphorous sea in the moonlight, John Park who painted his trees in cathedrals of light and oceans of flashing excellence. None of these should be ignored by the historian if he knows his stuff.

The feeling when it started in those early days was like not being able to tell others how it felt to climb Everest: to say what it was, was only to know what it was not.

Guido was locked into the pattern immediately, as though into one of his own formes.

It is in this way I want to present him: as a person of poetic vitality and belief, as an inspired printer, as a vulnerable but unique personality who, like most of us, carried his own destruction in his left hand. The rest about his work has been done better than I know how by John Farleigh in his book on creative craftsmen, and by Anthony Baker in his splendid article 'Quest for Guido' (Private Press, 1969). Although Baker seems not to have tracked Guido down till the very end of his life, and then for some reason avoided meeting him, yet found him far too elusive to imprison in facts alone, he still leaves us with a valuable chart of his whereabouts during the voyage, giving exact log data from 1936 to 1953 when Guido left St Ives; and, in collaboration with A.H. Brown, a 'tentative check list' of his printings, through all of which Guido passes like a spirit, with that faint smile and a fag hanging out of his mouth, leaving only footprints on the wet sand of their speculation. Since I always believed that someone like Guido, who insisted on bending destiny like a railway line to guide his life, would produce a unique last chapter, I have always hoped Anthony Baker would extend his Quest article into a book about this little genius even though he is now a ghost.

One of the extraordinary things about Guido's printings was their exact counterpoint to the pioneer work of the abstract artists, and they immediately saw its beauty because of his architectural use of space and form. In this it was completely pure like the painting of Ben Nicholson or John Wells, and by its sensitive power of incision, sculpturally parallel to either. Jock Graham's poems, although charged with dynamic content, have something of these qualities in their construction. The deft instinctive placing of a sail on the sea shows it to have been native to Wallis. Music for ballet composed by Stravinsky was only an octave away from Gabo watching the stars over Carbis Bay, yet had Guido Morris arrived in St Ives a decade earlier the artists would have ignored him.

During that first winter he lived in the vast empty room with a few packing cases and a bed built into one wall. I can only remember it in this sparse setting with the small, slightly stooped figure moving by candlelight casting huge shadows about him, but always with a flow of energy which seemed endless, unless he was depressed.

I was in my Tower and comforted to see his light burning, for I worked at night a good deal, hearing only the sea and an occasional sea-bird calling in the dark. If he was making tea he would signal with his candle from his window on the high rock and I would cross to the twisting path, past the geese hissing in the night and the old fishermen standing like ghosts by their huts watching the sea, to climb the escarpment and knock on his door, which he opened with swift movements, dressed in a red dressing gown and welcomed me by moonlight. We drank tea often for several hours and talked of our work, our friends, families, loves, with complete freedom from the beginning: a real friendship grew up, one that was matched only by my friendships with Bryan Wynter, John Wells and Jock Graham in the framework of what was to become the Cornish Saga and in earlier life, my brother, who was born almost on the same day as Guido.

How money was found to pay his rent and live till the press arrived in the Spring I have forgotten; nor can I remember how I found £2.10/- a quarter to pay for the Tower. His London friends helped him, I know, because I wrote to them to tell of his plight. Angus McBean the photographer appeared like an Assyrian king with his square beard and bald head. His luggage was full of bottles of youghurt, which made him very guilty lest it were thought he had stolen them and he took them empty all the way back to London when he returned. A quiet, recessive and sensitive person, he told me he could never live under the glaring limelight of St Ives: he preferred the obscurity of London.

This contact bought out a sophisticated side of Guido which belonged to a world I had never quite been able to engage with, and although I wrote to several belonging to the same circle – some of whom replied on tinted and flowered and even scented notepaper – I did not meet any of them, save the sad Angus, to whom the world had behaved quite brutally. All this seemed to indicate a certain inversion in Guido, though, as he said to myself and Bryan Wynter, 'I am not a homosexual: I was always too heterosexual for *that!*' This proved to be true. The women loved him and I never knew one to speak ill of him even after they had parted. Though it would not be unfair to say that his wives had a hard deal, even they do not seem to have pursued him with scorn. Behind the austere, concise and controlled printer there was a person of almost Dionysian delight in life, who loved drinking, women and sensation. Yet possibly this vicar's son was always haunted by guilt for his sins and rifts in his character, such as delivering a masterpiece of printing too late to be of use long after it had been paid for. In this connection I can remember the sinister figures of Jewish gentlemen in black homburg hats and beards moving about the Island against the glittering wall of the Atlantic, policing him while he worked on a text in Hebrew for them in the fortress of Carncrows.

Guido's great friend was Gordon Craig, who gave him the woodcut of a basket of flowers which he had found in Lucca many years before and Guido used as his colophon. Craig was still alive in Paris and they corresponded, which meant a great deal to Guido. As well as being an enlightened father-figure and guide Craig was a link with his other more sophisticated world. Also Nigel Heseltine, the son of Peter Warlock, was a close friend. Guido printed his poems, *Violet Rain*. Not always the great genius – like Eric Gill, but the offshoot of genius was the spark that fell towards him. Perhaps that was happening again. History will show. But it kept his own spark burning.

During these first months, as we penetrated through Winter to Spring, there was no heat and little food. It was a time in the desert when Guido took root in his new life. From the haunted face of which I had done drawings during those first days, there emerged a man of fine looks with a new light in his eyes and a fragile but tenacious figure that began to have more weight, even though he was always sparse. By April his Iron Soul had transformed him.

His improvement otherwise, and it was then his survival, was due as was mine to the two people, Mr and Mrs Keeley, who ran the *pension* called St Christopher's in Back Street West and gave us an open invitation to eat breakfast all the year round. And there in the mornings I found Guido at his table in the long dining room with the sea outside, reading Horace in Latin or a Hebrew text, after having helped himself to a medieval choice of food from the sideboard. We arranged to speak or not as we wished. Often he sat at the same table and said nothing, while I read Blake and he watched the sea. At other times we talked excitedly about our work. Guido was dressed nearly always in a cord suit and I in a fisherman's jersey and hat, which I found best for warmth and stone cutting in the open.

The Keeleys were people of great kindness and care. Their *pension* was unique. At different times I have eaten there with Ben Nicholson, Daphne du Maurier, Bernard Leach, Barbara Hepworth or glanced across at Gabo or Herbert Read. All this gave the atmosphere a little substance and one felt that here at least the unique genius of men and women with that gift of which I have set out to write chanced to foregather as ordinary people in a local place.

194

In *lieu* of payment I left a sculpture every now-and-again, with a note of gratitude for their kindness. Guido, I believe, did printing jobs for them and I know they gave him his first orders: others to follow while he was bathing in the sea during the summer. The Keeleys shall not be forgotten. The daughter, 'Copper', for whose eighth birthday I carved a horse's head; the son, Pat, who died young in a parachute jump; Sally with her large motherly form, genial face and cast in her eye behind her unexpected magnifying spectacles and Philip Keeley himself, who was smaller with a bald head, a stoop, a quick, friendly glance that made it seem he was looking at someone else. He was always in a hurry like the White Rabbit; thus called I him. He was a writer and had published a book in earlier days which went well. It was at his invitation that we held the formative meeting of the Penwith Society of Arts in Cornwall at St Christopher's. This was after the initial meeting at the Castle Inn, run by Endell Mitchell.

Guido was not involved with forming the Penwith but he did do work for them later, as he did for Leach, the Tate Gallery, Sir Gavin de Beer, Nicholson, Hepworth, John Wells, myself and so many others. He had printed the original *Catalo* for the Crypt Group started by myself, John Wells and Lanyon in 1946. I don't know if Lanyon paid him for that. I certainly didn't. He never charged me for a job because of my co-operation with his Iron Soul. Anyway I was broke. So was he. When we ran out of copies of the *Catalo* in the middle of the show he stayed up all night printing another edition and delivered it in the morning – for nothing. This time it was a broadsheet of Barcham Green on pink paper, just as original and beautiful as though he had known where there was another rare flower and had gone to pick it without telling us. Thus also his catalogue for the Crypt Group the following year, which he signed EXCUD. GUIDO MORRIS. ARCHITYPOGRAPHUS.

Once the press had arrived on a lorry from London, 'with about three tons of various impedimenta and a few hundred books', the room at Carncrows came to life. Which press this was I am unable to remember, but think it was the Albion on which he did most of his work. There was another press which I am sure came later: a larger, more imposing machine with an eagle on it which he treated with an awe-inspired respect, as though it were a royal personage. This was a Columbian, set up in the north end of the room and the Albion more centrally placed. He built work tables all around with shelves under them for handmade paper and racks over them to carry all the paraphernalia he needed and to store specimens.

Rollers and galleys were hung on shelves, everything was in order and the books were set up, especially in the original space by the window on the south side, which was shut off by a curtain and had become office, kitchen and bedroom in an area no more than six feet by four. He had to cut two feet off his bed so that he could fit it in to the bottom end, the desk at the top end and shelves all round. Indeed each thing fitted into the space like part of a format for printing, even to a chair or stool for me when I came over for tea in the night or to talk away some hour of loneliness, even to share a personal trouble. His current girlfriends made him the curtains and such, though I can't think how they managed on the shortened bed. There was a stove and, I think, gaslight later. A lone but truly inspired man who had a touch of genius in all he did – and fun.

Guido was understanding in human frailty, compassionate in grief, but dispassionately ruthless in going his own way. There was something monastic about him: a saint without a church who prayed to his Iron Soul.

Previously, he had been running a café in Northampton with his first wife, Doreen. A son was born to them whom he had never seen, but whom he insisted should be named Christopher Christian 'so that he could sign his postcards XX'. Doreen came down to St Ives for a visit: a good looking, down-to-earth woman who would be a fine haven even without a storm. She was obviously still in love with him and there was no animosity. I think she even slept with him while she was there. But there was no pact of reconciliation. Whatever the difference between them he was too intent on his new Odyssey to want to solve it. He was not cold. I am convinced he loved his child. He was simply unable to express that love by the personal sacrifice it demanded of him: a sacrifice he had already made to the Goddess who ruled his work.

His relationships with other women were not promiscuous. They lasted and always seemed to be happy on both sides. If it was someone else's wife, that was too bad, but it did not make any difference to Guido. One angry husband used to fly from the Isle of Wight and circle over Carncrows in a red aeroplane to let him know he was about and flew off to the nearest airfield at St Just, to return later in his Jaguar to Carncrows in order to beat Guido up.

One day this happened while Peter Lanyon and I were there. Guido simply did not mind. He said to the man:

'That's all right. I'm behaving rightly by my own standards. If you must give me a good hiding get on with it and get it over for heaven's sake!'

The man was very angry. When he started the beating Guido did nothing at all to defend himself. He simply curled forward covering his head and offered his back like an insect until it was over, sustaining some heavy punches in the doing which blacked his eye and bruised his face and hands considerably, before he curled up completely as if to fake death. Lanyon and I eventually pulled the man off for fear he would damage Guido too much, break his hands or smash up his workshop. He then turned on us and I remember a tall good-looking Lanyon stanced in Queensbury style, looking fantastically English against the man's more Oriental stamp, fighting on top of the great rock outside Carncrows to protect his friend, who afterwards was touchingly grateful, wiping the blood from his nose as he offered to make us some tea. His affair with the man's wife continued.

The lady in question was a close friend of mine. I was fond of her. One day after this conflict she called at the Tower and asked me to go for a walk in the snow, which we did, all the way to Bryan Wynter's Carn at Zennor. There we were entertained with cheap Algerian wine and seagull's eggs which Bryan had collected from the cliffs, and found ourselves cut off by a silent fall of snow as darkness came. We were marooned all night. We had been seen going by several people, including Guido. When we got back the whole town had been whipped into unrest and anxiety. The police and resident commandos were out in a search party along the cliffs and coves, believing we had made a suicide pact. Such were the emotions at the back of this, they could well have made a scene uglier than Guido's scene with her husband, had I not been more in love with someone else.

Our friendship continued unharmed. I went about with Guido like Paganini and his short German manager and drank a good deal of draught Bass when we could get it. We were content to share a half pint glass when we couldn't, going from pub to pub hoping to find someone to buy us a drink, me always a little behind because he walked at such an enormous speed I couldn't keep up. Here was a great companionship and a great deal of laughter. If all else failed, one particular barmaid who was an aunt to my girlfriend would 'tickle the old piano' for us, which meant rob the till, and a couple of pints fell out. These we would drink in a back room, and listen to the coarse wisdom and healthy humour of those on whom fortune had never smiled and posterity was not likely to remember – the rich in heart. Among them Guido never condescended or tried to pretend that he was not better educated than them. He remained elegant but shabby, like a courtier of a fallen palace. They loved him for it. And if I was quiet or depressed he would say to them, looking across at my girl, 'Take no notice. Sven is silenced by sex!' which had a humorous finality about it which they accepted with a smile.

I have known Guido drink eight or nine pints of this most powerful beer, which the hardened fishermen held in respect after four pints, yet he was never drunk. I never saw him drunk except on one Christmas Eve when he took me to Midnight Mass at the Catholic Church – he was white with it, like a small alabaster Christ but in perfect control. I don't think he drank to get drunk but liked the *sensation* of drinking. Drinking was a habit controlled by our lack of income and the discipline of work, but because we lived under the intense limelight of St Ives and were reluctant public figures, anything we did was magnified. Thus the folklore image grew up of myself as a drunken giant always hitting people in the teeth, instead of a serious and penniless artist in search of truth who despised fools and cowards. Guido was an ecstasy man. After a full quota he could and would sometimes go back to the Latin Press and work like a demon till dawn, the Albion going like the pistons of a steam train, at some important job he had left unfinished, without a single page spoilt. While alcohol would upset the manipulative powers of most people, it seemed to increase his efficiency and release that rhythm of spirit that gave unity to all he did. A dyed-in-the ink printer would laugh at such a statement, but there is a secret somewhere in a few of us that makes our work different to others.

> 'But God has a few of us whom he whispers in the ear:
> The rest may reason and welcome: tis we musicians know.'

The trouble was that the job was usually paid for and he was under some compulsion not to finish it till the money was spent. Which, of course, does not mean he was drunk whenever he worked. It was nothing to do with not doing the work at all or conning the customer: he was not that kind of person. It was simply the way his machinery worked and it was he who suffered most from it in the end. This was the quicksand that I said would swallow him like a mermaid: it did, and caused many a good soul also to lose out. Finally he went bankrupt for the second time.

Another printer of more sinister appearance, his skin the pale green of Pernod lighting his lantern face above a tall thin figure that approached you with an air of cautious amusement, was Anthony

Froshaug. We became friends and I introduced him to Guido, but they seemed already to know each other. For some reason we called him the Isomorph – probably a name invented by Guido.

Froshaug was an important and inventive typographer who has been sadly neglected. Though he was of the modern lower-case school that grew from the Bauhaus in Weimar, he learned much from Guido, the traditionalist with 'one foot in the 15th century'. As he himself said, that was the only way to become a good printer; in his case the broadsheets printed in sixteenth century Florence and Paris. It was a humble attitude of tall pupil to small, arrogant master – unique, even comic at times. Froshaug was of Norwegian extraction. A quiet sensitive person whom one suspected of carrying a private torture chamber somewhere in his soul, always courteous with something of Guido's recessive nature and tenacity for work, love of good beer and attractive women. His achievement in printing was of high standard, perhaps not so creative in the sense that it was 'like a piece of organ music', as Gordon Craig once described one of Guido's formes, but locked too tightly in new laws that had not had time to cool after their invention – one could not yet tell their sound. They had the stamp of honesty upon them and dignity in having created something new where before there was nothing. It was these qualities that delighted me when I went to London to open my second one-man show to find Froshaug had printed the catalogue as a surprise. That was his generosity. It was part of Guido's generosity in turn that would not allow him to condemn his contemporary but help him.

In many ways Guido was a scholar and prided himself on knowing Latin and Hebrew and French. Some said his Latin was not good. Yet it was one of his stated objectives 'especially to compile a Medieval Latin Dictionary on a new principle (Thesaurus Totuis Latinitatis) begun three years ago and maybe completed in another 22 years.' Guido told me once he intended to live in Paris when he was an old man and write a novel in French in order that it would have to be translated into English for his friends to read. A circumlocutory process characteristic of him, and Baron Corvo, who was in many ways his prototype.

He intended to give his son a Hebrew dictionary when he finally met him. He did so: I was there. His reading was otherwise in the direction of Corvo, whom he imitated in the itinerant eccentricity of his life, but his masterstroke of originality was in something quite unexpected which I will come to, and was part of his continuous journey into the unknown and into disaster.

I did not read much of his writings, only the concise article 'My Work as a Printer', printed in Denys Val Baker's *Cornish Review*, Autumn 1949 and the earlier article on his work in *Facet*. Poems he gave me from time to time. Two even dedicated to me.

For Sven

(How beautiful upon the mountains
are the feet of him that bringest
good tidings, that publisheth peace.)

You came when the ebb was low, love was outrun:
The bringer of good tidings, the speaker of peace;

You outwrought from my mind nascent images;
Like flames our spirits arose in unison;

You brought me the source at which I shall drink;
Now love dwells in the palm of my hand.

Carncrows Castle

High on the green headland, the white house:
Beneath, the ensanguined sea. . .

High on the deep-scarped rock, the great room;
Without, a disquieting sea. . .

High on four-square base, the white Tower;
Withheld, the pondering sea. . .

Above all, the lichen-covered chapel;
And fishermen spreading their nets
Against antinimous sky.

St Ives accepted Guido as they did other artists like myself, because the Cornish have that unique quality: they have not lost their identity. Even when one has long become a legend in their folklore there is retained a secret love for their tolerance, kindness and friendship during that other wilder life by the sea which has not yet been and never will be forgotten or repeated.

Guido owed a good deal of money and I suppose a lot of it was never paid, even to anonymous people who helped him and to those more famous ones who gave him orders which were fulfilled too late. He never did it to me. He designed the title page for my Wallis book, printed a folder brochure for my first London show at Lefevre Gallery, composed the startling little enigma for my Tower wall from a record of persecution by Wallis I had kept:

NORES
TINMY
HOUSE

He produced posters as a surprise for a show at Downing's Bookshop, large enough to have been done on the great eagle-crested Columbian press, and my famous Tower notepaper which was his first work as a jobbing printer after his Iron Soul arrived, done on off-cuts of handmade paper because he had no supplies.

Maurice Hill's translation of *Sappho* was Guido's last job in Cornwall. Maurice Hill was a war casualty – one of those incredible cases of a sweet spirit, imprisoned in a crippled body that was always in pain. I have never come upon worse. In the temple of daily life it brings a curse upon mankind whenever he comes to my mind. I used to meet him in the Sloop most evenings in winter, where he could just make his way from his studio behind the pub, to talk over a pint about books and painting and exchange notes about our different wars. It was simply that. He was not particularly articulate, but was looking forward to his Sappho, which dream it must have been difficult to realise. He died the night before the advance copy was delivered, long overdue.

The mermaid had swallowed one more into the quicksand.

That was in 1953, the year I left Cornwall for good on a great horse I called Atlas, who carried my world on his shoulders, and at a snail's pace made it to the New Forest.

Guido decided to leave also, but to satisfy his sense of form he waited two months longer, till November 5th, the day he first ran up my stairs eight years before and I had said, 'Survival for the artist is very difficult!' Every year in between that the ceremony had been re-enacted and he gave me a parcel of handmade paper for drawing to last me till the next year. This last time I was not there.

Perhaps it was this struggle of the artist with the inter-locking paradox of commerce and original creation that our friendship epitomized – that what was given as stipend was never equalled by what was withheld from us – leaving only our work that would last where the tracks in the sand had already disappeared.

On leaving Cornwall I forgot about Guido for a time and there seemed no sign of our unusual friendship recurring, which had ended just as suddenly as his unexpected appearance. My life in the Forest was silent and poverty-stricken. Froshaug came one night and slept with a young woman in a tent at the side of my waggon. He groaned mournfully in his sleep as though from some deep forgotten dream. In the morning, dressed all in black, they went off to get married.

I lived by poaching deer, pheasant, rabbit, trout and pigeon, and by horse dealing. After the first winter the Forestry would not allow me to continue and rather than go I set up in a field at the back of a smallholding owed by a countrywoman named Edie Gailor. Like most foresters she was tolerant of my condition and, for 10/- a week, gave me sanctuary. It was here with the help of some gypsy friends, that I built a little city of my own in a field, where Augustus John and Vaughan Williams both visited and Robert Graves sent his son to stay. The last of the wild roses still hung over the gate in the hedge as late as November. On November 5th, 1956 a small boy with fine delicate features, aged about ten years, came through the opening. When I asked him who he was he replied in a clear voice.

'I am Christopher Morris in search of my father.' His hair was fair like Guido's and he walked like his father.

In a little while Doreen followed. They lived near Bournemouth and had read in the paper about my being here. They had come to ask if I could find Guido for them. I promised I would try.

Because these things are probably operated by forces unknown there was no surprise at the uncanny form they had taken on their own, or that the first address I wrote to, in Chiswick – which Froshaug had probably given me – was the correct one. My letter brought an immediate and excited reply.

My Dear Sven

How delightful to get a letter from you again, and how wonderful this particular brief note of yours seemed to me. I opened it not knowing who it might be from, and was confronted by your dear signature – and the news you gave me, as miraculous as our first meeting; it was the Spring crocus repeated in the Autumn flower. . .

But to the business of a reply. Your cryptic message – of having met XX not only excited but intrigues me enormously. (And this was part of the pattern, of course . . .) For some years past it has worried me very very considerably that I have (I think perforce) remained quite out of touch with Christian, and his mother. What could I do?

Had I suddenly become rich I would have revealed myself, and invited Christian to stay with us. I would have done so years ago had that been so. I did write to him when I left St Ives at the end of 1953 – I thought of that Bournemouth address. But the letter was returned (I had put my own address on the outside).

So long has passed, it doesn't matter losing a little more time. Will you give me more details of your meeting with the boy? Was Doreen with him? How did it happen? Where did you meet?

In your letter you say 'he lives with his mother at. . .' She married and had another child (a daughter). Is she still with her second husband? Did you meet them all? I believe her name was Mrs French. When I write to the boy do I address him as C.C. Morris – or what?

Will you be a little more explicit?

Otherwise I am glad to be in touch with you again. I shall write back when you reply to this. For the moment the news of my son swamps all else!

I replied at once and was able to fix up their meeting at last in my own Berlin City without walls. There Guido Morris met his son, Christopher Christian, for the first time. True to his word he gave him a Hebrew dictionary.

I set a table up in the middle of a field with salad and wine on a white cloth. There we ate and talked till it was time to go. I don't think anything came of it save the working out of my friend's strange destiny.

Guido stayed for a time after his son had left with his mother Doreen, then borrowed £25 to get his press out of pound. He had tried everyone, even Lanyon. I was the last one. He was touchingly grateful. I never saw him again. Who better with whom to have shared a pittance than a man true to himself? I touch my forelock.

The strangest part of all – his masterpiece of originality – is that he was no longer working as a printer, but on the London Underground as a guard, training to be a driver.

'I used to watch the trains with their lights going over a bridge from my window as a boy. I always wanted to do that!' he told me.

'But don't you ever want to accelerate and have one almighty crash?' I asked him. He looked at me with the innocence of a child and blinked his eyes together, then gave that extraordinary belly laugh I was able to evoke in him. 'Yes, I suppose I do really.'

Now the imprint of his life was bound into one enormous Iron Soul of which he was both father and son.

GUIDO MORRIS: ARCHITYPOGRAPHUS

A name signed on the ocean where the Mermaid lives. Even the starlight has not washed it away, though his life-energy was used up. He died alone in poverty in a London high-rise flat on October 5th, 1980, aged 70. Run out of ecstasy, his spirit had died some time before.

GUIDO – SHALOM

THE PRINTER

GUIDO MORRIS

A Prince of Vagabonds

Before you took on your invisible occupation
Of walking on the bright wind,
Your head flashing in giant crystals
And your hands gathering oceans,
You once talked to me of death.
    'Who will be first?' you said
    'Someone will say: "Have you heard?
    Sven – or Bryan – is dead!"'
And smiling, you went your way.

I did not know it would come to you first
And leave me to spill sunsets of grief
Across an agonized evening.
I did not know that carns of understanding
Would spark starlight in your likeness,
And the sea's continuous music
Enclose your laughter
In waves drunker than time,
Ebbing from pools of pure and nameless beauty
Along the long shore where the curlews call.

I did not know I would wait here
Wondering what burning tear
Would cut like diamond
Through the screen of light
Under carn
Under cromlech and heather root
Over ocean where salt stings,
Gannet and gull-cry: and you
Locked forever
In a timeless clock.

I have spent many long starlit nights on Zennor Carn talking of
life and death to Bryan Wynter, who became in this way my very

close friend, as once I talked to Bernard Leach at the pottery while he cooked Japanese food in the early days of the Second World War.

It was at the pottery I first met Bryan. He was simply there one day in a huge mackintosh with a haversack, having flinked from London on a motor-bike now the war was over and he could give up his job with Solly Zuckerman at the Zoo, where both he and Guido Morris had been doing non-combatant work. My memory is that he was very tall with dark wiry hair – 'mossy' as he put it – and a rather loose skin to his face with large eyes which lit up every now and then with an illuminating smile. There was a kind of Rex Harrison charm about this unusual person dressed in low tones of brown, umber, sullen green and ochre. He sat in a chair in the middle of the room talking with great vitality and humour, every now and then flicking his cigarette ash into the turn-up of his cord trouser leg. He gave one the feeling of belonging nowhere, a classless traveller who spoke in a low cultured voice almost as though he were making it up as a satirical means of dealing with life's fantasy. There was a great gentleness and kindness that persisted into our later friendship.

He had got the cottage at Zennor Carn which he was setting up in a very simple way to make it liveable, with a big dark jovial man named Edward who had 'done a Gauguin on his wife' as he put it, who appeared in a red jersey carrying a new galvanized bucket containing some shopping. We walked to Carn, the motor-bike being no good on the rough moorland track covered with large boulders.

As the ground grew higher the great ocean appeared, receiving the universe at evening with its comets, its meteors, nebulae and sunsets as if it were the deep mind held in a sea reflector, forming, as it seemed to me, a timeless clock to record eternity. The long granite cottage was built in a nest of rocks worn by the sea, scooped out by centuries of winds, swirling particles of quartz, flashing felspar. Here Aleister Crowley still lurked. The ghost of D.H. Lawrence still haunted the plateau below where Frieda sang German songs. A place where anything could happen, built on an ancient burial ground shut in by the solid glass wall of the sea on three sides. It holds things men of the city have forgotten. The men who built the cromlechs in their gigantic simplicity and believed in the vision of our two worlds with an intuitive understanding still moved under the stones. It moved Sydney Graham also in this way:

Here this night this house held rockhigh dark
Over five lighthouses and the blind sea's horns
Keeps safe Nessie and Bryan and two gentle lamps
And my thankful self from the lightsleeping stones
And the visiting men under the stones.

What better setting for a young man already disillusioned by the world's muddle and the senseless slaughter of war, to set up his secret cell for research into life, into experience, into himself and interpret whatever heritage he might carry. He was already creating his own strange inner world peopled by fantastic birds and hands involved like the roots of a tree in the darkness of a fertile mind. Birds which were pterodactylic and sinister. Birds that had flown over scarcely remembered landscapes to the rocks at Zennor with claws caught in the gorse roots. Birds which a critic once referred to as his 'infantile traumata', giving Bryan a new phrase to use as a satiric weapon with which to protect himself and laugh at the world and if necessary at art, because he hated the desiccated language surrounding art. The birds were a tumult in his aviary of dreams, perhaps because death was within him, whereas my becoming a soldier had led to a friendship with death which extended it outside me like a friend walking at my side and talking to me.

'I am death!' he said.
'Life is but another name for me.
Flick yourself out of sight and pass.
Know your man: I who am he!'
And, tall as Eternity, with eyes of glass
There before me I saw him stand.

This was a vision from the battlefield.

The first time I saw Bryan's vision tie in with the outside world was his painting of curlews over Zennor: *Birds Disturbing a Town at Night*, painted in macabre browns and blues, brooding violets and morose greens, sudden whites. It was a painting that moved me very much and when I asked him about it he told me that he had been looking down on Zennor one night feeling suicidal. Suddenly the curlews flew over in the moonlight giving their fluting calls. 'After that,' he said smiling, 'everything seemed worthwhile again and I painted this!'

Bryan Wynter was not an 'intellectual'. Although he was influenced by Kafka when I first met him, it was but a shadow as though his light was obscured by an eclipse at that time out of which he was moving to self-realisation. He reached out for what he called 'wisdom-knowledge'. He was not logical or factual because he recognised the enigma of art and did not dispute the barriers of normal perception were a gateway to a further extension of life. He was serious about these things. I felt that he would have been the first to have become aware of the Presence at Emmaus, yet not allow himself to know it. I was not startled that he read *The Cloud of Unknowing*, as well as Jung's *Modern Man in Search of a Soul*, and he was as excited as was Bernard Leach with my copy of the *Secret of The Golden Flower*. He, like myself, was cutting his own way for his soul to emerge.

'Don't you feel there is something fierce inside you that wants to get out?' he would say, suddenly deriding something I had just said. Thus we laughed and drank together, deriding the very seriousness with which we worked and the claptrap surrounding art. In its own way each painting was a mystic notation about a unique inner experience of the external world.

The interior of his cottage at that time was full of dried plants, crystals, animals, a tame hedgehog which he fed on bread and milk, a jackdaw and later a raven. Shells, bones, skulls, skins, feathers and all *objets trouvés* of natural origin. There was a good deal of disorder until he married, and cheap furniture, an outside dirt lavatory, oil lamps for light. The open granite fireplace was a source of warmth and cooking. A Primus stove, as always in that sort of living, at that time, in that lonely storm-embattled place.

His genial friend, Edward, left after a time but I continued to go to Carn quite often and alternatively he stayed in my Tower as 'a grey sleeper' on my floor out of one of Henry Moore's Shelter drawings – under a grey blanket of course – if drinking or talking with Sydney Graham and Nessie had gone on too long. It was after one of these grey sojourns that we were woken at dawn by the crash of splitting boulders and on looking out found the box factory was on fire. I ran naked to help move some cars from the sheds and Bryan went for the fire engines. Probably our being there saved all that end of the Island being burnt out. It was thought to be arson.

But whenever I went to Carn it was more peaceful, with that kind of silence in which it seems you can hear the stars in their courses. And in the snow there was an almost primeval beauty and indeed mystery that contained one's own self and made you feel safe, because that was the beginning and the end at one and the same time. Otherwise time was not used as we are accustomed to use it, but put away like a smooth bone under a wave through which you could see it move.

We always seemed to eat seagull's eggs which he collected off the cliffs, with bread and butter and cheap Algerian wine. But all served with great courtesy like a medieval prince turned outlaw. There was a touch of Villon about him – and in another way, Fuseli.

One day Bryan told me how he was shut in a room with a cat which he had an overwhelming compulsion to kill. He told me with clinical curiosity how he did this. I remained dormant and said nothing. I had just returned from the war and recognised it as a confession of a truth that is in each one of us. I had seen far worse things done by men with flame throwers on the battlefields of France. Therefore I was not upset and because he told it without guilt, but as an almost clinically honest description of experience, with a detached interest in human emotion and behaviour, I accepted his story as a fragment of the spark that creates as well as destroys in a man. It is up to him. He was a pacifist and did not go to war. I had killed a man.

We shared our looking, our money, our food, ideas, drugs, troubles, alcohol and deepest thoughts about life. I think we shared these because I was never afraid of being serious, and probably he was. He would come back at me with a burlesque of what he called my 'wounded yak look', which was inherited from a story about Sven Hedin being charged by a wounded yak in the snows of the Himalayas. Thus most people knew nothing more of him than the charming satyr dancing before them with his pipes setting life up as an ever recurring joke, each time in a different way. Within this he was alone. He did not sit on committees or fit in with art politics or movements, take sides, plot to bring down art societies or harm other artists.

Bryan Wynter's originality of mind enabled him to move in the landscape as though it were a series of moveable parts he could adapt to his own use: the sea also. He gathered every object of interest – shells, crystals, bones – and drew them as he did the landscape itself. I experienced this very much at first hand because we worked so much together drawing the same images, passing our influence backward or forward to each other, like that old 10/- note I have mentioned. 'Drawing,' he said, 'organises your looking!' Looking of course is the secret of visual art. He moved a tree to let in an ocean, announced the moon, stopped a meteor with his hand. How he would laugh at my saying that! Out of this grew the gouache paintings of the 1940s. But growing already within this were the miraculous constructions I call his timeless clocks, organising the very essence of the lost planet on which he found himself and added to our perception of its kinetic and ephemeral beauty. It all proved to be a search toward finding a way to tapping the inner secret of life, to ambush beauty. One day I had lunch with him at his cottage in the town when he said suddenly.

'I'm going out in my canoe. Come with me, Sven!'

'Not on your life. You're mad to go out on that sea!' I said, hiding my fear and watching the rough pewter waves. He ignored me, and carrying his canoe down to the Lambeth Walk behind the church he set it in the water.

'Sure you won't come? It's terribly exciting.'

I refused again and he got in, pushed off and dipping between the waves, waved as he vanished beyond the granite pier, his hair blowing. I was very relieved I had not gone. This was his own adventure and the way he observed the movement of light and colour from the currents of the sea, and from which he produced many fine paintings. Later he had a canoe built with a glass bottom, making an observatory of the sea to complement his telescope at Carn with which he watched the heavens. On that particular day I refused to go with him, he paddled all the way down that rugged coast to Sennen where the lifeboat was launched to rescue him from a fierce squall which almost took him out to Seaman's Grave, where Augustus John lost his son, Elffin.

Patrick Heron did go with him on a later trip and got his leg severely fragmented when a wave took the canoe and smashed it against him while they were landing. It was no one's fault.

As far as I could see Bryan had no fear. He not only made these risky expeditions but I remember him facing a huge drunken man at the Helston Furry Dance, who was after his wife, calmly insulting him back and not flinching at threats till the man went away. Everyone was drunk. Even myself. At such an ancient festival the psyche is indeed disturbed.

Bryan was not a great drinker. He stayed on Carn for weeks and did not trouble about it, unless there was some Algerian wine to have with his gull's eggs. I don't know about drugs. I have already said I shared my benzedrine with him as with Graham. Both were close friends who shared the same mystical attachment and awe of the cliffs and the sea and it was mostly this groundswell that made us hang together; that, and the poetry and painting that came out of it, as much as a few. white devils that promoted our energy. I tried methadrine which works straight on the cerebral cortex, but only once. Perhaps it substituted old ways to ecstasy practised in earlier days by starving on the North Cliffs. The point about it is that the visual artist and the poet are both dealing with forces in them of which they know little, and use the whole personality and mind to bring about the transmutation of the experience into art. To the artist anything that clarifies and heightens the vision is as valid as prayer and meditation to the saint in quest of God. And the artist might well be nearer God than he thinks – fierce as a tiger – if God is about.

With Bryan I don't know. He was so interested in the processes of the mind and spirit that he would experiment far beyond the limits I set myself, as well as for the sensation and liberation of imagery it could bring, the heightening of powers. I was told later that he grew Indian hemp at Carn and progressed to mescalin about the time Aldous Huxley's book came out and made some calculated experiments with this drug in London, at Bill Brooker's studio. I was moving out of his orbit by then and had left Cornwall when he had his coronary and was carried down from Carn. I never knew if this was brought about by drugs or how extensively he finally used them. There are other factors that might well have affected him. I often wonder if he had taken the wrong antidote to something he was trying to cure in himself, a fleur du mal left behind by the sinister Aleister Crowley who had preceded him at Carn: something that cost him his life, for Bryan Wynter was not an evil person.

Each one of us was drawn to this one magnetic point in Cornwall, the only common factor being that we were humans, each with the magic shuttle active inside us. Each had to find his own way of making this factor work properly so that the best of original creation could be got from it: to take drugs was one way of doing this and therefore affected our human behaviourism, in which, being part of the process, we were also interested.

From early days there was something. I went to visit a fisherman friend who was dying in the local hospital and to my surprise Bryan was in the next bed. He was having tests, I think, but wouldn't say. I never thought of him as ill. Like a moorland goat he climbed the rock and drank rain with the moon between his horns and starlight in his eye. How could he be ill?

He had a son, Jake, by his first wife, Susan who was a tall, vivid young woman with hair as red as a Russian doll in a ballet – was indeed a toymaker. They had a cottage in town and he did not stay so much at Carn, but Bryan seemed restless between the two extremes and did not seem to settle down till after his coronary. At some point the marriage broke up. He went to live with his second wife near Land's End away from the disorientations of St Ives. She was devoted and gave him a new life and a new family.

He was always saying to me when I was complaining of my own family breaking up while I was at war,

'Yes I know family suits you, Sven. Terribly well. But not for me!' But the law of the family finally won and there is little doubt in my mind that this sanctuary, which we all need at some time, was to extend his life another 13 years, during which time he created his marvellous IMOOS (images moving on space), a distillation of the myriad fragments of rock, ocean, tree and star he had found moving around him in a sequence of pre-temporal beauty, becoming almost a part of evolution as they pass through movement in and out of time.

In the early 1950s he called on me in the New Forest, where I was building my little city in a field. He was very excited. Not only had he been left a legacy – 'more money than I shall ever want' – but he had with him the parts of what he called his 'polaroids'. They were cards of colour which he moved about on the table, creating the first of those poetic sequences for me to see. Now he would be able to make them properly and hold an exhibition entirely of his new work. These were the prototypes of what I later called his timeless clocks. When he did have the show in London I didn't go but sent a wire wishing good luck to the timeless clocks. I did not see him again.

Bryan Wynter once said to me, 'I believe the spiritual onus of mankind has fallen on the artist!' He believed each one worked in a little cell keeping the light going like the philosophers in the Dark Ages until the spirit of man emerges and is again free.

He died quite suddenly in 1975 of a further and unexpected coronary and is buried in Zennor

> Under carn
> Under cromlech and heather root,
> Over oceans where salt stings
> Gannet and gull-cry,
> Locked forever
> In a timeless clock.

He always seemed to me like a traveller who had suddenly found himself upon earth, as though he had fallen off a star and decided to make the best of it, investigate what he could see. He was probably more frightened of dying than I knew: that's why he so often talked about it.

'Strange, isn't it, Sven, someone will say to you one day, "Oh have you heard? – Bryan is dead!"'

In the centre of a complicated joke that was his each day's dying, he left a serious silence in which his clocks continue to live in newly created time. He whom I named soon after meeting him in 1945, Prince of our Vagabond Tribe.

ZENNOR

The Inner Circle

If Bach, Ben Nicholson and John Wells had met it is possible they
would have understood one another. Apart from Ben's wilful
incunabula against Bach's mature simplicity and Wells' 'deep
concern for truth', they were alike in many ways in their respective
arts. Priestly, intense, poised to interpret an abstract experience of
religious nature. All three reaching with great skill unexpected
heights, each on his chosen mountain, even though it was perhaps
for Bach alone to know it was only 'in heaven the perfect round'.
Yet it is possible that Nicholson was as near doing a painting like a
Bach fugue as John Wells, were it not for his absence of pity and
excess of delight. Ben Nicholson's differences were always mirror-
wise the same.

'The arm on the hip is a circle!' he said of a sculpture of mine,
Pregnant Woman.

'No, Ben. The space surrounded by the arm on the hip is the
circle and not the arm. That is the difference between you and me.
I start with an arm on a hip which might finish up as a circle, but
you start with a circle forgetting it is an arm on a hip.'

'The thought is the circle,' he suddenly insisted, 'not that by
which it is surrounded or what it contains.' He had whisked the
centre out of the world of images and placed it on a different plane
of ideas so that I was unable to answer because there was nothing I
could do except hold to my own sculpture.

This argument went on in my Tower one day in quite a friendly
way, but with a steel resistance on his side and a granite obstinacy
on mine. He had to have his own way. If he did not he never forgot.
With me he did not, even though he included me as one of his Inner
Circle of Artists.

On that day he called at the Tower in his long blue overcoat with
ARP stamped on the silver buttons which he wore long after the war
as though there could possibly be another air raid, but I think the
real reason was that he liked the buttons. He took 20 Player
cigarettes from his pocket and gave them to me, which was not
wholly a Greek present – he knew I would have none, and I
immediately lit up to feel that ecstasy of hot needles stab as I
inhaled my first drag of smoke. Such words now horrify the world.

'Thanks Ben, that's marvellous.' I said, and offered him one.

'No, I don't!' We went on talking.

He had come to get me to answer an article in the *Cornishman* newspaper which had sprung from the publication of my book on Wallis. It was written by someone who was angry at the neglect that sent Alfred Wallis to the workhouse. Ben was quiet and persistent, his lively blue eyes burning with intention. Like the argument over the arm and the circle he was certain I would give in. He thought it was up to me to defend him because I had written the book. For me, having at last got the book out after six years during which I had time to go and fight my way through Europe and return to correct the proofs, I felt my battle was over. In my book I had said what I had to say and felt he should defend himself against the counter attack. The trouble had arisen from my publishing (with his permission) part of a letter of his to Alfred Wallis. It had come into my possession when Adrian Stokes, acting as executor, gave me the kitchen table Wallis had painted. In the drawer I found three letters from Ben Nicholson to Alfred Wallis. The one I published read as follows.

20 Dulwich Common
SE.21

Feb. 18 1929

Dear Mr Wallis,

Many thanks for the paintings. There were some lovely ones among them, and we like them very much. Mr Wood and Mrs Nicholson both liked one of them as much as any you have done – one with land like clouds behind a ship with white sails, blue sky, yellow sun.

We have kept nine:

	s.	s.	d.
One at		3	0
Two at		2	0
Six at		1	0
		13	0
Post		1	6
		14	6

215

For two hours I watched Ben's circular head move against the square of my window with the blue Atlantic beyond, his sudden red jersey locking the two together. I listened to him argue that we were an inner circle of artists and should defend each other, that we were becoming so famous we would not be able to go out in the landscape to draw without being intruded upon and this article would make it worse, even aggressive.

I no longer had any axe to grind about Wallis because I had cared enough to write the book and was not really concerned about the artists at this juncture. Nothing after the Western Front presented me with real danger. It was a matter of valuation. I knew what he meant in quite a serious way.

When I was going to war Ben lent me a book by Hélion which belonged to Herbert Read. It tells of Hélion's life as a prisoner and how they formed an inner circle to protect themselves spiritually as well as physically against the enemy. It was the record of a very brave man and it affected me in depth. At war, in the isolation of the ranks I made friends with my Captain Harry Mainwaring. We met in secret by candlelight and talked about the spirit of man for he wanted to be a priest and I a poet. We read poetry together, and it has always seemed miraculous to me that the most sensitive of silver threads running through the human spirit should be so strong as to hold when men were blown apart and disembowelled. In this way we found the inner centre which became a source of protection and solace. Both Ben and Herbert Read wrote constantly to me at the front and I particularly looked forward to the playful collage Ben made of the economy envelope which carried his letter.

Gabo had told me how to survive. These people were a light in a darkness shattered only by shellfire and formed the outer crust of the inner circle which I had formed with my Captain – of the spirit searching for and holding to the precious spark that was life and the meaning of life when death was our only friend. It is from this obscure platform, which I have never mentioned before, that I write of Ben Nicholson, whose idea of an inner circle of artists dominated his life and art, but which seemed over-stated in this instance of the newspaper article. His letters to me are now in the V & A Museum and others in a private collection, and I hope mine to him, when they are released from his archives, will eventually find their way to be with them and complete the record of a friendship peppered with anguish over the Wallis saga, which he considered his territory, as with the political exigencies of the Penwith Society. There was a strong territorial sense in all the abstract artists. There still is.

This idea of the inner circle was not a new one. It has been used by the feudal system from which Ben emerged, for centuries. It could only be seen after the *coup d'état* in the St Ives Art Society that this was so and why the new governing nucleus was so complex and unbalanced – not only by the abstract apartheid, but by the nepotism of the governors. For years after, meetings of the abstract artists were called weekly with Barbara Hepworth as queen of the hive and later, after her death, the spiritual magnetism of this centrifugal force continued.

I could not alter my work on Wallis now but I had allowed the manuscript to be with Ben and Barbara, and adjusted paragraphs and sentences when the pages were returned annotated all over and cut by scissors to such an extent that some had to be re-typed. There were many meetings between us in which he described in detail being driven from Falmouth by Kit Wood on the day they discovered Wallis. I was religiously accurate. So when it came to the meeting in the Tower I remained inflexible, and Ben walked away that morning with defeat in the nape of his neck and the shoulders of his ARP overcoat.

At the early Penwith Society meetings, of which I wrote earlier in this book, it was the same. I was diametrically opposed to the rules I found myself helping to form, after seeing Barbara and her young artists heckling while Ben, watching the old Society fall, stood in that same long coat like a peregrine on his cliff, silent and pale. It had been my belief that we had joined the old society to revitalize it, even cut out the dead wood and bring great strength to what was a deeply rooted and healthy tree. What I saw that night was a sudden attack with high explosive and I was horrified.

I am reluctant to stir this ocean bed after so long and am well aware that some fearsome creatures might be disturbed, but my old age has been so aggravated by historians, television producers, museum keepers, architects, trustees and keepers of great galleries and other art writers and artists getting it wrong, that I might as well set the record right according to my own feelings and memory. Then let the rest be silence, I hope.

Ben Nicholson told me of how once he had formed a group called Unit One. 'I continued showing with it until I had seen everyone off,' he said, 'and then closed it down.' This seemed to delight him. I saw it as the negative aspect of his inner circle, the penumbra, and that he had to be the centre of that which described the circumference and what it contained until there was nothing left but empty space.

The propaganda of all he did as a team with Hepworth was everywhere thorough and far-reaching, permeating the very structure of people's thoughts and habitation. His unique vision of using the bare bones of construction and liberated colour entered the whole fabric of our civilisation: from influencing the shape of a lipstick holder, about which I found him highly excited one day in 1940, to the shape and decor of high-rise flats, ships' interiors, television productions and furniture, after the war. He was the Nuncio of the New World. This was illustrated so well in the story of Adrian's Wall: the saga of Nicholson's getting Adrian Stokes to paint his walls white, as he did later with Alan Bowness and others, to go with the painting Ben had sold him, which led to a quarrel that continued during the war and ended in a split between the two.

I suppose Adrian, who had been instrumental in getting Ben and Barbara down to Carbis Bay and was M'sieu Le Patron in more than one sense, was greatly upset, as indeed was Gabo with the theft of 'zee egg'. Ben had to win. To have his way. To see everyone off, except for those who got on the show boat with him. He succeeded. With Barbara he constructed the first abstract satellite to circle the world of art, with unprecedented effect even to the point of having complete control with ruthless seriousness. Even the law of change seemed to be suspended.

For me the human drama went on. The agonizing destiny of man was of vital importance. The consequence of love between man and woman. The secret life of creatures and the beautiful performance continuing behind the stage set of civilization. The conflict of good and evil and the symphonic experience of man against a mountain. The poetic power of the spirit must be engaged in a creative purpose: to construct an edifice for all this – a cathedral of light, a palace of colour, a window of creation – which would contain man and woman, creature and planet. This was my burning need. I did not want it to end in a town turned to a stone sarcophagus, a Pharoah's tomb, so I went away.

The early effects of this *nouveau art* upon me were extraordinary. I first called on Ben and Barbara at their house in Carbis Bay in 1940 before I knew the battlefield. On the walls were abstract paintings and drawings. I had never seen any before and it seemed, as I followed her upstairs, that the air became thinner with its stratospheric blue, celestial white, ultimate red and crashing yellow. My senses were actually affected. I began to levitate and feel curiously weightless – indeed, sinless. I was shown into a room

painted white and covered with abstract paintings. I was at once
uplifted and frightened because of their direct invasion of the mind.
Ben, dressed in his shirt of mist grey with a red tie and blue eyes,
was vital and greeted me with great friendliness. Immediately
excited and inspired he told me about his work, the liberation of
colour and form, the new visual world that was being discovered.
Barbara was more silent and a little self-conscious I thought, but
perhaps she was nervous of this passionate soldier back from the
war. I could not tell. Both were extraordinarily kind and outgoing
as priests of their own denomination or, indeed, as a dentist might
be who was about to extract an old tooth no longer of any use. My
vision was reorientated in less than an hour and it was a long time
before the anaesthetic wore off. Some young artists never woke up
after such an experience.

Suddenly I remembered why I had come to see them – to ask if I
could see their collection of Wallis paintings about which I had been
told by the headmaster of the school up the road where I ran the
kitchen garden. In fact, it was at this school that I had first met
Barbara. She had a rather flat oval face and wore a snood. It made
her head into a sculptural whole like an African carving in ivory,
not unbeautiful but not in the other way of women attractive to me,
because she was withdrawn and rather cold. She sat staring at a
white flower in a silver vase. Her remarks about its beauty of form
seemed to me self-conscious, perhaps because of nerves.

We talked through lunch and, being an intense young man with
all the arrogance it takes to make an artist, I poured out my ideas
which probably made her flinch and more withdrawn. She spoke
little and when I asked if I could see the Wallis paintings, invited
me to the house. After this a friendship grew both with her and Ben
Nicholson which was kind and generous and more than helpful, but
fraught with difficulties for which I was partly responsible in my
obstinate pursuit of my own tiger of truth.

'Can I see the Wallis paintings?' I now asked. They looked at one
another, then Barbara got out a large portfolio, opened it and
passed to me, one after the other, on irregular bits of cardboard,
paintings by this old seaman whom Ben and Christopher Wood had
discovered painting in his cottage just 12 years before. The impact
was tremendous, in a world changed to an abstract utopia under
which the powerful seas and turbulent history of this wild old
mariner surged. I was profoundly moved. It was like meeting
Coleridge in paradise. Seeing these paintings of great primitive
simplicity was like hearing great music for the first time and I think

the experience plucked a chord in my own orchestra that warned me off the celestial beauty of the stratosphere shown to me by my two new friends. Like Chuang Tzu's Sacred Tortoise, I would rather wag my tail in the mud than be stuffed in a glass case in the Emperor's Palace.

For a time, though, I made constructions and Euclidian paintings, sprung from the growth of flowers by the sea, with clean precision catching the stress and strain of gravitational force against the thrust of creation. I was at once eloquent and stalked about preaching the new gospel with none of the insight of those who had invented it and, unlike them, using the hand-jive gestures of the intellectual, as though the world was deaf and daft. But it faded and finally vanished when I saw a Miro for real of the battlefield, made from a human foot, a telegraph wire, a blown cow and a man's face: *objets trouvés* of war. After that I saw Beauty in a rubber mask until I had no positive vision at all. One thing that did remain with me was the memory of the old man of the sea painting his memories, and I was able to complete my book on him with a deep groundswell of feeling that finally brought me through the terrible experience of war, which *is* what happens when you don't create. And I went to the Islands to see John Wells. There I found my vision again, beautiful and intact.

I often saw Ben Nicholson, a lone figure on a rock drawing on the moors at Towednack or Zennor, a cloud sliding down a hill, a church locked between a hedge and a cromlech, propped by a dustbin, planked by the sea, wedged by square fields in which his incunabula of animals grazed under a sudden tempest scrawled in the sky – quite different perhaps to his father's, Sir William Nicholson's *Square book of animals*, but a somewhat timeless artist of the inner circle which I had the privilege of knowing and the distinct advantage of belonging to for a short while.

Like the Georgians and the architects of ancient China he was able to place a hole in a rectangular surface and make it work. Thus he changed the square face of our time. But only Cimabue could draw a perfect circle by hand without a compass.

I remember Ben Nicholson for his help in getting me my first show in London which established me as a painter, for his kindness and concern when I was in battle, his skill and integrity as an artist and for his continuity. Not for his ambition to be king at all costs. As he said to David Lewis near the end of his life, 'We are exactly the same as we were. We don't change. We simply paint our hair white!' His death was the invisibility of the inner circle, the face of time under which the pendulum must finally swing back and mark another age, in spite of the glasshouse history that follows and is sometimes created by unusual men to perpetrate their exquisite flowering.

With Barbara I had an almost co-operative relationship and no doubt her directness and passionate defence of Ben at all times irritated me and awoke the rage of Oedipus in my heart. Unconscious memory held the secret that my mother, who was also from Yorkshire, was prevented from being a sculptor by an attack of rheumatic fever which left her with a weak heart. Perhaps I was angry and jealous because of this. I shall never know because self-knowledge can never be complete. But it made for a restlessness in my friendship with Barbara which blinded me to some of her values and did not obscure all her faults.

Entering the almost clinical interior of their house, and indeed of their art, was like having administered a new kind of caponizing drug which rarefied the atmosphere and purified the forms and colours of ordinary daily life. Their lavatory seat was electric blue and lit by some device which seemed to make it float. So beautiful was the experience one was even frightened of farting.

Ben was dressed in several grades of grey and had electric blue eyes and a circular bald head which against the box frames was like one of his own paintings. Barbara wore a white overall like a hospital registrar. They talked articulately about their work and I went away that evening with an edition of *Circle*, published in London, compiled by Nicholson, Martin and Gabo, under my arm, loaned to me by these two completely dedicated people. After that I often called.

In spite of their total commitment to a new religion which they themselves had discovered and the manufactured history that came out of presenting work of skill and originality, the one factor I missed in both Ben and Barbara was greatness. What greatness is I cannot say but Vaughan Williams had it, Gabo, Jacob Epstein, had it. So did Augustus John, Robert Graves and Mai Zetterling. Each of these artists I knew personally and each gave me a feeling they had been touched by the Gods when no one was looking and did not themselves know. They were not precious or puffed up but naturally taller than other people. I never forgot meeting them in a world of dwarfs.

One day when Ben was there alone I remarked on the many Henry Moore sculptures he had in the house, over which, while I had been waiting, I had run my hands and my eyes with the real

221

pleasure only sculpture can give, taking the body and the mind on a journey which was also a discovery.

'But why so many?' I asked.

'Not Henry, Sven – Hepworth!' I had already learnt that this was the way he liked to refer to his wife in matters of art. 'Every time Henry does one she follows with one of her own. They were at art school together. Hepworth is to be the most important sculptor of our time.' He spoke with authority. His electric blue eyes were switched on. 'She is held back just now because the triplets are still young. Later, when the war is over, you will see for yourself.' He was right – I did.

It was not till after she got free from Henry and had also absorbed what she had culled from Gabo that she found her own vision, largely in the Cornish landscape.

I was under the powerful influence of the Cornish land, honey-combed with mine shafts and caves, crowned with granite, bejewelled with amethyst and quartz, robed in oceans. It was now that my flat vision as a painter started to extend into the round image in space, landscape that can be entered like a woman, journeyed over, interlocked with eye and spirit and body which is the prerequisite of the sculptor in stone, as though suddenly I had started to grow antlers and could see through as well as at a form and turn it in space.

Meeting other sculptors like Gabo and Hepworth, later Moore and Epstein and Frink, helped me to translate this newly awakened vision into terms of stone. Hepworth was never ungracious in showing me her things, even though she would not comment on my own work save to remark on the nature of the stone. Perhaps because I was immediately concerned with more dramatic arche-typal images that stirred in the deep mind like a boiling ocean, I was never able to touch her arctic classicism or evoke her sympathy.

But why, I often asked myself – and ask myself now as a very old man – why did no one come right out and cut from a stone the immortal sensation of the human fusion locked in the conjunction of Love? I think that is what Henry Moore was after but avoided saying so, and his vision gave the theme a cosmic meaning.

When my wife became pregnant and we were asked to leave the school, I hired a horse and cart to take us out with our few possessions and our young son to the cottage lent to us by Robin Nance, and we settled to a life of terrible poverty on those strange moors near Zennor.

There we lived among the cromlechs and menhirs, stone beds of prehistory, ithyphallic rubbing posts, Ogham stones, the forts and foges that had such influence on Hepworth in the years to come, drawing her away from Moore and Gabo to her own vision of these ancient monuments and their unique existence over oceans, against nebulae, leaning across centuries, heather root and charred gorse, even though she said she could not carve the granite of which Cornwall is made. And there is sometimes the fear that her classical intellect, heightened consciousness and consummate skill could transmute these forms with controlled emotion, but could not transpose the magical content which they carried in the deep soul – that a snake might have bitten where a star should have pierced.

I know the terrors that lurked behind these ancient stones where in darkness and candlelight I had slept and starved. One day I was returning across the moors when I saw a bombing on the ocean and went to war because I knew the face of evil was uppermost. In the words of Xenophon

> It was the reply of Zeus
> That he should leave with the rest.

The poet's prophesy in John Heath-Stubbs' poem, *Mermaid of Zennor*, that also came true thirty years later brings me now to a standstill.

Whatever the conflict between myself and Hepworth before, during and after the war, neither one lost respect for the other as artist working beyond creed and time in that danger zone which is creation. The friendship continued whether by exchanging a stone and trying to get her into my 1924 Morris car to drive to my Tower to choose it, or finding a rubber ferrule in wartime to fit a walking stick for Sarah, one of the triplets who had osteomyelitis; quarrelling in committee, competing for the Festival of Britain after the war and hating the result which placed me second, especially as I knew her assistant, Denis Mitchell, had cut out her entry while she was in London and he himself came third.

Finally, the St Ives Arts Ball, with Hepworth as a prehistoric woman dressed in skins with her hammer in her hand and her muscular arms showing. I knew nothing of Brody-Berlin then but I went as the Wandering Jew with a bottle of rum in my cloak dancing the jitterbug with a pretty girl – the same one by whom Augustus had been enchanted. We won first prize: a Lanyon painting, which I gave to my partner on the floor.

It was by some chance that a friend lent me the costume with skull cap at the last moment. Endell Mitchell had a pair of roe deer antlers on the wall of his pub and had laughingly suggested I wear them to go to the dance as the Devil.

'Le Satan conduit le Bal!'

But everything in me opposed the idea. I said at the time, to wear the horns would be to identify with evil and dangerous. I felt a deep resistance for, although I believe we should be touched with evil, the stain must not be a dye: only a smudge of understanding to protect and not to be consciously used, as with Christ. But looking back now after more than 40 years and a lot of research for this book it is uncanny how to go as Mephistopheles was the alternative given to going as the Wandering Jew, when, as I have said earlier, my ancestor Brody-Berlin was living out the theme of Faust at the time Goethe was writing it. It is no doubt true that this impulse remained down the centuries if only as a dull throb in the main symphony.

Even though such images might be reversed by legend and history they remain absolute in that they marked the difference between myself and Barbara. It was this difference that enabled me to stand aside. I refused to work for her when my comrades did: four men my own size were employed to help cut the Festival images out of Irish limestone, conceived and conducted by Hepworth. I remember how moved I was when I saw them half-finished against a grey running sky and the tower of the twelfth century church from her walled garden, where one of her assistants had taken me. Although I would have learned so much had I gone with them I did not want the Medusa touch, her abstract shadow so strongly upon me that it would stunt my personal vision at a time of growing. I knew even then that the only uniqueness we have is ourselves, although each of us was inspired by the same ancient places and stones.

The end of war brought the younger artists back to the magnetic centre of Cornwall where an act of creation came about – the 'Disturbance in the West' in John Wells's words – superimposed on the traditional nucleus which had kept things alive while we were away, long before that also. Barbara became queen bee at its centre. For the first time I saw a hard and more ruthless side to her which rode like a Boedicean chariot leading the Icene across any opposition and got the young men to fight at her side. The blades of her wheels were sharp.

But she did influence me in one thing for which I have never forgiven myself. I told her of an idea I had conceived in granite of a Man to be placed on the top of Rosewall Hill above St Ives so that the fishermen returning at dawn would see it rising out of the sea.

Sven Berlin working on a lion's head for the St. Austell Brewery Company, a commission undertaken 1947–1949.

The Song of the Tower

vain merlin
lonely stone
sven berlin

Outside the Tower, St. Ives, 1948 (Photo: Gilbert Adams, Tate Archive).

John Wells in his studio.

Tambimuttu.

Sven Berlin, at the Castle Inn, St. Ives, 1945.

. . . If I paint what I see (I try sometimes) the result is deplorable. But how can one paint the warmth of the sun, the sound of the sea or the journey of a beetle across a rock or thoughts of one's own whence and whither? That's one argument for abstraction. One absorbs all these feelings and ideas and if one is lucky, they undergo an alchemistic transformation into gold and that is the true creative work . . .

. . . I cannot, nor do I want to, make copies of nature. But everywhere watching and studying natural rhythms and processes (within as well as without) till very humbly one begins to create entirely new things as nature does – when the idea and the material are in dynamic sympathy growing together towards the same end . . .

Part of John Wells' famous, and much borrowed from, letter to Sven Berlin, April 1945 (Tate Archive).

St. Ives 'old guard': Leonard Fuller (in 1970), and Borlase Smart working 'en plein air' in 1940 (Tate Archive).

The famous St. Ives Crypt Group, 1946–48: Peter Lanyon (with Bryan Wynter behind), Sven Berlin, Willie Barns-Graham and John Wells (photo: C.O.I.)

A later Terry Frost (photo: Dean Wilcox).

The author's drawing of Patrick Heron, 1945 (Dopita).

W.S. Graham by Sven Berlin: 1946
pencil drawing now in the National
Library of Scotland, and an earlier ink
sketch.

From a letter to the
author from Nessie
Dunsmuir.

And I remember the songs at the
caravans. But even I had forgotten
that it was you who asked Sydney
to write the poem for your book on
Wallis. And what a great poem
your request brought forth!
But I have not forgotten that, morning
about six o'clock on a beautiful
day, when you led the procession of
the goats and luggage, Sydney
and I following, walking from the
caravans to the common opposite
The Falmouth Packet, where our good
kind friend, Bob Wills and his wife
lived, who were accepting the
goats from us, because we were
moving on, I think to Mevagissey.
It must have been a fine sight to see!

Poet Arthur Caddick: drawing from life by Sven Berlin, 1951.

Endell Mitchell, cartoon by Segal.

Denis Mitchell in later life (photo Richard Henty).

Mermaid and Angel, *carrara marble 1946.*

Head of a martyr, *granite 1950.*

Bird, *marble 1946/7
(photo Studio St. Ives).*

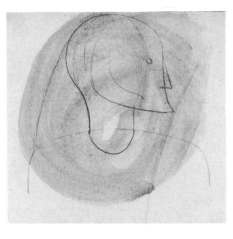

Serene Head *drawings and finished alabaster sculpture, 1950.*

Peter Lanyon in 1949 (photo Michel Ramon).

Sven Berlin's drawing Miner at work, Geevor, *1948 and* Composite man, *oil 1945.*

*Family man: ink drawing of
Janet, 1946, photographs of Janet
and Paul, and oil wash drawing
for carving* Man with children,
1948 (photo Studio St. Ives).

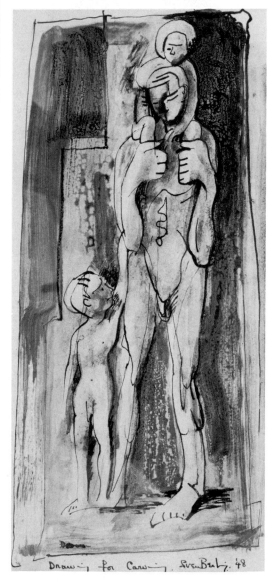

Unknown political prisoner, *alabaster,
with drawing 1952 (photos: Gilbert
Adams and Dopita).*

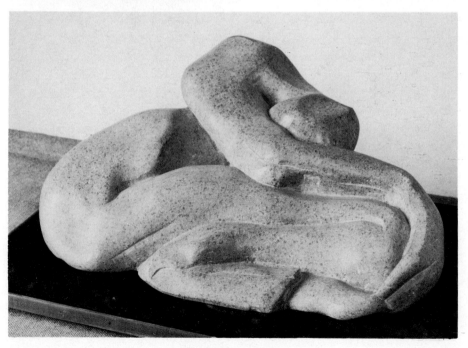

Sleeping figure *1946.*

Augustus John; Jacqueline Moran, ink drawing by the author 1949 (photo David Brown); Adrian Ryan, c.1949 and his artist's proof of Augustus John.

Guido Morris with his Albion Press,
1949 and drawing by Sven Berlin, 1945
(both Tate Archive).

Jasper sleeping, ink 1954 (Dopita).

Bryan Wynter in ink drawing by
Sven Berlin, 1945.

Ancestors *in newsprint and marble*
1948.

Mother and child, *granite 1950 and* Dark
Monarch, *ink.*

In my innocence and enthusiasm I had not realised it would weigh several tons and would take me some years to carve. It was to be the final image for Wallis and for all the Cornish, and Cornwall, have given to the artists. She talked me out of it. How, I don't know, but the negative side of her personality was powerful enough to do so. Perhaps it was her reply to my not wishing to take her Medusa touch. I was young and able enough to have cut it out. Perhaps, knowing more than I, she wanted to save me the heartbreak.

I think there was a deeper politic kept secret and that was the driving force. It seemed she became more remote, the human contact had gone: if we met in the street we were friendly but talked mostly about stone. As Ben said: 'We are an inner circle of artists working for a common end: we must keep together!' which recalled Hélion's inner circle during the war. When she died, a Cornishman told me local people said 'We scarcely knew her!' But I had long lost contact by then and don't know the truth of this.

After the war, for those of us who came back there were conflicts of family and love, drinking and dancing to the Harry Lime theme over the ashes of the old world and, for those of us who understood, the vibrations of the Dark Monarch who lived in the spectre-ridden hills down to the end of the land, which ended in tragedy and death and deep sadness. I took my caravan elsewhere to lick my wounds and re-orientate to other stars, lucky to have got out with my life.

The Priestess was now with her own temple and walled garden at the back of the town where the huge images were cut out standing among tropical plants: her own flowers to gaze upon. Her court was the new society which, with dear Bernard Leach and others, I had helped to form, and of which I was the first secretary. From there the nucleus grew until the branches fell away and history was made by a woman of extraordinary talent, ambition and power, for which she was deservedly dubbed Dame of the British Empire.

But one thing was forgotten: the brooding Presence in the hills that troubled our souls in a deep and mysterious way, and was understood by the poets and by the Cornish. Early in 1975 many artists died, my great friend Bryan Wynter, quite near to Roger Hilton whom I met only once. This prevented my returning as I had planned. On June 4th of that year I received a letter from Eric Quayle, who was advising me on a cottage at Foage. I found it disturbing.

You know by now that your erstwhile friend, Barbara Hepworth (1905–1975), was charred to a cinder after setting fire to her bed above her studio in St Ives. A three-quarters full bottle of Johnnie Walker exploded during the conflagration and ensured that survival was quite impossible. Her housekeeper was unable to approach close enough to save her.

We seem to be living in troubled times here in West Penwith, and on a recent starlit night the Carn above Zennor was criss-crossed with moving lights – shooting stars – and the villagers talk of ominous tidings. For me the worst has already happened.

My friend had recently lost his own wife under tragic circumstances. Bertrand Russell's daughter was burnt to death soon afterwards. I recognised this as one of those areas of destruction I had myself experienced in the same country and knew what had happened. I wondered if the poet, John Heath-Stubbs, half-blind like Tiresius, saw in his fierce vision of the Mermaid of Zennor all those years before, when he wrote in 1946

> . . . the villagers
> Remember burnings by the hewn stones . . .

stones of which classical transmutations stand in her walled garden as her own memorial. From the unconscious mind only can the oracle be spoken and the speaker not know the meaning, yet here was the sacrifice in all its horrifying truth performed in this land of quartz crystal, radium and granite, never giving up its secret or only to the timeless ears of the sea and the early sculptures that litter the land where my friends are resting.

The much younger woman wearing a snood whom I first saw staring at a white flower in a silver vase could not have foreseen what destiny was before her or I would have known. Those who take hammer and chisel to create beautiful form and space out of stone awaken the Dark King from his slumber, and fires are lit in the hills to tell us he is abroad and to avoid his rage. He takes no one for his Queen but the starlight.

Hepworth is remembered by the hewn stones. Let this be her epitaph. And Ben in some curious way, is the square root of her destiny, Keeper of the Inner Circle.

But the Inner Circle did not stop there. It had been centred first with Gabo and his brother Pevsner in Russia, then Paris and

Weimar, to London with Nicholson, St Ives with Adrian Stokes, also Hepworth, and like the eye of a hurricane working by centrifugal force through Lanyon and the Crypt Group to Johnny Wells, Wynter, myself to the explosion that made the Penwith – followed by Terry Frost, Barns-Graham, Heron, Hilton, Mitchell and many others who usurped the originals. To this umbrella came others.

I left in 1953 with a horse and was long considered dead. But I cannot quell the disturbance until I have cut a niche for my friendship with Bernard Leach because it was unique and influenced my life. This book is about that life, to try and show how the first illegal entrance of a wandering Jew into eighteenth century Sweden started a great family from a trickle of melted ice in the snow-covered mountains and lakes of a distant past, and like Bernard from China and Japan, I came to be part of an extraordinary movement of the forces of history in Cornwall.

The Ceramic Horse

This sequence of memories has been written down with the feelings and thoughts that have collected round them like sea weed containing strange or beautiful creatures over the years, not to be amputated by the sharp blade of hardened fact which cuts away so much of the truth and leaves dead matter, but examined with love and not a little sadness for the passing of a distant friend. I had been trying to salvage these memories when a friend of Leach who was writing about him, Takashi Tanahashi, wrote to me from Japan, saying this:

> I am writing you because I wish to listen to your comment on Leach. You were the best friend of his in a sense. Most friends of his were potters or critics, but you were not such a specialist. You must have been a *friend* of his in a pure sense. A few years have passed since Leach's death so his complete figure must have been modolld up in your mind. Would you please tell me something about your great friend? Your memory of him.

I was moved by this unexpected appeal from the other side of the world. Tanahashi had written to me some years earlier about my work on Alfred Wallis whose work he wanted to introduce to Japan. He told me then he was meeting Leach and getting material for a book entitled *Conversations with Bernard Leach**. And then we lost touch. He was ill and I was involved with a large sculpture which took all my time and energy. Now this new contact released the stream of difficult and unique memories from the bed of my ocean, particularly because I had been writing about Augustus John, by whom Bernard had been influenced in earlier years.

In the early days of World War II several young painters and poets gathered around the hills of Zennor mostly because they were pacifists and therefore fugitives from society and quite often then from the law. They found this timeless clock formed of rock crystal and piercing blue light, of heather root and gorse burnt black on the

---

* This was published in 1992 under the title *Vase of the Soul* by the Shincosha Company.

evil side of the hill above the Atlantic Ocean, to be an austere but truthful sanctuary where they might survive and work. At the foot of the moorland hills before descending into the town, Bernard Leach had built his pottery in the 1920s, with Hamada.

When I worked at the private market garden run by the writer and painter Adrian Stokes in Carbis Bay, on the long low roof of his house was a pottery horse and rider which I admired. When I asked Adrian about it he said:

'Bernard Leach made it for me. I think it has something to do with the first express post!'

'With the influence of Tang.'

'Possibly. You would know better than I. The Tang is there, I'm sure Sven. But it's very much Bernard's own,' he replied with his polite smile and shut me up. I said I would like to meet Bernard and went back to my gardening. I was more excited by this than I was by the advent of the abstract movement at my side.

I had been influenced by the East for some years through a friendship and tuition with Dr Turk, one of the great sinologues of our time lecturing in Cornwall for Exeter University, which gave me the chance to learn something of religious and artistic cultures in the East, particularly China and Japan, though I never became a sinologue myself, as he was – and of course Bernard, although Bernard was not so much an observing scholar from the West as a Western artist who entered the creative activity of the East. One of the most pregnant things Bernard said to me was in those early days of the war when I expressed my horror at fighting the East.

'We fight ourselves, Sven!' he said, looking straight into me with those intense pale eyes trapped between a head of startled grey hair and his Schweitzer moustache. 'We are fighting our own westernization of Japan!' This remark opened up a whole world of understanding. I was able better to deal with the wound this had inflicted on all of us who loved Eastern cultures – particularly in my case, Zen.

But I think I met Bernard Leach's son, David, first. I was building some clay dryers at the back of the pottery to earn some extra money in the evenings. Bernard was probably away, either abroad or at Dartington Hall. David and I used to walk home together to Carbis Bay in the late evening and became close friends. I suppose we were the same age. He lived at the Count House (once the house of a tin mine manager) with his wife Elizabeth and young family.

And his mother, also Bernard's first wife, whom I remember as a gentle Edwardian lady in a black dress, always courteous and kind, and Bernard's attractive daughters Eleanore and Jessamine. I loved going there. David told me about his father on our long walks home when we discussed the enigma of the creative spark. David said that he was convinced he had not got it in the way his father had: so much so, that he had gone to technical college to learn the more advanced chemistry of potting and so build up a background knowledge that would be helpful to the pottery his father had established, and save many of the good pieces of works he saw lost through the lack of this knowledge. I recall being impressed by the dedication of a man who had done this, especially in my full blown arrogance as a young painter, who could never have worked under the shadow of a famous father in that way. Bernard himself was rather cautious about his genius and did not like to spill too much into another's cup, though too many stole from his sacred urn when he was not looking. Since then David has done work that stands well against the towering beauty of pots his father made.

Bernard was separated from his wife, Muriel, and lived alone in a small cottage beyond the pottery under a hill called Rosewall, which dominated the landscape like Mount Fuji. I went there once: he lived in quite primitive conditions. The house built at the side of his pottery had been blown up by a land-mine dropped from a German plane. The local people, who did not agree with his life-style anyway, said he had been signalling to the enemy with his furnace. But the furnace was not being fired that night it happened. He was nevertheless in dudgeon. The Cornish are always very difficult in wartime. Earlier I had been arrested for drawing a church which, unknown to me, was a military headquarters. D.H. Lawrence was expelled from Cornwall in the First World War for singing German songs under the windows of the people in Zennor. Coming home one night across the moors I was reported for 'signalling to a German submarine with my torch'. This wild country which attracted the stranger and wandering artist rejected him when the enemy was near.

Bernard was very distressed by this antagonism. But he had extraordinary tenacity and sense of justice (which probably came from his father who was a judge in Colonial China), both qualities which enabled him to shoulder the huge responsibility to rebuild, and it took him years to re-establish the house and pottery under war time restrictions when the creation of beautiful objects is secondary to killing other men and women. The pottery itself was not hit by the bomb. It became the nucleus of his life and his belief in so many ways. I remember standing late at night watching the moonlight through the slats in the roof of the ruined house like a drawing by Paul Klee, and thinking of the broken marriage, the broken building, the social split, the larger inter-hemisphere schism and warring humanity: they were all emblematic of this struggle.

It was at this time I used to stay on in the evenings to spend them with Bernard in the pottery itself, through the door leading from the open room where the cold furnace stood silent like a sleeping dragon, built 20 years earlier by Hamada and Leach: possibly Tomimoto also. Here there was a small fireplace built of glazed bricks and clay with two little Gothic niches above and an iron fire-cradle below. He held conferences with his clutch of apprentices and David by day. After they had gone there was only the potter's tables and wheels and tools and pots drying to make an austere but honest background, with a peculiar silence of its own, to sit and talk and watch him cook simple meals of Japanese food on the open fire. Being the younger man I listened a good deal because there was a certain authority that demanded it so, not in the sense of being at the feet of the prophet but a friend who had an eagerness to be heard about the East, which was his obsession. As an old man he even looked Chinese. When we were to first meet, my friend Turk was excited. 'Ask him,' he said, 'who was the seventh Kenzan.' This I did. 'I am!' was Bernard's unexpected reply. 'When he was at the end of his life the sixth Kenzan had no son. He passed the mastership on to me.' That was the only time I heard Bernard mention an honour bestowed.

My fragmentary knowledge of the Orient was being re-awakened by meeting Bernard, and by reading Wilhelm's translation of the *Secret of the Golden Flower*: a Chinese Book of Life with a European commentary by Jung. Here for the first time I saw the East touch fingertips with the West. It was my copy Bernard borrowed to read; we discussed it and here, in the midst of a disintegrating world, was a flower opening in the silence of the night. Through it I became friends with this man of great personal integrity and truth who did so much for English crafts.

I was never a potter. I did try, and threw one or two very thick asymmetric pots and even fired a heavy horse in clay, to Bernard's anxiety because he thought it would blow up in the kiln. He sometimes came to my side with sound advice but I told him to go away. 'I am the Alfred Wallis of pottery, Bernard. It's no use trying to teach me!' I think this irritated him. Few people find humour in the thing of which they are master – except comedians. But I often watched him at the wheel when he did not know and he was working alone, his tall figure in shirt sleeves and apron, moving with the rhythm of the foot pedal, his strong, slender hand directing the clay and his head moving in its own orbit over the turning wheel. At this point he was the complete man unforgettable and forgetting himself.

After a time my work as gardener with Adrian Stokes where I met so many people now part of history, came to an end and I was in for a very rough time. I went to live in that remote cottage on the Zennor moors lent to me by Robin and Dicon Nance, where I existed with my family in great poverty. I used to go researching for my Wallis book among the Cornish people and working on the land as well as at the pottery. The link with Alfred Wallis was another link with Bernard. I used to discuss my work with him and he read the first manuscript of my book. He was helpful. Although I took note of what he said that evening, being obstinately a lone voyager I stayed with my vision. I was nonetheless grateful for his care about what I was doing, as I was later moved by the lighthouse in glazed tiles he was to make for Wallis' memorial. I tell of this elsewhere in this book.

That was the night, returning to my moorland cottage on foot, I saw a battle going on at sea. Planes were bombing a Merchant Navy convoy: everything was alight, men were falling into the sea, ships sinking. For me it was a moment of *satori*. I realised in a flash there was no escape, the destruction was within me and only by becoming involved could I become a complete person and artist of my time. My family was starving. I went to war.

It was during this crucial time my friendship with Bernard was vital to my sanity, for he knew better than anyone else how deeply my convictions went and that being taken over by the objective psyche was no easy matter. There were also practical problems to resolve. Through his help I got my family into the cottage he was vacating and he kept an eye on them, helped and advised with matters of welfare from the military which was so niggly, and when his house at the pottery was rebuilt he was near enough to see no harm came. I was able to store things at the pottery, especially the table that Alfred Wallis had painted, which was given to me by Adrian Stokes acting as executor for the authorities, and which I wished to preserve and present to the Tate when the war was over. But when I came back in 1945, on army pay of 10/- a week, I was forced to accept an offer from Eardley Knollys through Stokes to sell. He came to the pottery with the painter Edward le Bas, and I remember how little I was able to laugh when I watched them saw off the legs of the table, throwing them aside with the joke that they must remember to present those to the Tate, before fitting the table top with its great lighthouse and ship into the boot of their car and driving away. I don't know what happened to it after that, but it certainly would not have been saved had not Bernard allowed it to be in his house during those difficult years.

Bernard was not always aware of his best things. When I did casual work at the pottery, I found a rubbish dump at the back lower end of the site where a small stream called the Stennack ran down the hill, always reminding me of Hokusai. It was here the old pots were discarded and pots indeed that had failed at the time or were disappointing after a firing. Among these, even in the river,were some that had fallen on the bank first and were not broken. Among them a beautiful square teapot with a fish upon it I took living from the water. I built up a small collection of these, some of them quite asymmetric, which I kept on the mantleshelf in my cottage. When I was away at war Bernard made one of his regular visits to see all was well. He took them down and examined them with some excitement.

'Where did he get these?' he asked.

'From your rubbish dump!' my wife replied. 'I thought you knew!'

He smiled and nodded his head in a way he had of letting you know he understood the unexplained, without saying anything. He knew as I knew that the best art happens without knowing. That art like faith is in the forgetting, even sometimes in the failing. It was perhaps this that made him sometimes the great artist, whereas at other times his western self-consciousness was too strong to make him more than the great craftsman: he was never less than either at any time. Hamada seemed to work straight from the unconscious behind reason and let the pot create itself. In a television programme in later years Hamada said: 'Leach could not draw!' But he could draw a fish. One day he drew for me a John Dory which he was going to cook for our supper. I was very excited by the sharp spines and black spot and he gave the drawing to me. Later it went on to a dish he was making. We ate the fish. I gave him a drawing of a magpie I had done that day. I have lost the John Dory now and the magpie will have flown away, but it was these close parallels running alongside our spontaneous creations that contained our joy and delight in being friends and in living, showing the ephemeral nature of both life and art outside any philosophy or fashion. Had Hamada (co-founder of the pottery) stayed, the result might well have been a revelation for both men and for the world, since each man was the other half of the other – or a disaster for one, for each great artist must reach this point alone.

I am reluctant to speak of his private life for fear of hurting anyone and will mention it only as it enters my memory with any of the feelings that make it part of 'his complete figure that must have been modolld up in my mind' – and with loving care.

After Bernard's first marriage was dissolved he married Laurie Cook who lived at that time in a long wooden chalet at Dartington. During this transition he was in a state of continuous nervous exhaustion. He had a high moral waterline below which he did not like to sink, which made it difficult for him to accept himself as a full male animal as well as a questing spirit. I used to listen at length to his agonies to which he could not find a solution. I went to Dartington with him to meet Laurie, a highly intelligent intense, dark haired person who sought perhaps domestic peace and love for her own sake as a pre-requisite to happiness. I even prophesied the difficulties of taking her into a family concern as the pottery then was. There was no question of his going to Laurie. I think it was a source of considerable distress to Bernard that I turned out to be right. Laurie came to live in the pottery above St Ives but could not deal with it and had to go away again. He was completely naive about women and had not the faintest notion what they were about and what they wanted, yet he was always surrounded by women at the pottery, mostly of the *artistica nervosa* type. As with all innocent people his problems were always a surprise – at least in this field – and he just could not understand why his marriages would not work.

When I was going on one of these journeys to Devon I used to go to the station early in the morning to watch the sea washing round the little fishing town and wait for his tall lean figure to appear, dressed in a loose overcoat and old Trilby hat. On his shoulder, from a long leather thong, was slung a receptacle made of cord and leather and net which he told me was a Japanese head-basket once used by Japanese warriors – Samurai perhaps! He had it stuffed with a change of shirt and his writing gear. He looked like a travelling Chinese monk. On the journey he talked a lot, leaning across the carriage and sometimes sat watching the landscape through the window and the steam from the train. The rest of the time he spent writing letters. There was a great sense of purpose in all he did: no time was wasted. When I tried to write I had to give up because the movement of the train made it impossible. When I was at war I received letters from him with drawings which helped me to see my friend against the landscape through which he was passing. I made such journeys again when I came back and it was through Bernard I met the Elmhirsts and stayed at Dartington Hall as their guest, among the Picassos, the Wallises and the Henry Moores. They were generous people, who gave me a grant to work for my first show at Lefevre Gallery in 1948. They were also very gracious people, and I remember on Dorothy's birthday Imogen Holst gathered under a Gothic archway singing Tudor court songs with her pupils to celebrate by surprise, looking like a medieval sculpture herself.

Leonard Elmhirst held a special meeting of the whole community while I was there. It was to mark the end of the war and restate their principles. They argued and quarrelled all the time and he could not understand why this was. Afterwards he asked me. I had just returned from being a front line soldier and could only say one thing. 'Because they are not soldiers and you are too good a king. It takes a frontline soldier to give his life for you. Soldiers are peaceful creatures.' Bernard said nothing.

But another unexpected thing happened when I returned from the war in France and Holland. Like so many I was nervously exhausted; and my little family had disintegrated, for reasons which Bernard would not have known and would not have been able to correct if he had. There was nothing for me to do but live alone and I moved into the shack on the Island at St Ives which I called my Tower. I worked hard and lived and drank hard, which distressed my friend. I saw him less, for no longer was I able to keep up to the earlier religious and moral standards, because war had replaced them with a new realism. Perhaps I felt he judged me harshly. As with his friend, Mark Toby I was closer to the joys of drinking than he. The coarser reality of life, out of which death and destruction had come, now formed a deeper humanism and wider humour than Bernard understood. He told me once that he always envied me for being able to fight alongside the frontline soldier, and for this honesty and for so much more I loved him. Perhaps my full life had started on the night I saw the battle at sea and death became a friend. I had passed the fear-barrier.

During this time those who were to make the nucleus of the new creative emergence in Cornwall after the war had come together from different parts – Russia, Japan, Italy, Sweden, London, Scotland and the north of England, France, Holland, Germany and

Africa. By their being together such a force was detonated as to form a spiritual explosion – it wrecked the old St Ives Society of Artists overnight. I was there, but not Bernard. The next morning was Sunday and I met Bernard cycling down an empty street in the little town like a man in a Dali film, tall and remote as a dream.

'Have you heard about the Society?' he said looking through thick pebble glasses as he dismounted. 'It was destroyed last night!' He looked anxious and over-wrought as though he had not been sleeping.

'Yes. I was there!' I said.

'What shall we do?'

'Start a new one, Bernard!'

The rest I have told.

Gossip has it that in the early days before I was there and before the pottery was bombed, during the 1920s and '30s, Bernard was looked upon sideways by the locals and was not welcome in St Ives' social life which was set against a narrow Methodist backcloth and middle class snobbery, because of his way of life. This was a source of great discomfort to him and the fall of the old Society was of great importance. Also the building of the new one which went along with his third marriage and the final re-establishing of the pottery as a vital world force both here in England and in Japan. The house was now whole, no longer with the moonlight through the slats of the broken roof. He even lived in the town in later years and was no longer the stranger on the hill. He had refired his links with society.

It was a strange time. A time of the movement of deeper patterns, like a geological change, bringing with it a charge of energy in which we were all caught. Even though this full creative force was behind it, the place was still caught in the waves of violence and abandon, its native magic disturbed, families broken. There followed wild parties, drinking and dancing. In the midst of this, in the crowded little seafront of the town one evening, I saw Bernard standing on a soap box denouncing immorality and preaching the Bah'ai religion, with an amanuensis, Marion Hocking, who was also a student of Arthur Hambly, assisting him and carrying his papers, amidst the shouts and catcalls of the local fishermen. This seemed to be a time of imbalance when the great potter and the man of God were fighting for supremacy, not a little marked by the image of a Judge of the Supreme Court, until he finally settled in the new movement among the artists, when he became an outstanding force. The slip-stream of time displaces the order of things but the poise seemed to come about after a chance meeting on the return trip from Dartington. When he got to St Erth there was no connection to St Ives. He had a travelling companion whose name was Hepworth. She had arranged for a taxi to meet her and asked him to share it. So Bernard the saintly potter joined with this priestess of stone and they became friends. It seemed to me that after this his power in St Ives grew greater. The gentler politics were discarded and the strands of our secret friendship were obscured though never broken or betrayed. His growing fame led to the highest honours: Commander of the British Empire, Companion of Honour and several doctorates in the West and the Order of the Sacred Treasure in Japan.

There was so much I could not agree with in the pattern of the Penwith Society of Arts and Crafts in Cornwall – to give its full name – that I resigned a year after I had helped to form it, and was left out of the pattern after that. It was my own destiny I was intent on following: not theirs. I took the consequences.

My broken home did not repair. I was under heavy fire from society as a whole for this, but we had arranged not to say anything for the sake of the children. No one knew the truth: it was not their business. Bernard housed my family at the pottery for a time. Finally I left Cornwall to pitch my waggon under other stars. When I left, Bernard made a mug with my name on it and sent it down to me for my beer. Because of all these things my friendship with him was left in the other room. The grinding of megatons of rock over the years has not destroyed it, but left a saucer of radium that shines unexpectedly in the dark every now and then. I realise the earlier talks through the night, the trust and care for each other and the effort to find the great creative force behind East and West, and indeed all mankind, was for all time. Perhaps I was mistaken to think the Divine Man in my friend had shifted centre toward the power to judge and away from the power to create, because he did not spill glaze on a dish or fire a pot out of centre without he threw it away.

I retained a great affection for the pottery itself. In those wild days by the sea anything might happen. One day in my Tower I was visited by a madman who threatened me with a knife. It took a long time to pacify him. By the time I had done so, and I had made him some tea and got him to sleep in the little wooden bed, it was late and I had nowhere myself to sleep. I walked through the empty town and climbed the hill where the Stennack ran. When I got to the top I walked like a shadow into the pottery, took the key where I knew it to be hidden in the furnace room, where I had often watched them fire and Bernard wait impatiently for the furnace to cool enough to unpack it, and unlocked the door into the workshop. The little fireplace had a few ashes as if to remember me by, and the potter's wheels stood still like mandalas. I walked through to the end room where there was a long table and lay down on it like a warrior sculpture in a church fully clothed in the moonlight and slept safely in the silence of this little sanctuary. I had returned to a still centre from a raging world. I rose and left before dawn, telling no one. In the night I had listened to the little stream which reminded me of the lifeline between two worlds formed by Hamada and Leach and was explained for me in the *Hui Ming Ching*: 'The subtlest secret of the Tao is human nature and life!'

Bernard also had a Man of Sorrows in his soul.

A year or two later I returned to Cornwall to help my daughter out of an *affaire de la coeur*. While I was there I drove up to Bernard's house on the hill. He was cooking breakfast and pointed to me with his outstretched arm and piercing eyes through the window. 'Sven!' he exclaimed. I had breakfast with him and his American wife, Janet, who was a student of Hamada and a more positive person, enough it seemed to dominate him. I got on with her immediately and we had a long conversation about the gypsies and the American Indians which sparked off quite spontaneously. As Bernard did not know anything about either he was forced to be silent, until he could stand it no longer and insisted on telling me of a visit to Japan he had made recently and how he had stood on a hill in America with (I think) Suzuki and Janet, looking both ways – East and West. I left after several happy hours with close friends. It was the last time we met.

A final contact with Bernard came in the 1970s. A member of The Buddhist Society in London asked my sister, Alma Berlin, if she could find out if Bernard Leach would write something on Suzuki for the Society. Bernard was now blind and very old. I did not hold out much hope but said I would write and ask him. He replied quite quickly enclosing a pamphlet he had already written on Suzuki which Judge Christmas Humphries, the Head of the London Buddhist Society, had overlooked. He added that he had that day been talking about me to a mutual friend and had forgiven me for something I had written about him – or someone he thought was him. He remained friends. I was comforted. 'I think I am a Zen Buddhist!' he said. Bernard Leach had a touch of greatness.

THE CERAMIC HORSE

I wonder: had I not seen the ceramic horse and rider on the roof of Little Park Owles when I was digging potatoes would I ever have met this rare spirit for part of his journey into the unknown, with his Japanese head-basket, his shoulder washed smooth by the moon?

Deep Seasaint

During the hurricane of October 1987 I sat in my workroom watching the glass panes in the windows bend, just as I had done in The Tower on the Island at St Ives in an Atlantic gale. Suddenly the lights failed, and I was plunged back nearly fifty years to the world of candle and lamplight with their golden beauty and deep shadows. It was in this light that I learned about Alfred Wallis, sitting by the firesides of old Cornish fishermen and their wives, as they told me stories of his life at sea and the little town he retired into to become a marine rag-and-bone merchant. The anecdotes conflicted but were only different versions of the same story and the same man. It was from these I pieced together my book on the old sailor before I went to war in France. When I came back the old people had gone, and with them an ancient world. Only this gold dust they had given me remained.

I had signed a contract for publication on D-Day, and went from London to the marshalling areas at Gosport straight on to an LTC to join the invasion of France, never expecting to see England again. Because of paper shortage and an internecine war among the artists for territory, publication was delayed for five years after the book was completed. One day in 1949 the postman dropped a parcel on the stair of the Tower, the door of which was always open, and there it was. I opened the first copy and read the great poem that W.S. Graham wrote especially for it in 1945, and I wept with joy. I held the first book ever to be written on Alfred Wallis taken from the mouths of his relatives and friends of his own generation, and plucked from the golden shadows of the past and, as it happened, from the flames of war.

In March 1986 after Sydney Graham's death I had a beautiful letter from his wife Nessie, remembering

> . . . well the richness of those days when we first met, the fierce joy and love of everything around us.
>
> And I remember the songs at the caravans. But even I had forgotten it was you who asked Sydney to write the poem for your book on Wallis. And what a great poem your request brought forth.

Graham seemed to have that exact imaginative equivalent needed to interpret Wallis's life and unconscious art, and through it he struck a poetic instance of great beauty and power.

When Graham wrote his poem for my book, little was known of this obscure painter save among a small knot of people who collected his paintings for a shilling and sometimes only sixpence each. By arrangement Graham was to be paid a fee. He got a copy of the book sent to him, 'but no money', he wrote to me. 'I don't bother about being paid for it any more and resent being irritated about it. If you can get the 3 guineas from them without much effort, fine, for as usual I'm broke.' I wrote to *Poetry London* but it had gone into liquidation and I don't think he was ever paid.

Wallis had died in the workhouse,

> His poor house blessed by very poverty's religious
> Breakwater, his past house hung in foreign galleries

Graham and I lived at this same level of existence. Perhaps it took this kind of simplicity to present Wallis to the world, as he did his paintings. Since then a lot has been written about the paintings but except for the vivid recordings among the St Ives people made by Dr Roger Slack about Wallis himself, nothing as though he had become nothing more than the strange old Cornish fisherman who did extraordinary paintings. He became a cult and influenced everybody from Ben Nicholson and Christopher Wood to Patrick Heron, Barns-Graham and John Wells.

When I first called on Ben and Barbara in Carbis Bay in 1940 it was to see their collection of Wallis's paintings. Each was a mystery of his past memory locked into an instinctive form. 'Paints what used to be,' he wrote. 'Guessed. I guessed it all!' Ships of religious black in fog-grey seas that contained a porpoise; sails of gull white and duck egg green of evening skies. Dragons of land roared on shore where sea snarled, as they crashed over domino cities being played with by a giant. Ghost ships under chocolate skies. Icebergs that threatened an orange steamer in seas of deepest puss green. Seine nets surrounding a miraculous draught of fishes and Brunel's bridge reconstructed like a mind that is about to crash into disaster. The experience plucked a chord in my orchestra that warned me off the abstract beauty, at best like Bach shown to me previously by my two unique friends, as if they had hidden away a tiger who suddenly roared.

Alfred Wallis was *not* a Cornishman. His father was Devon and his

241

mother, Jane Ellis, was from the Scilly Isles. Alfred was born in Devonport in 1855.

The day I was going to see Wallis himself he was not there. He had been taken to the workhouse the day before. I went to the cottage in Back Road West and looked through the dirty lace curtain, rubbed the glass free of grime and saw the room as he left it. Packed with things he used. Parts of a meal still on the table and a painting covered by a newspaper. Other paintings were on the floor. In the shadows he looked out from a photograph with a sad face and drooping moustache. The Devil had silenced his wireless. He had gone away to the Big House where soon after he died. As I stood there I listened to a simple but untranslatable sentence that turned into a book.

He had come out of the country and seafaring people of England with no trimmings or pretence. He was the most real, the most honest spirit I have brushed shoulders with – tough, humorous and independent. The ships he painted were 'his kept beating painted heart' and not a tick-tock intellectual metronome. This remained so even while he was gibbering in the workhouse garden, as an old man, frail, resentful and angry. He was only defeated – not conquered.

When William the Bastard got as far as Devon after having put to death or subjected to serfdom all the people on the way, he was stopped at Exeter by one who bared his arse to the King. It cost the man his life because the bowmen shot an arrow up it, but the King went no further. This kind of defiance in the Devon people was also in Wallis. It caused him to let his donkey bray in the streets of St Ives at night where he was a foreigner, and to send to Okehampton for an old English fighting cock to kill his neighbour's roosters that had been coming on his patch. It was the toughness that took him as a sailor through icebergs like the one that sank the *Titanic*; to later walk from St Ives to Penzance with his pony Fairyfoot with a load of old iron – he was known as Old Iron – and that over rough moorland and Satanic hills, hewn stones black with magic, and millions of years spent under the sea. Ravens, sea-birds and passing ships.

> Falls his homecoming leaving the old sea testament,
> Watching the restless land sailrigged alongside
> Townful of shallows, gulls on the sailing roofs.

He taught himself to read and write at sea and commit the Bible to memory. Taught himself to paint at the age of seventy by allowing the experience of a lifetime to change places with the soul of a child. Somewhere in him there was a fountain of energy that would spout like a whale in the arctic night. A freedom of spirit, and the secrecy of a seaman on his lone voyage, which was completely his own and original, unaffected by trends of art of which he knew nothing. This was something for which those who imitated him would have given their eye teeth to possess as their own. Like radium he gave a touch of truth to all that happened around him.

When the local grocer said of him: 'Mister Wallis was always held aloof from those interested in his work by what they called his 'queerness!' he was not trying to say that Wallis was a homosexual. The word 'queer' used to connote oddness, unusual person, eccentric, misfit, as indeed Wallis was. And a good deal of this oddness would be self-protection, some of it devilment and clowning to make his admirers hellish – who were after all a pretty unworldly lot. He was taking the piss.

When the intellectuals and painters of the day found him at work in his cottage he was doing what he was barely conscious of doing, painting to ward off the lethal boredom and loneliness of old age. He just happened to be doing it better than anyone else, prompted as he was by the spirit that walked upon his past oceans in robes of ice.

> He's that stone sailor towering out of the
>   cupboarding sea
> To watch the black boats rigged by a question
>   quietly
> Ghost home and ask right out in jackets of oil
> The standing white of the crew 'what hellward
>   harbour
> Bows down her seawalls to arriving home at last?'

Unknown to him his work was already in the Museum of Modern Art, New York. 'O yes!' he said when Ben showed him a reproduction, 'I've got one like that at home.' His work has influenced many painters and had a warm rejuvenating influence on the emergence of primitive painting in our time, causing the unconscious vision to melt the intellectual icebergs that float about in national establishments and direct art to a sharp frozen point north, instead of letting it happen.

As an old man he was troubled by persecution both by the Devil within and the children without. The children stoned him as indeed

243

they stoned my Tower, breaking the windows, until I made a mask of the Devil out of copper and nailed it to the front door to protect me. But Wallis had no such devices other than shouting at them. He was the Lubie who was the butt of children's fun. The Mayor's car ran him over. He believed the woman next door was trying to poison him when she brought food for him to eat. He shouted that some had made thousands of pounds out of his paintings.

NO REST IN MY HOUSE

He wrote in a unique utterance of agony. Deep down he was a foreigner, for a man even from St Just is a foreigner to a man from St Ives.

Wallis died in the workhouse in 1942. I remember the August afternoon when I was walking along the Wharf at St Ives and suddenly saw Adrian Stokes coming towards me, looking distraught. Apart from that he was so seldom seen in the street publicly I thought there must be something wrong.

'What on earth are you doing here?' I said.

'I'm looking for you but was not sure where your place is. Wallis has died and, as I am executor of his affairs, the authorities are sending his body to me. It is on the train for Carbis Bay now. I can't do with it at Little Park Owles and I don't know what to do.' We were standing outside the Salvation Army headquarters.

'Go in there, to the Salvation Army, Adrian. I know his wife was a devoted member. Probably Wallis was too. They will fix the funeral.'

'Well can you deal with the flowers, Sven? It's awfully good of you. Tell them to send the bill to me,' said the perfect English gentleman. He looked very relieved as he went into the brick building. There he arranged the matter, although Wallis was a lapsed member, and paid an extra £4.10/- to save him from a pauper's grave. I arranged the flowers with a grocer named Anthony for whom I had worked on the fields. I did not go to the funeral because I was in London arranging the publication of the book but Bernard Leach took my place and George Manning-Saunders, both of whom told me about it afterwards. And on my first leave from the Army I started the subscription for a gravestone on Rosewall Hill. As I have said elsewhere, I had hoped to carve this myself, but circumstances did not allow. In the end Bernard Leach did it. He offered to make the golden lighthouse out of large pottery tiles with the inscription:

ALFRED WALLIS
MARINER
INTO THY HANDS O LORD

It took Bernard's unassuming sincerity to realise that Alfred had gone back into the fold that held his wife and his ancestors and made something simple and beautiful to mark the place where he last passed by.

It was not, though, 'that stone sailor' as I had hoped to see against the grey Cornish sky; an image Jock Graham finally immortalised.

When he married the Devon woman, Susan Agland, she was twenty one years his senior with many of her children older than himself, which perhaps made up for his never having had a mother.

By some trick of destiny, fifteen years after I had published my book on Wallis, I was to meet and marry a descendant of Susan Agland: both came from Beer near Seaton in Devon. I was 52 and my Julia, 19, was of the Agland family. One of my children by my first marriage was four years her senior. With me as with Wallis they said, 'We took't en in, my dear and gave en a home. E were good boy. E worked hard and earned a livin!'

It was in this way I came to know these beautiful tough, fierce and defiant people who grow out of the same seafaring stock as Wallis and his Susan, a strict Salvationist and to realise how little those who discovered Wallis understood him or knew anything of his real nature. Having worked on the fields for some years in the family smallholdings around Camborne and St Ives I knew also the Cornish peasant stock at first hand and loved them. Bound in their Bible of golden light they handed me his life as a kind of legacy for my labours.

When he was given a show at the Penwith Society prior to one at the Tate Gallery I sent him a telegram, though it was many years after his death.

GOOD BYE DEAR GHOST LOVE SVEN

To which sadly he could not reply. But that is how I knew him – as a dear ghost.

A man's work is the sun that lights his eye and transmits its beauty to our souls, adding a cubit to the stature of Man while he rots into creation. Without this painful process in the end nothing can be achieved, even by the establishment.

A lone voice is heard in the distance: it is the voice of the poet, who understood and somehow tells more than we know by asking a question.

> What shipcry falls? The holy families of foam
> Fall into wilderness and 'over the jasper sea'.
> The gulls wade into silence. What deep seasaint
> Whispered this keel out of its element?

I knew him as a silent ghost. In my book I told about a man of gentle light, who was the most misunderstood and exploited artist of our time.

The Voyages of Alfred Wallis

Worldhauled, he's grounded on God's great bank,
Keelheaved to Heaven, waved into boatfilled arms,
Falls his homecoming leaving that old sea testament,
Watching the restless land sail rigged alongside
Townful of shallows, gulls on the sailing roofs.
And he's heaved once and for all a high dry packet
Pecked wide by curious years of a ferreting sea,
His poor house blessed by very poverty's religious
Breakwater, his past house hung in foreign galleries
He's that stone sailor towering out of the cupboarding sea
To watch the black boats rigged by a question quietly
Ghost home and ask right out with jackets of oil
The standing white of the crew 'what hellward harbour
Bows down her seawalls to arriving home at last?'

Falls into home his prayerspray. He's there to lie
Seagreat and small, contrary and rare as sand
Sea sheller. Yes falls to me his keptbeating, painted heart.
An Ararat shore, loud limpet stuck to its terror,
Drags home the bible keel from a returning sea
And four black, shouting steerers stationed on movement
Call out arrival over the landgreat houseboat.
The ship of land with birds on seven trees
Calls out farewell like Melville talking down on
Nightfall's devoted barque and the parable whale.
What shipcry falls? The holy families of foam
Fall into wilderness and 'over the jasper sea'.
The gulls wade into silence. What deep seasaint
Whispered this keel out of its element?

W.S. Graham

A Box of Jewels

'You are our English Van Gogh, Mary!' said John Wells looking at Mary Jewels' painting of *Cornfields with Peasants*. She smiled with pleasure and took others from the room at the back of the cottage where she kept them – everyone a jewel. To sit in the front room of Vine Cottage at Newlyn with the stream and the big tree outside, with this dark woman whom I always thought to be a gypsy, was an experience to revitalize anybody, let alone two artists like John Wells and myself who were bitten by the mad dog of creation after the war. She wore long skirts, a coloured diclo, gold in her ear shining against her black Irish hair. The room was bright but with that glow deep colour takes on when muted by heavy Edwardian furniture. Her sister, Delia, once married to the sculptor Frank Dobson (the Henry Moore of those days) was a counterpart of the person but not the painter, equally as dark and vigorous.

Their origin was County Waterford. Their family came from Dungarven and started a brewery and fishing business in Newlyn in 1750. Mary's husband was a carpenter, killed in the First World War. Their darkness was that of Celts, but I have seen Romany women moving with the tinkers in the west of Ireland who looked just like these two sisters. It is possible some of Augustus John's passion for the gypsies had wiped off on them or theirs on him. Jewels is also a Cornish and a Breton name. And there was a West Country gypsy named Joules, which could well fit – so like was she.

In 1920 Cedric Morris put a brush into Mary's hand and told her to paint. Augustus John encouraged her.

On the other side of the Cornish peninsular in St Ives, Alfred Wallis had started to paint in 1925 because he was lonely after his wife's death. Ben Nicholson and Kit Wood on a painting expedition made that now famous trip to St Ives in a T-Model Ford and found the old man painting in his cottage, completely unknown. At the same time Christopher Wood, through Ben, met Mary Jewels and became a friend and admirer of her work.

In 1945, when I returned from the western front and met John Wells I had already written my book on Wallis who was now dead three years. One day I went with Wells to visit Mary Jewels. It was through this I suddenly realised what had happened: there had been a disturbance in the west much earlier and this vigorous war was part of its source: another part was Augustus John who had swept his romantic cloak across Cornwall when he had come here when Dorelia was a beautiful young woman and painted her on the seashore and dunes in that haunting manner which was uniquely his. The last of the great portrait painters still painting with his heart and, as Renoir put it, with his prick. When classic walks in at the door the love goes away. That is why Picasso remained supremely romantic.

Mary Jewels was a primitive of a different order and degree to Wallis – less naive and in a sense more skilled, with more luminous and less opaque, muted colour. Augustus John writes in a letter:

> I don't think she cared much for Wallis's work. Mary Jewels has a natural original talent owing nothing to art traditions of any kind. Her drawings have an instinctive gift for decoration.

In my 1945 notebook for 'Disturbance in the West', I find this:

> She understands the beautiful proportions of the cottages in which her people have always lived, built out of stone and everywhere to be found; also the little fields bordered by stone hedges called 'Little Hundreds', fitting into the side of a hill like the structure of a single stone; and the grotesque armies of corn stooks, the figures of men shaped by centuries of work; the incandescence of light on water, boats that float and do not get stuck in a sea of paint; yet boats seen from the land and not ships articulated at sea by a ship man such as Alfred Wallis was. All largely unconscious.

Kit Wood, in spite of coming from the sophistication of Paris and working with Picasso, Cocteau and Diaghilev, as did Gabo, still retained an ingenuous way of painting which his opium eating transmutes into a dream that drugs the mind – as with Keats:

> My heart aches, a drowsy numbness pains
> My sense, as though of hemlock I had drunk,
> Or emptied some dull opiate to the drains
> One minute past, and Lethe-wards had sunk.

'I see him every day,' he writes of Wallis. 'I am influenced more and more. Even Picasso mixes his paints on box lids . . . doesn't he?'

Kit also knew Mary Jewels. It is this naive quality that runs like a sacred thread through him – childlike as in Ben's vision, not primitive but adding to the main stream that produces the beautiful paintings of another Cornish Primitive, Bryan Pearce, half a century later. Kit Wood was more complex and, perhaps because of his public school upbringing at Marlborough, he carried the seeds of destruction like bullets in the heart as seen in his *Self-Portrait* with the huge self-murdering hands. He also reminds me of Lanyon, even in his looks and the wilful childishness they both shared with Nicholson. Kit Wood was a far greater influence of original genius on British painting than has yet been realised.

Of those early days in the twenties Winifred Nicholson wrote to me in 1946:

> It takes something tremendous and nothing to do with oneself to break through so that the subconscious influence of one creative thought upon another as effortless as the tides of the sea, makes others begin to see as you say. John Wells began to see – and Kit did too. We all did. Even Wallis got larger pieces of Post Toasties boxes to paint on. It was magic. A time on the crest of the wave. The breathless held poise before the long inevitable crash. . . how one struggled to prolong it. I suppose if such a moment is prolonged the word 'Classic' is used: those marvellous periods when all artists worked in a common knowledge of the unconscious.

Soon after this Kit went to his death under an oncoming train. Wallis went on painting for another 14 years.

There is no reason to believe that Mary Jewels and Wallis had an influence upon one another, except, perhaps for Mary to say to herself, 'I can do better than that!' and for the old man to ignore her entirely, for country people have a deep independence among themselves. They met but Wallis was very difficult and they did not get on well or admire each other's work, Mary told me.

More recently Hazel Berriman wrote of Cedric Morris and his pupil, Mary Jewels: 'The former claimed to have come across Alfred Wallis, who began painting at the age of 70, some time before his

250

'discovery' by Ben Nicholson and Christopher Wood in 1926, which was to have such an influence on the St Ives School'.

Although Hazel Berriman's dates differ slightly from mine calculated 50 years ago, I think it is very likely indeed that Cedric Morris did come upon Wallis first and introduced him to Mary Jewels.

Prior to this the ground had been ploughed and harrowed, and indeed sown, by more conventional artists in the twenties, which was a very exciting time. Encouraged by Augustus John and Cedric Morris, Mary Jewels had started to paint in Newlyn. In St Ives, under the encouragement of the watch-maker, Mr Edwards and the antique dealer, Mr Armour, Alfred Wallis had done his first painting of 'Lands End, the Longships – all the bloody lot!' Kit Wood met Wallis and Jewels. The seed, however long it took to germinate, now burst and took form as a plant. At that time Wood was staying in Feock with Ben and Winifred Nicholson, and a young doctor who wanted to paint, John Wells. All were influenced by Wallis.

Soon after this, in 1930, when Kit Wood went to his death, it was as though the first counter-blow had been made to terminate this creative emergence which was taking hold, in 1928, a long time before it became so apparent in 1945. I remember asking Ben about Kit's death one day. He was showing me a painting Kit had given him, of a deep green pool, a few cottages and a flag staff carrying a Union Jack. As always it cast a curious spell over my mind.

'Why did he kill himself?' I asked Ben. With that quick decisive mind of his and husky, high-pitched voice, he answered at once.

'Because he couldn't get any more opium. Quite simple really. He came in one day very excited by this painting. "Would you like it? Have it!" he said. I of course said "Thank you very much!" and took it. But I wondered afterwards when I looked at it again – where do you go from here? Then I heard he had thrown himself under a train.'

It was probably Cocteau who introduced Kit to opium. Kit Wood had been to see his parents who lived at Salisbury, with whom there was conflict over his painting, I was told later by Leonard Elmhirst at Dartington Hall. We stood before another of Wood's paintings of a Frenchman in Brittany driving his horse and trap straight at us out of the canvas hanging over the mantelpiece. It was a frightening moment.

The Nicholsons returned to London. In 1933 John Wells bought a doctor's practice on the Scilly Isles. Wallis was painting in St Ives and the traditional artists were everywhere at work in Cornwall in 1934 when I first went there and joined Redruth Art School under Arthur Hambly. Ben Nicholson, now with Barbara, returned to Cornwall at the start of war from London. Gabo, the creator of the Constructivist group who discovered invisibility, came from Russia, via Berlin, Paris, London, now under the wing of Stokes. After the war Wells returned from the Scilly Isles to the mainland as a maturing painter with a passion for the sea, awakened on that long ago holiday with Kit and Ben – and for the islands.

The slow pavan of the octopus had started to be born.

Kit Wood was fervent about these artists whose direct vision and lack of pretence led him back to his own sources, thankfully still coated with a layer of innocence. Through their influence he produced his best Cornish paintings and had a positive effect on English painting. Emphatically on Ben Nicholson.

'I don't know,' writes Augustus John, of Mary Jewels, 'if Kit Wood was influenced by her work. He would certainly have had sympathy with it. It is possible that he found it stimulating.'

Looking at the painting *Mousehole 1943*, by Mary Jewels it seems likely it was both ways, counter currents in the same tide.

Nicholson was very much under Wallis's spell and John Wells has suggested that Cedric Morris influenced Mary Jewels. So it goes on. Each artist is part of an organic process of the psyche, is coloured by the earth and the people out of which he grows. He is part of his own season in his neighbour's fields. He touches forces and rhythms about which he does not know. A Primitive takes fewer influences than anyone else. This was the case with Mary Jewels, and Wallis none at all, except for a large book on sailing ships, which I think Ben gave him. Both had direct and forceful vision which is the only reason for painting at all.

Augustus radiated his magic over the early scene as he did when I met him in the Ship Inn at Mousehole as an old man, giving out light like Noah and was a little drunken.

Mary Jewels' friendships with artists such as Cedric Morris, Frank Dobson, Augustus John, Nicholson, Wood, must have opened doors of sophistication that were not for her. At a party in Bloomsbury someone said, 'How nice to exhibit your paintings. And what profession is your husband – is he a painter too?' Mary replied, 'He's dead. He was the same profession as Christ – a carpenter!'

This rude unadorned quality protected her. An honesty we find in her paintings. Tacho, as the gypsies say. Truthful.

She claimed to refuse to go to art galleries or to look at books on paintings. The way to such wide development being open placed her in a perilous position – on the hill watching the cities of the world. Refusal of the voice at her elbow left her safely within her limits. A genuine Primitive who could paint, not only with passion, but with wisdom and love.

Her importance as a painter was that she preserved this natural richness and strength which came from the Cornish people. John Wells understood this when he compared her to Van Gogh. She painted Cornwall as Cornwall is to the Cornish. She painted the things loved by the Cornish Celts living on their strange thigh of land, built up in a structure of paint that is at once rocky and alive. And he who knows nothing of the rock knows nothing of the people that grow from it – their austerity, simplicity and primitive insularity.

Vogue 1928 carried an article by Augustus John called 'The Woman Artist'. In it he said. . .

> Mary Jewels' Cornish landscapes are remarkable for their intensity and earth-feeling. They blaze in the sight and are almost menacing in their hint of place magic. The colour and design carry something of the wonder of primitive vision and the luxuriance of barbaric nature.

It was as though the roots of the big tree outside Vine Cottage, and the vine itself, spread through the earth of painting in Cornwall and drew together the richness which formed that strong opiate we feel in the mind when we look at those paintings. That curious uplift and delight I always experienced after a visit to Vine Cottage to be shown 'The Paintings' again, to the sound of their excited voices as though the work had that minute been done, as though each time I had discovered a new box of jewels, sparkling through the slow insanity of a whole bottle of sloe gin and the slower disorientations that followed on the way home.

God bless you Mary Jewels!

Battle for the Tower

My first show in London at the Lefevre Gallery and the second at
the Grosvenor established me as a painter and sculptor and one way
and another I had made quite a name, partly helped by the Crypt
shows and the disturbance going on around me in which the art
world was interested. The Arts Council sent a man named Jack
Wood-Palmer to choose and collect work regularly for their
travelling exhibitions in Britain. Unesco for Europe, British Council
for the world.

Then came the travesty of the Penwith Society with which I could
not agree and, after being proved right by having all my work,
except for two drawings, rejected from their first exhibition, I
resigned. I was asked to come back several times. Arnold Forster the
diplomat who lived at Eagle's Nest, before Patrick Heron, interviewed me at length but I did not think he could see the situation in
depth from his rock and we came to a friendly disagreement. I was
painted by Leonard Fuller to 'try and find out about Sven', as he
put it to someone else. In a few sittings he produced that fine
portrait, now in the St Ives School of Painting, working with great
excitement, the brushes flashing through his hands, looking fantastic
with that Magritte-like image in shirt sleeves. I thought he worked
on it too long after the last sitting and lost a lot of the vitality by
overworking and trying to get it right, which is one deadly trap the
traditional painters fall into – even Augustus John. But I saw it
recently and I was surprised how good it was and how well
constructed, with mellow colour, well drawn, even the fag was still
alight. Myself looking out at me after more than thirty years in no
way a stranger. But it was a strange experience when I lectured at
the School with it looking over my shoulder as an old man. I don't
know what Fuller found out, except that years later before he died
he said to my son Paul, 'Tell Sven he was right!'

Also my friend Tom Heron came to my workshop at
Cripplesease after I had left the Tower, and tried to persuade
me to go back to the Penwith. He said that Patrick wanted to join
and that Peter Lanyon – who had also resigned after me – said he
would return if I did. I suppose I was obstinate, but granite is
hard to carve and once given shape, even harder to change: that is
what I was doing and I could not change myself either. With his

gentle wisdom my friend went away without taking a sculpture he had started to buy.

So it was left to Denis Mitchell who, with brother Endell and his incomparable mother Blanche, was my close friend. He came to the Tower before I left and asked me to return to the Penwith Society telling me that the Tate, the Contemporary Art Society, the Guggenheim, the Arts Council – in fact all the top brass – were coming down to buy. If I did not return I would be left out. He did this in all friendliness but I don't think I was very friendly about it. And I didn't believe that my opinions could influence interest in my work. It did not seem credible, but the only institution I had served in was the army and there was no answering back. The truth is I did not know that this is how it worked. In one word I set the course of my whole future for the next thirty years, and even longer. I said 'No!' It has been said that this was some sort of a death wish. To me it was a simple act of truth. Whichever way, my sentence was exile. No more did Jack Wood-Palmer come to the Tower to choose work for the Arts Council travelling exhibitions. Not the others either. The national, public and corporate galleries left me out of their collections here and in America. I lost my place in the Festival of Britain, which shocked even Mitchell, Wells and Lanyon. The London galleries dropped me. People stopped buying my work and I was relegated to the status of provincial artist who never quite made it.

I was ONE IN A TOWER. It is an indictment of the Establishment that these silent sanctions were imposed upon me and my exile was to last 30 years, until in 1985 I was represented by one sculpture and one drawing at the great St Ives Exhibition at the Tate Gallery, but left out of the roll of honour.

The exclusion was complete. I was left only with a fame for being a rebel, committing acts of which I know nothing, uttering words I have not spoken, with the unenviable task of following my star and doing my work unrecognised and with no income. Yet nobody could tell why. It was a strange experience to be a folk image living out my own legend on an island which I had made for myself by a bid for speaking the truth in a movement of which I was at the recognised centre.

It happened to John Clare. He went mad. To Dreyfus also. He was reprieved.

At this time my life was fraught with far more terrifying tragedy that I can dare remember: partly a slip-stream of the war and partly the result of the opening up of the unconscious mind by the forces surrounding me. I can't believe that this tremendous happening was only to change the status of man's psyche from romantic to classic, which it successfully did, but also it was to reorientate the spirit of man facing the universe after a war, fulfilling his place in evolution. But to do this the whole globe of truth is needed, not just the shadow side of the moon. The forced discrepancy brought fragmentation to the heart and destruction to the level pavements of daily life and we were trapped by history, crushed between its metal plates like disused cars. It would be further waste to feed the gossips, enlighten the fools and hurt the innocent at this late stage when the tide of history is about to swing back to re-orientate our creative purpose and our broken moralities. Nothing can stop it.

I was five years in the Tower which meant five winters with Atlantic gales to live through, as well as five summers of unspoilt magic, both in work and love – of great experience, unique friendships, unrecorded joy from love, for the pendulum swings between seasons as well as between the groins of history.

When I was first asked to write about Adrian Ryan I hesitated, because for a painter to write about another painter he has his own vision in the way, but Adrian has that rare gift of being a painter's painter. He does not talk from any pulpit of theory but from the paint directly on the palette and the brush rooting about in it, which you can *hear* because the sounds still stay with the tension and apprehension of the impossible task of throwing a sunset or lighting a moon over a French village where a sinister curé walks alone. Painting a church like a Titan in the sky. No wonder the shouting eye is nervous and wants to screech with excitement when suddenly it is done, and silent beauty of the moment is before you with the honest facility of a true painter. Even a great painter, if greatness consist in content of a haunting beauty like an opium dream, as in his paintings of Mousehole, or the wonder and awe of moonlight. My own vision is no obstacle, because he got there first and has done it direct as no other painter can do, though many will pray at his altar and copy perhaps some of his liturgical brilliance.

One of the memorable things of my years in Cornwall was a visit from Adrian Ryan to the Tower. I had first met him on Exeter Station when I was travelling to London with John Wells in 1945. A short, black haired Irishman who always seemed to be smiling at a joke he never got round to completely telling – it was life. Always generous and kind, a fine painter with a touch of Soutine that betokened a macabre streak. He could paint a calf's head fresh from the butcher, day after day, until it was teeming with maggots, yet produce a landscape as gentle to the eye as a Ruysdael. A painter whose every brushstroke is the centre of the universe he is creating.

He called on the day the children were finishing their wall paintings and was as much interested in them as in their creation of a tiny Sistine Chapel in my Tower. We went drinking with his girl Polly Walker, and talked of all that was going on, among them of Augustus John – or Gus, as Adrian called him – whose friend he was.

'Would you like to meet him?' he said suddenly.

'Christ, yes. How marvellous. Do you really mean that?' I exclaimed.

I had seen Augustus the week before on the wharf at St Ives looking up at the Copper Kettle Tea House with Dorelia who was an old lady by then but with a fine figure in her long dress and head scarf. Augustus wore a Shantung jacket and one of those straw hats they sell on the Camargue at Les Saintes Maries like Van Gogh used to wear. Sandals showing his beautiful feet. His white beard filled with butterflies as the afternoon sun shone through it. Now I was going to meet this man who had been a legend through my whole life from boyhood.

In the afternoon of the next day I got the bus to Penzance with my girlfriend and walked from there, till by early evening we descended the hill with the mysterious and slightly sinister harbour of Mousehole swirling before us like an opium dream. We walked along the narrow wharf where the houses almost bend over and touch you and into the Ship Inn.

'They're in there!' said someone who knew me, and pointed to a room on the left called 'The House of Lords'. Augustus sat on a settee along the wall with Adrian and Polly, giving out that indefinable light that comes when you are in the presence of a great person – a complete personality in a real sense, as distinct from the ego doll of an individual. Something quite unconscious and very beautiful. It was like meeting Noah. Adrian introduced me.

'This is Sven, Augustus!'

He looked up, not at me but my girl Jacqué Moran, who was a person of rare beauty, grinning all over his face and his eyes starting out of his head.

'Who is that beautiful woman?' he roared. He took her hand, not mine and drew her down to his side, glaring with delight, with Polly Walker at his other side.

'A thorn between two roses!' he said.

After shaking his fragile but tenuous hand I stood him a gin –
double Plymouth, neat, as he instructed – and got through to him
by talking across. But he was only interested in Jacqué and Polly –
not me.

Tall friendly archetypal Augustus John
I see you always between Hell and Paradise
With your delicate hands and feet
Bleached by a century's tide.

They make you Dionysus in a sailor's hat
And place upon your thin blue shoulder blade
A drunken parrot – sex this and sex that –
But do not see you living now you're dead.

You were a vivid man acting Silenus
For the girls, to waken their crimson lilies
Out of mind: courteous as a king
Who played his own court painter to the death,

Till all those portraits growing from your hand
Were made more beautiful – rejecting the tear, and,
Even when beauty was most near,
Praying with passion, praising Pan,

Hating religion, despising fear.
Dear magnificent Augustus John
Worn out by trying to record
The tall ithyphallic human form.

You are like a city on a hill
In a portrait of an old Italian Lord,
And vagabonds outside your fortress wall
Crowned you their King with only their love for sword.

Thus I approached him from outside and was never part of the
inner circle that was the family, but rather from the women and
later the gypsies who crowned him. Although he was so little
interested in my presence that evening it somehow sparked off a
friendship that lasted fifteen years – not as the sex maniac who had
to jump every woman he saw including his own daughters – but as
a kind and sensitive creature who was searching for a haven which
his obsession with creation would never allow him to find, until his
fragile being had fallen· and split open in his childhood grass to

fertilize the future. Greatness is a rare content to find in a formalized world. He completed the whole tapestry of his life and work in the way he had set out and did not flinch from the consequences. For me this is the one quality that defined Augustus. That was where the light came from – and the feeling of Presence – something that is now depersonalized. The greatest draughtsman of his time: the last of the great portrait painters. And, at this point of history, equator to Nicholson's cold north.

Quite soon that evening he was taken off to supper in the village, probably at his son Edwin's house and I did not contact him till later when I needed help with my writing on Mary Jewels. She had told me to ask him to show the article he had written in *Vogue* about Mary Jewels, Marie Laurenson and Berthe Morisot, which I did. It helped me with my work on Disturbance in the West and to resurrect her work at the Penwith Society, to whom I suggested her membership, which was accepted.

Among the many people I knew there were one or two unique friendships I have always valued. One was with a woman named Pat Chambers who lived in Teetotal Street where I used to go and talk and drink her gin and dubonnet. She preferred for some private reason to be a man, and did it with such simple elegance and charming humour that it removed the squeaking gate of sex from our friendship and I was able to teach her Zen, that was a discipline of the mind which, like good oil, made it move at a warm viscosity and revealed the truth without intruding on her Catholicism. Out of this I was asked to carve a *Serene Head* which I did beautifully from a still centre, in alabaster, and set it up in an alcove on a gramophone turn-table with a low light to use the translucence of the stone. When the battle for the Tower came she tried to buy the building. When she went away I kept the sculpture safe for her for 25 years until she died of bone cancer and it went to her beneficiary, Monica Askew who loaned it to the Tate for their St Ives Exhibition in 1985. Thus I remembered a unique friend who tried to save the roof over my head so that I could go on working.

The Battle for the Tower which had been in the air for so long continued. My friend who had tried to buy the place and rent it to me, lost the day because the Council stepped in with a compulsory purchase order: they wanted to turn it into a public urinal. I fought this in the national newspapers with the help of artists and writers who were willing to get behind me to save the place where I lived and worked. Since the patron saint of St Ives, St Eia, had a public lavatory built over her sacred well there did not seem much hope, but both friend and enemy tried their hardest to help.

Augustus replied from Percy Street in London to a friend who had written on my behalf, but a little late.

> I have been away in France and have only lately got your letter after much delay, as I had left my studio in Chelsea. I thought it was too late to write to those St Ives Council buggers, but if you think it will do any good I will do so. Perhaps they have already turned Sven's Tower into a Public Convenience. I was about to write and ask him. I did not know the inner meaning of this move but I see you are up against a gang of religious bastards and there is very little hope for you here or in the next world. Let me know if it's not too late to send a polite letter.

The result of the battle was that I got a six months' deferment of the order to quit and then the Council built their urinal – not in the Tower, but on the plat at the side where I cut my stone, with a foot space between the end wall of it and the wall of the Tower. The lavatory attendant lived in the Tower. After that the glory had departed, the magic gone. The Tower still stands.

> Black rose, dark flower, Tower of a single turret
> More simple than where Helen lit her fires!
> Tower of the stars and lone comet -
> Tower of Love and insatiable desires!
> Unshackl'd, stormbound dark Tower.
> I hear your raintorn sound over ocean graves
> As the sweet ghosts die – and I, the Sorrower
> Shout my agony before the shattering waves.
> Stand on the fractured rampart to receive
> This spear, this torn heart, this place
> So dear, where I have gone secretly to grieve
> And draw from the phosphorus wells God's face,
> So near the mind's hidden tear, the Murder Cart
> And the broke battlement of art's disgrace.

I remember the last evening of the summer in 1949. All my friends had gone and I walked alone by the shore, kicking the sea: it was like mercury, the phosphorus gone. I walked quietly into it until

I felt the waves through my clothing searching my secret skin. It brought life into me and the feeling that I belonged to the rocks and the silver sand, to the salt waves, the loving ocean. As I progressed the waves broke over my chest, crashed in my face and lifted me off my feet, the current dragging at my legs. A slow ecstasy rose in me and the moon broke from the clouds making the water iridescent and full of white fire. At this point I felt something jog my shoulder and I turned to see the familiar face of Bryan Wynter's brother, Eric, floating near me with an army gas cape trailing out behind like seaweed. He had a silver case in his hand, offering me a cigarette.

'Don't you think you had better come in?' he shouted. 'It's getting a bit rough out here.' I nodded, and started to turn back, not really realising what had happened. I was in a kind of dream in which the other levels of the mind were taking one over. But for the incongruous image of my friend appearing in the moonlight with a silver cigarette case I would have continued on my way and been washed out beyond the Mermaid to find my own cavern in the friendly loins of her ocean, not having committed suicide but died as the result of what I was doing.

After I left the Tower I re-married. We went to live in the hills over St Ives at a place called Crippleseas where I kept an old English he-goat to carry the Life Force called Billy Death, and I learned further to carve granite from my old one-eyed friend John Craze who came and gazed at the stone like a surgeon till he almost split it with his eye. There were many other human compensations, among them the birth of my son, Jasper, who was first man at my second wedding. My fortunes changed a little, the hills closed round me and were kind, until one day when I was out my cottage burnt down and I knew I must go.

I left Cornwall in 1953 with a new family. Each day as we progressed east I looked at the blue hills over Zennor, where the granite was worn with starlight and the silent land had laid herself down in stillness, no longer torn by the tempest or other disturbance. It was over. But I knew you can't be One in a Tower and forget it: it is forever. I knew that the transformation of material by the spirit was possible and that was my purpose in life and work, before the emulation of the immature, or reserving a place in the Kremlin Wall. The way was difficult but filled with a simplicity of excellence in harmony with the universe.

Dolmen

There are a few stones strewn along my window sill under the sunset on a winter afternoon in Dorset so many years later to remind me of Cornwall: among them a hexagonal quartz crystal through which I can see the fingerprints of early man holding it, wondering at its beauty, also a grey water-worn oval stone with black lines like the linking of tides over centuries, both given me by John Wells: 'To remind you of the islands, my beauty!'

I remember those who were the sacrificers and those who were sacrificed as I hear again the reverberations of our music – the slow pavan of the octopus spread over the underwater world with its tentacles sweeping everywhere, aggravating the seabed, causing a groundswell in other oceans, dancing in a gentle ballet of fish – solo for the shark, mazurka for the moray eels, symphony for storm, all conceived when chugging in the doctor's little boat from island to island about his tough business of healing the human body and sometimes perhaps the spirit, in the same act as searching for the components of pure beauty and new structures for the universe.

There to the north east of us was the granite thigh of Cornwall plunging in the sea – the sculpture that was never finished. Like the great rock outside my Tower window I see it now as the reclining figure of a huge goddess with her head ground smooth by centuries of storm and spars of salt filing her face, articulated against wild skies. She moves only with the slow motion of the ocean sliding over her huge torso – carved by comet, sawn by the edges of the moon, polished by waves, voiced by sea birds and seals entering her to open echoing chambers everywhere.

> Sirens sing as drowned men reach
> To pull them under
> Thunder
> And wonderland with each.

I see her neck as a male column passing right through her and her mouth a quarry frozen into jewels of rose quartz, flying buttresses of gold and the silences of blue behind the green moss down her great thighs, between yellow and aubergine of dying suns.

She is a peninsula, half encircled by herself and the everlasting magnet of her moon. Aeons enter her, she is fecund with a million dawns and storms that hammer out her isomorphic forms and the meteors that ream her groins. All our dreams are shipwrecked between her colossal legs and burned into their essences. And a spiral wind has worn a saucer in her belly from which a handful of radium shines into the ancient darkness of tomorrow.

Those who are drawn to her shores by treasure in her deep ocean should not betray her secrets. She is death to any who adulterate her wisdom or make little of her everlastingness, misconstrue her beauty, devalue her spirit. She will dismember those who are false, burn those who ignore evil.

Continually emerging into new forms being created like the folding of water, she keeps vigil at the doors of the Creator whose palace is the sun. The reclining woman who is always awake, supine on the shores of time, the sculpture that is never done, by an artist who remains unknown. A hole of stone.

DOLMEN

I who saw, rising from the sea,
A granite man mastering my despair
Know now that I at last am he
Of whom I ask this last gentle care:
To give sanctuary from storm again,
Create another century of Love,
In this rough coat contain my own domain,
Cut from tomorrow's dawn a sleeping dove:
There is no other opiate I desire
Than to request from peace her white fire.

EXODUS

I looked across the bay to the hills and the houses sleeping below them extinguishing their lights – Little Bethlehem, the Unholy City, where my heart was still caught under a stone as I made my way, once more a vagabond. Perhaps I had more than a touch of my distant ancestor whose garment I wore – the Coat of Many Colours – and would take with my children into exile, as the sun, like a burning bush, went down behind those blue hills.

INDEX

INDEX

INDEX